Economic Policy and Planning in the Netherlands, 1950–1965

ECONOMIC POLICY AND PLANNING IN THE NETHERLANDS, 1950-1965

by James Goodear Abert

New Haven and London, Yale University Press, 1969

Published with assistance from the foundation
established in memory of Philip Hamilton McMillan
of the class of 1894, Yale College.

Library of Congress catalog card number: 69-15439
Standard book number: 300-01108-3

Designed by John O. C. McCrillis,
set in Baskerville type,
and printed in the United States of America by
the Carl Purington Rollins Printing-Office of the
Yale University Press, New Haven, Connecticut.

Distributed in Great Britain, Europe, Asia, and
Africa by Yale University Press Ltd., London; in
Canada by McGill-Queen's University Press, Montreal; and
in Mexico by Centro Interamericano de Libros
Académicos, Mexico City.

Preface

This study is an interpretive history of economic planning in the Netherlands from 1950 through 1965. Its purpose is to examine the economic and political structure within which Dutch economic policy is framed and the main institutions and tools used in the policy-making process. Its focus is a decision-making process as tempered by the technical economic constraints embodied in an econometric model.

For the most part an institutional orientation was selected because it was felt that such an emphasis would best portray the changes that have taken place in the Dutch political and economic systems during the years covered by this study. It also serves as a convenient point of departure for an inquiry as to whether there is any discernible relationship between the structure and form of the planning organization and the results obtained. Both the institutions involved in Dutch planning and the issues with which they have dealt are described. In several instances the actions of the policy-makers are cast directly in terms of the problems with which they are faced. In the sections that are developed in this manner, the political circumstances of the day are set side-by-side with the salient economic arguments in order that the reader may better understand the forces that shaped particular courses of action.

It should be made clear at the outset that while the Netherlands authorities practice economic planning, the Dutch economy is not centrally directed nor does it exhibit a high degree of hierarchical control. In fact, the Netherlands has a number of characteristics that would be difficult to reconcile with a monolithic and centralized organizational structure. These include a belief in local autonomy, a rather individualistic orientation, a deep attachment to personal liberties, and a strong democratic tradition. Planning as practiced in the Netherlands is simply a pragmatic approach to the formulation and attainment of national goals in the economic sphere, an approach that, for the most part, has proven to be workable during the period covered by this study.

In slightly different words, Dutch planning represents a process by which problems of national economic policy are identified and evaluated in an attempt to formulate a consistent economic policy. In analyzing how this process is carried out in the Netherlands, one finds that the planning process itself is really a combination of two processes: the political process and the technical process. The technical process is directed toward the quantitative economic analysis of the main issues of economic policy, while the political process is directed toward the determination of policy objectives and the selection of means for attaining these objectives. This study attempts to show that close links exist between the technical process and the political process in the Netherlands and that the technical process plays a significant role in the framing of Dutch economic policy, or, stated somewhat differently, that the quantitative analysis furnished by organizations associated with the technical process exerts a strong influence on those political decisions that have economic undertones.

The first chapter outlines the Dutch economy and the influence of Holland's demographic and geographic characteristics on the economic development of the Netherlands and on the types of problems encountered by the policy-makers. A brief description of the Dutch concept of economic planning follows, after which the groundwork is laid for the body of the text with a short discussion of the objectives of Dutch economic policy and the means available to the planners for achieving these objectives.

In the second chapter government economic policy is discussed in terms of the objectives of Dutch economic policy. Each objective is described in some detail, and emphasis is given to the significance of external economic forces. Many of the peculiarities of Dutch planning arise out of the need to reconcile internal objectives with external balances, as illustrated by the policies designed to maintain Dutch costs and prices at levels that would ensure a strong competitive position for Dutch exports. In essence, Chapter 2 deals with the problems of planning in an open economy and, in particular, the effects of balance-of-payments deficits and of balance-of-payments surpluses, often called "imported inflation," on the attainment of domestic economic policy goals.

The political process is described in Chapter 3 by focusing attention on the political parties, the parliament, the cabinet, several influential extra-parliamentary bodies, various pressure groups, and the institutional apparatus within which these institutions function. It is shown that the lack of an inherent political consensus has resulted in a broadening of the political process and a strengthening of the connection between policy decisions in the economic sphere and quantitative economic analysis.

During the period of this study, the government, through a policy of wage coordination, attempted to keep annual wage increases within the bounds of estimated annual average productivity gains. In theory this practice should have prevented increases leading to higher prices, with adverse effects on the Dutch competitive position in the world market. However, as shown in Chapter 4, theory and practice do not always agree.

In Chapter 5 the technical planning process is introduced. Two government agencies, the Central Planning Bureau and the Central Bureau of Statistics, play important roles as official staff organizations of the policy-makers: the former is charged by law with the coordination of economic policy; the latter provides data essential to the planning process as a whole. Chapter 5 shows that these organizations, although they do not have the power to make policy on their own, narrow the range of subjective argument and aid in the rational selection of economic policy by providing information and analysis of the main economic issues. The chapter contains a discussion of how an annual economic plan based on an econometric model of the Dutch economy is developed by the Central Planning Bureau. The model is used to predict future economic developments and to contrast the likely results of alternative policy measures, while the plan enables the authorities to appraise the financial and economic situation of the country at regular intervals.

In Chapter 6 several examples of the influence of quantitative economic analysis on Dutch economic policy demonstrate how the model and the drafting of the annual plan play an important role in determining the current objectives of Dutch economic policy and in selecting the measures necessary to accomplish these objectives. In Chapter 7 there is a detailed description of the 1955 and 1961 versions of the short-term macroeconomic model used by the Central Planning Bureau. Chapter 8 contains an analysis of the accuracy of the forecasts prepared by the Central Planning Bureau aided by models of the sort described in Chapter 7.

The final chapter discusses the influence of the Central Planning Bureau and the central economic plan on government policy and the likely effects of forecasting errors on the direction of economic policy. The appendix describes some of the more technical aspects of the 1961 model.

While this study provides an account of economic policy formulation in the Netherlands and the Dutch approach to economic planning, the reader should note at the outset that the objective is to provide an historic narrative of an ongoing socioeconomic process rather than a normative evaluation of Dutch planning. Although a great number of institutions, policies, and practices are described, no attempt is made to cover all aspects of the process by which Dutch economic policy is formulated and executed, nor to evaluate completely the results attained. Tariff policy, taxation, and cartel policy, among others, have been neglected in favor of an extensive discussion of wage policy coupled with a less exhaustive discussion of price policy and monetary policy. The study does bring together a variety of descriptive information that heretofore has been available only in scattered sources. Throughout the text, Dutch citations are given English titles if they are available in English translation; if no English translation is available, the Dutch title is used.

While it is not possible to record the names of everyone who responded generously to my inquiries, I would particularly like to thank the following for extending the facilities of their organizations to me: P. de Wolff, Director of the Netherlands Central Planning Bureau; E. de Vries, then Rector of the Institute of Social Studies in the Hague; L. J. Zimmerman, Dean of Programs, Institute of Social Studies; and Jan Tinbergen and H. Bos of the Netherlands Economic Institute. Financial support for this research was provided by the Earhart Foundation, the Duke University Graduate Council, and the Institute for Defense Analysis, which also provided secretarial and research assistance. I would also like to express my thanks to Diane Verona and Anne G. Rhodes, who read the entire manuscript and made many useful comments, and Mary Lee Rech, Shirley Phillips, Laura Cain, and Melissa Carter, who typed the draft and final manuscript. Special appreciation is due C. E. Ferguson, Stuart G. Schmid, and Ann S. Barber, whose thorough and incisive reading and comments substantially improved the clarity, focus, and direction of the study. The usual disclaimers are of course in order. Finally, I wish to thank the silent partners, my wife and children.

J.G.A.

Washington, D.C.
January 1968

Contents

Tables and Figures

Tables

Figures

CHAPTER 1

The Economy of the Netherlands

The Dutch economic system is characterized by a considerable amount of freedom in production, distribution, and consumption of goods and services. With a few exceptions, one of which is public utilities, production and distribution take place in privately owned firms. Consumers are free to choose the sorts and quantities of goods they wish to buy with their incomes and savings. Government rationing of consumer goods has not existed since the early postwar years. With the exception of residential construction, producers may provide those goods and services they feel will be most profitable.

The economy is highly industrialized, but Dutch industry is primarily of the processing and finishing variety. Almost all raw materials are imported and a good deal of the product is exported. Sales abroad are important for several reasons: first, Holland is a small country and the domestic market for finished products is limited; and, second, there is the need to acquire foreign exchange to pay for the imported raw materials. The result is that the Dutch economy is one of the most open in the world. In recent years the value of imports has amounted to approximately 50 percent of national income. Exports are almost as large, with the proportion of exports to imports running about 85 percent.

As an open economy, the Netherlands is extremely sensitive to economic events abroad. Consequently, Dutch economic policy is never formulated in isolation but attempts to take into account the competitive position of Dutch products in the world market. In fact, during the years covered by this study, most of the economic policies of the government were conditioned by the necessity to keep the

Dutch export price level competitive. In addition, a number of demographic and geographical characteristics and certain aspects of the economic development of the Netherlands have had a particular influence on the types of economic problems encountered by the Dutch authorities and the ways and means chosen to overcome them.

DEMOGRAPHIC AND GEOGRAPHIC CHARACTERISTICS

The Netherlands is a small country with a population of approximately 12 million people in only 36,330 square kilometers. The population density of 351 people per square kilometer is the highest in Europe, exceeding that of the United Kingdom (219) and France (86). Surprisingly, it is also higher than that of India (148), Japan (257), and even Nationalist China (315). By contrast, in the United States population density is 20 per square kilometer.[1] In addition, more than one half of the population of the Netherlands is concentrated in about one fourth of the area. This area, known as "Rim City Holland," contains the largest cities: Amsterdam (pop. 866,800), Rotterdam (pop. 731,000), and The Hague (pop. 604,000). It comprises the provinces of North Holland, South Holland, and Utrecht, and it has a population density of about 800 per square kilometer.[2]

The already high population density is compounded by an annual birth rate of 20 per thousand which, coupled with a death rate of 7.6 per thousand, has led to an average increase in population over the decade 1950–60 of 1.3 percent. This increase considerably exceeds that of Holland's Western European neighbors. For example, during the same period Belgium increased in population at the rate of .6 percent, Germany at 1.1 percent, France at .9 percent,

1. United Nations, *Statistical Yearbook 1962* (New York, 1963) pp. 28, 32, 36, and 37. The figures cited above are for 1962.

2. "Quarterly Economic Review" Annual Supplement on the Netherlands, *The Economist* (London, May 1964), p. 2.

the United Kingdom at .4 percent, and, for comparison, the United States at 1.7 percent.[3]

Between 1950 and 1960 the working population of the Netherlands increased by approximately 12 percent,[4] and the need to accommodate the increase in the work force brought about by the ever-increasing population was one of the main concerns of economic policy. While trade and services were expected to absorb some of the excess work force, the policy makers felt that industry would have to make the most important contribution to the creation of employment opportunities. Hence, as discussed later in this chapter, postwar Dutch economic policy was designed to facilitate industrialization.

Geographical considerations have also played an important role in the economic development of the Netherlands. The country is located on the lower reaches of three important rivers: the Rhine, the Meuse, and the Scheldt. The Rhine is an important European trade artery and the focus of an intricate network of inland waterways that has been built throughout Northern and Central Europe. Indeed, Holland might be said to be the northern gateway to the European continent. As a result, the economic structure of the Netherlands has been determined, to a considerable extent, by the relatively easy access to the interior of Western Europe provided by these rivers and canals.

Long ago the Dutch turned to trade and shipping as a means of livelihood. In the early seventeenth century the Netherlands was the leading commercial and maritime nation of the world. In spite of frequent wars with France and England, Dutch trading activities spanned the globe. From countries bordering on the Baltic, the Mediterranean, and the Atlantic Ocean and from countries in Asia, Dutch merchantmen brought goods to the Netherlands to be

3. Ibid.

4. J. E. Andressen, "Economic Development in the Netherlands," *Planning and Development in the Netherlands, 1*, No. 1 (1962), p. 30.

transported up the Rhine, the Meuse, and the Scheldt into the heart of Europe.

In addition to trade, agriculture also represented an important means of livelihood for the early inhabitants of the Netherlands. The humid climate, coupled with the rich delta soil, gave rise to cattle breeding and intensive farming. Even today land use is quite intensive, inasmuch as over 70 percent is cultivated; only eight percent is forest, and a mere six percent is unused.[5]

Industrialization, the bulwark of the present-day Dutch economy, came late to the Netherlands. Throughout the seventeenth, eighteenth, and nineteenth centuries, trade and agriculture remained the chief sources of national income. It was not until the closing decades of the nineteenth century that there were signs of real industrial activity, and even these were comparatively moderate. The slowness of industrial development can be partially attributed to the fact that the Netherlands has a scarcity of raw materials. Only coal, some oil, natural gas, and salt are found within its boundaries.

ECONOMIC DEVELOPMENT OF THE NETHERLANDS

The lack of raw materials notwithstanding, industrialization, once begun, proceeded rapidly. From the meager industrial base that existed in the late nineteenth century, industry grew to be the most important economic sector. During the last twenty to thirty years in particular, the economic structure of the Netherlands has undergone considerable change. As an illustration, Table 1 shows the change in the distribution of the labor force among the primary economic sectors over the last half century. Note in particular the decline in the percentage of persons employed in the agricultural sector and the rise of employment in industry, commerce, transportation, backing, and insurance.

5. Netherlands Central Bureau of Statistics, "National Account of the Netherlands, 1960," *Statistical Studies*, No. 11 (The Hague, December 1961), p. 58, cited hereafter as "National Accounts, 1960."

TABLE 1. Employment by Economic Sectors in the Netherlands (in percentages)

	1899	1960
Agriculture	30	12
Industry	33	43
Commerce, transportation, banking, insurance	18	29
Other	19	16
TOTAL	100	100

Source: L. M. Koyck and G. K. Boon, "Post War Holland and the Impact of the Common Market," *The Common Market Economies* (London, District Bank Limited, 1962), p. 70.

World War II interrupted the industrial expansion of the Netherlands. After the liberation, productive equipment had to be rebuilt or renovated in all branches of industry. The employment, monetary, and budgetary position of the country had to be reorganized, and it was necessary to bring prices, wages, and profits into equilibrium. In addition, trade and capital exchange with foreign countries had to be resumed.

One of the first problems was to rebuild the prewar industrial base of the country. The necessary modernization of agriculture, however, was expected to reduce the number of workers employed in this sector. This, combined with the population growth that had taken place during the war, compelled policy-makers to plan for an even larger industrial sector than existed prior to the war.

In view of the limited home market and the need for imported raw materials, the Netherlands directed its industrialization efforts largely to the manufacture of products that would find a ready market abroad.

During the early postwar years, completely new export markets were needed to counteract the structural deficit in the balance of payments caused by the loss of Indonesia. Dutch investors had suffered large capital losses, and the

Netherlands lost a market that in 1939 absorbed about 9 percent of Dutch exports of goods and services.

Shortly after the war, the Minister of Economic Affairs issued a *Memorandum on the Industrialization of the Netherlands* which is illustrative of the philosophy adopted by the Dutch government for dealing with the nation's postwar problems. The basic tenants of economic policy outlined in this memorandum were supported by all elements of Dutch society well into the decade of the fifties. Only recently have new leaders emerged, particularly in organized labor, who have questioned the institutions and procedures, and perhaps also the objectives of economic policy, that grew out of the early postwar experience.

The *Memorandum on the Industrialization of the Netherlands* stated:

> The future standard of living in the Dutch nation, as well as the stability of its economic and social structure, is largely dependent on the way our problems [the balance of payments, increasing population and employment opportunities] are solved. A satisfactory solution is only conceivable if it is based in an important, if not predominant, degree on a vigorous further development of Dutch industry. . . . If this absolutely essential policy of industrialization is to be realized, the entire population of the Netherlands will have to make sacrifices. Our people will, above all, have to be prepared not to use the expected increase in productivity and production to expand their own consumption, but to devote a considerable part of it to increase industrial investment. . . . . It is, in effect, a question of austere living and of exerting our energies to avoid greater adversity in the future.[6]

6. Netherlands Minister of Economic Affairs, *Memorandum on the Industrialization of the Netherlands*, English translation of Annex IV to the Explanatory Memorandum to Chapter X (Economic Affairs) of the 1950 Budget (The Hague, Ministry of Economic Affairs, September 1949), pp. 1, 41.

In the *Memorandum*, the balance-of-payment problem received special attention: "The redress of the balance of payments, without a drastic lowering of the general standard of living, is only possible by a considerable increase of the national productivity, especially of such goods as will find a market abroad or will render unnecessary the import of capital or consumer goods."[7]

That the overall industrialization policy of the Netherlands has borne fruit is indicated by the increase in industrial exports. In the period from 1949 to 1960 the volume of such exports rose by some 400 percent. In the latter year industrial products constituted roughly 62 percent of total exports, in contrast to 55 percent in 1949.[8]

The figures in Table 2 show how the increased employment in industry has been accompanied by a rise in the contribution of industry to national income. Table 2 shows the origin of national income by sector from 1950 through 1965. During this period the net national income at market prices rose from 17.06 billion guilders to 61.69 billion

TABLE 2. National Income by Economic Sectors (in percentages)

	1950	1955	1960	1965
Manufacturing	38.9	40.4	42.5	40.8
Agriculture, forestry, and fishing	14.8	11.5	10.8	8.4
Trade and transport	25.1	26.3	25.4	26.5
Government	10.5	10.5	11.1	13.7
Other	9.1	9.0	9.1	9.5
From abroad	1.6	2.3	1.1	1.1
TOTALS	100.0	100.0	100.0	100.0

Source: "Nationale rekeningen, 1965," p. 68.

7. Ibid, p. 4.
8. "National Accounts, 1960," pp. 80–82.

guilders.[9] According to the national accounts of the Netherlands, the contribution of industry was 31 percent in 1938. From the table it can be seen that the proportion attributed to industry had risen to 42.5 percent by 1960, although this figure fell to 40.8 percent in 1965 as trade and transport and government increased their proportionate share in the national income.

Accompanying the structural shift in the Dutch economy has been a growth in real national income. This has been particularly evident in the postwar years, as depicted in Table 3, which also shows the increase in real per capita national income over the same years.

TABLE 3. Indices of Real National Income (1953 = 100)

Year	Real National Income	Real National Income, Per Capita
1900	29	60
1930	67	89
1939	69	82
1945	35	40
1950	89	92
1955	118	116
1960	145	132
1965	186	160

Source: "National Accounts, 1960," p. 50, and "Nationale rekeningen, 1965," p. 68.

In terms of per capita domestic product, the Netherlands ranks somewhat below its closest European neighbors and trading partners, Germany, France, Belgium, and the United Kingdom, but above Austria and Italy. Table 4 shows this comparison for the years 1953 and 1964.

During the decade 1950–60 real gross domestic product measured at constant market prices increased at an annual

9. Prior to March of 1961, when the guilder was revaluated, 3.80 guilders equalled one dollar. Since the revaluation, the exchange parity has been 3.62 guilders to the dollar.

rate of 4.8 percent, while real per capita product grew at a 3.4 percent rate. While these ratios were exceeded by Western Germany (7.9 and 6.7 percent), it was considerably above the rates achieved by the United Kingdom (2.8 and 2.4 percent), Belgium (3.1 and 2.4 percent), and the United States (3.3 and 1.5 percent). From 1960–65 Dutch real gross

Table 4. Per Capita Gross Domestic Product at Factor Costs (in dollars[a])

	1953	1964
Austria	$471	$1,033
Belgium	839	1,462
France	861	1,579
West Germany	812	1,766
Italy	494	1,032
Netherlands	780	1,431
United Kingdom	832	1,698

a. Calculated parity rate conversion
Source: United Nations, *Yearbook of National Account Statistics 1965* (New York, 1966), p. 501.

domestic product grew at a 5.0 rate with the per capita figure increasing by an average of 3.6 percent. Comparable figures for Western Germany were 4.9 and 3.6 percent, the United Kingdom 3.3 and 2.5 percent, Belgium 4.9 and 4.2 percent, and for the United States 4.7 and 3.1 percent.[10]

Dutch Economic Planning

In Holland, planning is not considered the hallmark of a particular social order but rather a method of arriving at decisions. Dutch planning is primarily a process of co-ordination by which the political aspects and the technical aspects are combined in such a way as to provide a general framework and the instruments by which a consistent,

10. United Nations, *Statistical Yearbook 1966* (New York, 1967), pp. 572–74.

overall economic policy can be obtained.[11] In fact, the annual Dutch plans are not really plans at all, but are most accurately described as forecasts for a coordinated economic policy.

Hence, economic planning in the Netherlands is significantly different from planning in Communist countries. The Dutch authorities do not set concrete targets or means for achieving them, as is done in most Communist economies. Nothing in the Dutch planning method implies the rigorous exercise of the authority of the central government over the allocation of economic resources or, consequently, on the course of economic events. On the contrary, as this study indicates, the government's authority is severely limited by the institutional arrangements within which the government must operate and also by strong countervailing economic, social, and political forces. In fact, it can be said that the economy of the Netherlands is not planned, in a strict interpretation of the term, but guided, with the state playing an important, but for the most part passive, role.[12]

11. For a discussion of planning methodology, see the *International Social Sciences Journal, 11*, No. 3 (1959), in particular the "Introduction" by John Friedman, pp. 327–38, and the article entitled "The Politics of Planning" by Robert A. Dahl, pp. 340–50. Also on the concept of planning, see Yehezhel Dror, "The Planning Process: A Facet Design," *The International Review of Administrative Sciences, 29* (1963), pp. 46–58.

12. A number of survey articles dealing with various aspects of Dutch planning have been published. They include: C. van den Beld, "Short-term Planning Experiences in the Netherlands," and Willem Hessel, "Quantitative Planning of Economic Policy in the Netherlands," in Bert G. Hickman, ed., *Quantitative Planning of Economic Policy* (Washington, D.C., Brookings Institution, 1965), pp. 134–78; F. Hartog, "Economic Policy in the Netherlands," in E. S. Kirschen, ed., *Economic Policy in our Time* (Amsterdam, North-Holland Publishing Co., 1964), pp. 3, 68–137; William Fellner et al., *The Problem of Rising Prices* (Paris, Organization for European Economic Cooperation and Development, 1961), pp. 61, 175–80, 247–52, and 359–90; J. Tinbergen, "Central Planning in the Netherlands," *Review of Economic Studies, 15* (1947–48), pp. 70–77; Pieter de Wolff, "The Scope, Methods, and Tools of Planning," *Planning*, paper read at the Conference of Business Economists, New College, Oxford, April 1962; Pieter de Wolff, "Central Economic Planning in the Netherlands," *Weltwirtschaftliches Archiv, 92* (1964), pp. 181–207; G. M. S. Verrijn, "Economic Policy in the Netherlands," *Lloyds Bank Review* (January 1953), pp. 34–43.

THE OBJECTIVES OF DUTCH ECONOMIC POLICY

Dutch policy objectives have never been explicitly defined. They have only been stated in rather general and, in fact, somewhat vague terms. One list of policy objectives detailed in 1956 by an independent organization known as the Social and Economic Council set forth the overall goals of Dutch economic policy as follows:

1. To maintain equilibrium of the balance of payments;
2. To achieve an acceptable distribution of income among relevant groups of the population;
3. To promote a stable price level;
4. To maximize the national income and to achieve full employment of all factors of production, particularly labor; and
5. To promote a level of investment in fixed capital which enables an improvement of the standard of living of the growing population.[13]

Clearly, the decision-maker should, if he is able, take into account the importance or priority of each objective prior to formulating policy, i.e. prior to selecting the means to achieve policy goals. However, while it is rather easy to state objectives in broad terms, it is much less easy to define what these objectives actually mean or to make comparisons among them in terms of their relative importance. This is made even more difficult by the fact that no objective is really sought for its own sake. For example, the achievement of balance-of-payments equilibrium, or a stable price level, or even maximum output and employment are only instruments for attaining higher, but virtually unquantifiable, welfare targets. Thus the authorities seek equilibrium in the balance of payments because when the balance-of-payments is high, a country has too large a portion of its savings in an

13. Netherlands Social and Economic Council, *Advies inzake de bestedingen* (Advice on National Expenditures), (The Hague, Sociaal-Economisch Raad, 1956).

asset that yields no return (gold or creditor position in the International Monetary Fund) or only a small return (foreign exchange balances). On the other hand, if the balance is too low, the country may not be able to meet its external obligations without borrowing or taking policy actions whose secondary effects often increase the level of unemployment or have other economic consequences not generally acceptable to the policy-makers.

There is a further difficulty in evaluating objectives and in selecting means for their attainment that should be kept in mind if one is to understand Dutch economic policy during 1950–65. This is the fact that it is rarely possible to achieve all objectives at the same time. For example, full employment generally leads to some price inflation while equilibrium of the balance of payments is often inconsistent with full employment and growth. In the latter case, full employment and growth often stimulate a high and expanding demand for imports, which in many cases produces a deterioration of the balance-of-payments position. Thus the policy-maker is faced with a situation in which it is impossible to obtain more of one objective without sacrificing some part of another objective. In determining which objectives should receive priority, the authorities, in effect, trade the attainment or near attainment of some objectives for the attainment or near attainment of others.

THE INSTRUMENTS OF ECONOMIC POLICY

In the Netherlands the means for attaining goals of economic policy are limited because the economic system is based upon free private enterprise. Neither the volume of consumption nor the pattern of expenditure is directly determined by the government. The government can, however, attempt by indirect means—such as taxes, subsidies, or government spending—to cause changes in income and expenditures and thus mitigate cyclical conditions. At one time tariff policy was also useful in controlling imports of finished products and raw materials, but as a result of Benelux and European Economic Community commitments, the effectiveness of tariffs as an instrument of economic policy has been greatly reduced. The government has one additional instrument of policy, the institutionalized wage negotiation apparatus that can be tightened or loosened, at least in theory, depending on the economic situation.

In the publication of the Social and Economic Council that outlined the goals of economic policy, the following instruments were set forth for Dutch economic policy: (1) the general wage rate; (2) indirect taxes and subsidies; (3) direct taxes; (4) government expenditures on commodities; and (5) instruments which are specifically monetary, such as a restrictive credit policy or changes in the rate of interest.[14]

As will be seen in subsequent chapters, each of these instruments has been used at one time or another by the public authorities.

Since all desirable objectives can seldom be realized simultaneously, decisions must be taken as to the objectives to receive priority. Finally, decisions as to the means to be employed to achieve the selected policy objectives must also be made. Conflicts among objectives and among alternative means are resolved through the political process. Indeed, deciding among objectives and means is the very essence of politics in the economic sphere. Because of changing economic and social conditions from 1950 to 1965, the Dutch government shifted from a strong reliance on wage policy to a greater use of fiscal and monetary policies.

14. Ibid.

CHAPTER 2

Government Economic Policy

The Netherlands, like all countries, strives to achieve both internal and external equilibrium; that is, the authorities attempt to keep the foreign accounts in balance and at the same time aim for an internal level of aggregate demand that will maintain acceptable domestic economic conditions. Unfortunately, economic forces from abroad often cause conflicts between internal and external goals, and the extreme openness of the Dutch economy renders it especially vulnerable to external events. Thus the coordination of economic policy is more difficult for the Netherlands than for an economy less dependent on foreign trade.

For the most part, government economic policy actions from 1950 through 1965 were dictated by short-run considerations, especially the need to combat inflationary developments. Since the war Europe as a whole has had only two relatively mild recessions, one in 1952 and one in 1958. After the initial recovery period in the Netherlands, there has been a relatively high level of employment, sometimes even tension in the labor market. The scarcity of labor has led to continuous pressure on the domestic wage level; and as wages constitute the main component of industrial prices, this wage pressure has led directly to pressure on the price level. For an open economy like the Netherlands, a rising price level has serious implications with regard to maintaining both internal and external equilibrium.

In theory, the initial impetus for inflationary conditions can be generated domestically or can come directly from abroad. A domestically created conflict can be illustrated by actions designed to expand aggregate demand in order to reduce domestic unemployment. The more demand is stimulated, the more the price level is likely to rise. In addition, the growth of consumer demand tends to stimulate increased capital investment which reinforces the pressure on domestic prices.

However, rising prices undermine the Dutch competitive position in the world market. This tends to reduce foreign demand for products at a time when, as a result of the increase in domestic aggregate demand, imports are stimulated. The result is to reduce a surplus or increase a deficit, whichever is present, in the balance of payments. Continuing deficits in the balance of payments would, in the long run, require the adoption of policies designed to force the country to adjust its spending to the available resources. It is possible, however, that the equilibrium in the balance of payments would be restored at an inadequate level of employment because of losses in sales as a result of increases in export prices, which in turn were brought about by the domestic inflation. Thus, although external equilibrium had been restored, aggregate demand might be insufficient to achieve the objective of full employment, the policy goal the authorities set out to obtain.

Conflicts between the dual objectives of internal and external equilibrium can originate abroad as well as domestically, as illustrated by the phenomenon of "imported inflation" brought about by increased foreign demand for domestically produced goods and services. Such an increase can be caused by a difference between the levels of domestic and foreign prices, changes in tastes, or as the result of inflationary forms of financing in foreign countries. International price differentials can result from many causes, such as, for example, a relative improvement in domestic labor productivity, by differences in industrial pricing policies, or by differences in the organization and aggressiveness of the labor movement.

Imported inflation brings policy problems, particularly

for an economy that is at or close to full employment. The natural mechanism of price equalization tends to transmit price changes very rapidly from one country to another, especially when exchange rates are inflexible. Thus export prices in the country experiencing the imported inflation will tend to rise in conformity with the prices of competing foreign countries. Profit in the export sector will tend to rise and, as a result, the export sector will probably expand, with the consequence that export sales will increase. Finally, as exports increase relative to imports, the current account of the balance of payments will acquire a surplus. The resulting influx of foreign exchange will lead to an expansion in the money supply, which in turn will lead to price increases for goods that are not in direct competition with foreign goods. In effect, imported inflation means that resources have been exchanged for a current-account balance-of-payments surplus, and while aggregate demand has increased, the domestic supply of goods and services has decreased. Thus the economy is in a state of "overspending," the same situation as that resulting from inflation caused by domestic impulses.

Whether inflationary impulses come from domestic sources or from abroad, in theory they can be offset by monetary policy, by a conscious budgetary policy on the part of the government, or by a combination of the two. In actual practice, however, the strength of the impulses often renders it impossible to offset them fully. For example, if the government should try to dampen inflation through fiscal policy, it might call for more flexibility in expenditures than is possible. It might also entail a substantial reduction in spending that is neither practical nor politically feasible. Thus in reality the government must often choose between balance-of-payments equilibrium and price inflation. When faced with this choice, the Dutch authorities have often sacrificed some measure of price stability in order to achieve balance-of-payments equilibrium.

BALANCE-OF-PAYMENTS EQUILIBRIUM AS AN OBJECTIVE OF DUTCH ECONOMIC POLICY

The concept of balance-of-payments equilibrium as a target of economic policy is somewhat nebulous. It is probably more meaningful to say that the policy objective, although expressed as equilibrium in the balance of payments, is to maintain a fixed exchange parity at some acceptable level of gold and foreign exchange reserves.

In fact, it is the depletion of reserves and not necessarily the deficit in the balance of payments that represents a danger to the economy. The balance of payments is only a flow over time which, when summed from a certain date, changes (increases or decreases) the stock of foreign exchange. If reserves increase, at some point the marginal utility of additional reserves will become lower than that of alternative investments at home or abroad. At the other extreme, too low a level of reserves may, because of the importance attached by the public to reserves, endanger the strength of the national currency in the exchange markets.

Nevertheless, it is equilibrium in the balance of payments that receives direct attention.[1] Inasmuch as the balance-of-payments account consists of two parts, that pertaining to current transactions and that recording capital transactions, it should be made explicit that the object of Dutch policy is an equilibrium that takes into account both current and capital transactions. In the Netherlands, equilibrium in the current account is not sufficient to maintain a constant stock of foreign exchange as the capital account has generally shown a structural deficit. During the early and mid-

1. The balance-of-payments account can be calculated in two ways: a transaction basis or a cash basis. On a transaction basis, the account is calculated on the basis of deliveries of goods and services rendered to and by foreign countries. The account on a cash basis shows the related payments. Thus a difference between payments and deliveries, due, for example, to an increase or decrease in the amount of credits supplied, leads to different results in the two types of balance-of-payments accounts. A reconciliation between the two can, however, be made.

fifties the capital account deficit ran about 350 million guilders a year. This deficit resulted from loan repayment, the export of capital for development aid (particularly in Surinam), direct investment abroad, and lending (commercial credit) with a view to promoting exports. During those years a surplus on current account of that amount was required to offset the structural deficit on the capital account. However, in order to keep abreast of increased foreign payments resulting from the growth of the export sector, larger quantities of gold and foreign exchange were needed for transactions balances. For this purpose, an annual increase in reserves of approximately 130 million guilders was considered necessary.[2] Thus for the reasons outlined above, authorities set a rough target of achieving a current account surplus on the order of 500 million guilders each year during that period.

In recent years, this so-called norm representing balance-of-payments equilibrium has been raised to 800 million guilders, roughly 2 percent of the national income. This increase was due to the fact that after 1959 capital outflow for investment and credit increased to a figure approximately double the annual flow experienced during the years 1954–55. It should be noted that even this increased target does not allow for increases in capital exports in the form of aid to underdeveloped countries, nor for continued export of capital through sales of foreign securities in the Netherlands, both of which are increasing.

Since 1950, current account balance-of-payments surpluses have slightly exceeded the norms described above. The authorities discovered that when the percentage of imports of goods covered by exports of goods (the balance

2. The size of desired increase in transaction balances is estimated to be between 10 and 15 percent of the rise in national income. From about 1960, the latter rose on the average of 4 to 5 percent per year, which means that approximately 200 million guilders' worth of foreign exchange were added to the reserves per year. Netherlands Bank N.V., *Annual Report*, 1961, p. 55 (hereafter cited as Netherlands Bank,) *1961*, or whatever year is appropriate.

of trade) falls below 80 percent, the surplus on the balance of payments current account disappears completely. In order to maintain the current account surplus at the desired level, exports of goods must cover imports of goods to the extent of approximately 84 percent, which is roughly the average maintained during that period.[3]

INCOME DISTRIBUTION AS AN OBJECT OF ECONOMIC POLICY

The relative position of labor income vis-à-vis other income has received considerable attention, particularly during 1954–55 when the Social and Economic Council was discussing the so-called lag in the rise of wages behind the rise of the national income.[4] One notes, however, that even though the government officially endorsed the principle of equitable income distribution as an object of economic policy, no government spokesman has ever explicitly defined what equitable meant. Expressions such as the allocation to the workers of a "justifiable" share of the increase in national income or an "acceptable" distribution of the national income among relevant groups of the population were used to express the government's position.

The reluctance of the authorities to define equitable is not surprising. During a series of debates in the Social and Economic Council on this issue, there was considerable controversy simply over the selection of a statistical series to be used to show movements in the share of labor. In calculating such a series, it became apparent that labor's share of the national income could be expressed, for example, as (1) wages and salaries, including contributions to social insurance, as a percentage of national income at factor cost; or as (2) the average amount of wages and salaries, including contributions to social insurance, per worker in enterprises

3. Ibid., p. 42.
4. This topic is discussed in more detail in Chaps. 4 and 6.

as a percentage of the average national income of factor cost per person gainfully employed.

For the Netherlands the share of labor expressed in terms of the first measure averaged 59.1 percent during 1950–65. Year by year figures are given in Table 5. Several distinct cycles are discernible from the data shown in the table. Starting at 53.3 percent in 1950, labor's share fell slightly from 1951 through 1953. It rose in 1954 but fell again in 1955, reaching a low point of 53.6 percent in that year. During 1956, 1957, and 1958, labor's share rose more than 1 percent per year. However, in 1959 and 1960, the share again fell. From 1961 onward, the employee's share in national income rose at the rate of approximately 2 percent per year.

The second measure of income distribution has received more attention in the Netherlands than the first. This measure is defined as the quotient of wage income per employee in the business sector and national income at factor cost per head of the active labor force. The term active labor force means "not unemployed." When the numerator (the wage bill divided by the number of wage earners) and the denominator (the national income divided by the working population) show the same percentage change, it can be inferred that, to the extent that earnings measure welfare, there has been an equal distribution of any increase in national income between wage earners as a class and the active population as a group. Each year the Central Planning Bureau calculates the employees' share in the national income according to both definitions; these series are reproduced in Tables 5 and 6.

One should note that the two series are not equal nor are their fluctuations consistent. Nevertheless, their basic pattern is essentially the same. By both measures, labor's share declined during the inflationary period of 1950–52 and the post-Korean War recession of 1953–54. As economic activity increased during 1955–57, both measures likewise

TABLE 5. Labor's Share in National Income, 1950–65 (First Definition)[a]

	1950	1951	1952	1953	1954	1955	1956	1957
Labor's share (%)	55.3	55.0	54.5	53.9	54.3	53.6	55.4	56.8
Percent change		–.3	–.5	–.6	+.4	–.7	+1.8	+1.4
	1958	1959	1960	1961	1962	1963	1964	1965
Labor's share (%)	57.9	56.7	56.5	59.0	61.4	62.9	65.2	66.6
Percent change	+1.1	–1.2	–.2	+2.5	+2.4	+1.5	+2.3	+1.4

a. National income is measured at factor cost. Labor income includes wages and salaries from enterprises, government, and the rest of the world, plus employers' contributions to social security and pension funds.

Source: Netherlands Central Planning Bureau, *Centraal Economisch Plan 1965* (The Hague, 1965), pp. 172–77.

TABLE 6. Employees' Share in National Income, 1950–65 (Second Definition)[a]

	1950	1951	1952	1953	1954	1955	1956	1957
Employees' share (%)	71.5	70.0	70.5	69.1	68.5	66.7.	68.0	69.2
Percent change		–1.5	+.5	–1.4	–.6	–1.8	+1.3	+1.2
	1958	1959	1960	1961	1962	1963	1964	1965
Employees' share (%)	70.3	68.2	67.3	69.3	71.4	72.5	74.3	75.0
Percent change	+1.1	–2.1	–.9	+2.1	+2.0	+1.1	+1.8	+.7

a. Employees' share is defined as wage income per employee in the business sector divided by national income at factor cost per head of the active labor force.

Source: Centraal Economisch Plan 1965, pp. 176–77.

increased, and both fell, with about a one-year lag, during the recession of 1958–59. Since 1961 labor's share has continued to rise along with the increased levels of economic activity in the Netherlands.

Some theorists have suggested that the relative share of wages and salaries in national income would be expected to increase during a fall in economic activity because entrepreneurs are usually not able to decrease employment in proportion to the slackening in economic activity. When economic activity picks up, the share of labor should tend to decrease because industry is usually able to increase output without a proportionate increase in labor input. Thus entrepreneurs are able to keep a larger proportion of the initial revenue gains from increased sales for themselves. If output continues to expand, however, additional hiring will be necessary and at some point a scarcity of labor will develop. It is then that labor can be expected to exact a larger proportionate share of the increased income for itself.

During the earlier years of this study the hypothesis described above seems to have been borne out in fact. However, during the economic expansion of 1956–57, and the one that began in 1960, demand conditions in the labor market were such as to enable labor to obtain an almost continuously increasing share of national income. In fact, changes in the share of labor have been procyclical rather than contra-cyclical as hypothesized. The share of labor has increased the upswings and fallen during the downturns or pauses in economic expansion. The decrease in labor's share during the slight recession of 1958–59 most probably reflects a slackening in new employment rather than a lag in the reduction of the labor force. The latter appears to be valid only in cases of less than full employment.

Other conditions of course have also played a part in the upward movement in labor's share in national income. Changes in factor shares are often caused by changes in the relative size of sectors, by changes in the composition of the labor force, and by movements of income per head in different factor groups. For example, agriculture usually has a low content of wage and salary payments; therefore any tendency for agriculture to become less important relative to other sectors would be reflected in an increase in labor's share for the economy as a whole. This played some part in the increase in labor's share in the Netherlands. In addition, a rise in the share of labor may be caused by a decline in the proportion of self-employed in the economy. The latter could be due to a relative decline in an important sector where self-employment is large, such as agriculture, when some who formerly worked on their own account are led to take up dependent employment.

Fluctuations and shifts in the distribution of income cause both short-run and long-run policy problems. For example, if labor's share in national income lags too far behind that of other income, a condition is created in which consumer demand is not likely to rise enough in relation to the general increase in wealth. However, if increases in wages cause labor's share of the national income to outrun that of entrepreneurs, both the propensity to invest and the savings ratio (i.e. the supply of investment funds) will be lessened.

In a growing economy, and using the second of the two measures described above, an increase in relative shares represents an increase in real wages. However, to the entrepreneur, in the long run a higher level of real wages calls for a substitution of capital for labor. Thus when the distribution of income shifts toward labor, employers may find that their sources for new capital investments decrease while their need for such funds is increasing. Structural decreases in the savings and investment rates are particularly serious for the Netherlands' economy, which has to create employment for a population that is growing rapidly by Western European standards. Thus the capital widening implications of a possible decrease in the funds for investment must be considered along with the capital deepening aspects.

The Maintenance of a Stable Price Level as an Object of Economic Policy

Price stability, like equity in wages, is a nebulous policy objective. One basic reason is that there are any number of price indices whose stability could be selected as a policy objective. Moreover, these indices usually do not move in perfect or even near perfect conformity with each other. Another reason for the difficulty in interpreting price stability as a goal of economic policy is that as long as the authorities peruse the objective of full employment, interpreted as levels of unemployment below, say, 3 percent, it appears that some price inflation is probably inevitable. In fact, the more unemployment is reduced by policies that expand aggregate demand, the higher will be the price that is paid in terms of inflation. The effect of inflation on external equilibrium measured in terms of surpluses and deficits in the balance-of-payments account has already been discussed.

One might also note that for countries heavily engaged in international trade, price stability might better be treated as an instrument rather than a target of economic policy. This has seldom been done because of the current reluctance to let exchange parities vary.[5] Given that exchange rates are fixed, only differential changes in international price can bring about international equilibrium between countries with surpluses and those with deficits in their balance-of-payments accounts. In surplus countries, prices must rise and in the deficit countries prices must either be kept down or, if possible, made to fall. By this means the possibility of the latter selling in the world market in comparison with the former can be improved with concomitant improvement in their balance-of-payments accounts.

5. The evident desire of the Dutch authorities to adhere to a system of fixed exchange rates, coupled with the goal of a stable price level, has consequences that bear on the functioning of the international price system. Literally interpreted, if all economies which engage in international trade were to achieve a stable index of domestically produced goods and services, there would be no possibility of changes in world prices. In this event the international economy would not be able to efficiently adjust to changes in taste and technology. Under such circumstances the pattern of international production, consumption, and investment could hardly be expected to conform to what an appropriate price system would bring about.

In fact the Dutch authorities have used prices as policy instruments, although neither as extensively or with as much flexibility as they have employed wage policy. By law the government has the power to establish maximum prices and to prescribe methods for calculating the highest permissible price of any individual item. It can require businesses to keep records that enable the government to discover how prices have been determined. Under the Price Raising and Hoarding Act of 1939 and the Economic Competition Act of 1961, the government has been given statutory powers to back up its price directives by fines on violators. The threat of legal penalties, however, generally has proven sufficient to insure at least a measure of cooperation, and the government has seldom used formal coercion to enforce price regulations.

Rather elaborate rules governing price increases have been established. The first of these is the "external cost rule," by which a firm is allowed to pass on increases in the cost of raw, basic, and auxiliary materials. Conversely, a reduction in the prices of such imports is supposed to lead to lower commodity prices. A second rule, relating to traders' margins, is called the "money margin rule." It states that when there is an increase in the cost of goods purchased by a trader, the absolute amount of the traders' margin may not be increased although the increased purchase price may itself be passed on. This rule means that price may not be recalculated so as to yield the same percentage margin as before; profit can be maintained only in terms of guilders per unit. The third rule is the "non-charging rule," by which wage increases must not, in principle, be passed on in price rises.

The actual rules followed in attempting to maintain price stability have varied, depending on the government's estimate of the extent of pressure on the price level, i.e. on the cyclical situation. During one period in which a policy of differential wages was favored, one of the conditions under which wage increases were granted was that they would not result in price increases but that wage increases would be justified solely by increased productivity. In some cases, prior to the approval of specific collective agreements, the employer was obliged to make a public declaration that he would maintain the existing level of prices during the length of the collective agreement. In other cases, again depending on the cyclical situation, price increases had only to be reported to the Ministry of Economic Affairs, although this sometimes led to consultation between the government and the enterprise over the anticipated price increase. If the authorities found objection to the announced price increase, the government had the power to intervene and, in effect, set the price to be charged. In recent years there have been orders fixing maximum prices or trade margins for a number of goods and services, including bread, some dairy products, house coals and bricks, potatoes, and items sold in hotels and restaurants.

One measure of success or failure of the government's price policy is its ability to resist the upward pressures on prices as a result of upward tendencies elsewhere, for instance, in connection with wages. Unfortunately, in the Netherlands the cost of living index rose an average of 3 points per year during 1950–65, and part of this increase can be laid to wage increases in excess of productivity gain. In industry, wage costs per employee rose by an average of 8 points per year. During the same period productivity rose by only an average of 5 points per year. Thus it is probable that per capita wage increase in excess of productivity gains have been a major cause underlying a rise in consumer prices, which averaged 3.7 points per year.[6]

6. Figures in this paragraph are from the Netherlands Central Planning Bureau, *Centraal Economisch Plan 1965* (The Hague, 1965), pp. 176–77. This Plan is published annually, and is hereafter cited as *Centraal Economisch Plan* if it is available only in Dutch and as Central Economic Plan if it is available in English translation.

This wage–price spiral has caused concern in official circles. For example, in 1963 the president of the Netherlands Bank stated in his annual report:

> Wage increases averaging 7 percent per annum, such as those now common in the Netherlands, . . . mean doubling the nominal income in ten years . . . [and] the effect would be to multiply incomes by twenty within one worker's active lifetime. Even if per capita productivity continued to rise at the same pace as during the last ten years . . . the price increases which would in the long run be inevitable would cause the cost of living to rise more than fivefold during the same period. . . . No society based on private entrepreneurs' initiative, and on a high degree of personal responsibility for safe-guarding the individual's future, can accept with impunity such a fall in the value of its currency.

The Bank report went on to say:

> Entrepreneural production finds its economic justification . . . in the fact that the enterprise has to bear the risk of profit or loss, this being the best available criterion for judging whether the service rendered is economically useful. . . . Where currency depreciation releases the enterprise (usually a debtor) from the risk of loss, and relieves it of debt, an essential precondition for the entrepreneural production system is destroyed. In such circumstances highly inefficient production can be established without detection or can be continued for too long, and the pursuit of speculative gains is promoted rather than the rendering of useful economic services.[7]

In 1964 the president of the Bank again warned:

> The danger of a continuation of the inflationary spiral . . . must not be underestimated. . . . In a strictly

7. Netherlands Bank, *1963*, p. 21.

> economic sense . . . the expectation that price inflation will continue affects more and more strongly the actions of the . . . business sector, especially in connection with investment in fixed assets, and influences the determination of prices for real assets. The increasing difference in yield as between monetary claims and real assets is evidence of this. The inflated assets in their turn form the basis for a part of the credit system. Thus there is danger of a position arising in which the stopping . . . of the spiral would remove the basis for numerous expectations of profit. . . . The final result . . . could be a credit crisis which might induce the deflationary spiral that is so rightly feared.[8]

While the dangers of a wage–price spiral are clearly pointed out in the quotations, the argument is often cited that stable prices may be an unreasonable goal in an open economy because international price increases cause the domestic price level to rise even if exchange rates are adjusted to attain external equilibrium in the balance-of-payments account. This holds, the argument goes, because a changing domestic price level is a function of per capita productivity changes in the marginal export industry. The marginal export industry is defined as the industry with the lowest per capita productivity engaging in international trade. Further this industry must sell abroad in order to maintain external equilibrium in the balance of payments. Then, it is maintained, if changes in the per capita productivity of this industry are larger than changes in the national average per capita productivity, some rise in the domestic price level is to be expected.

Pursuing the argument further, suppose that in the Netherlands during a period of full employment, labor productivity increases in the marginal export industry while international prices and exchange parities remain firm.

8. Ibid., *1964*, pp. 16–17.

Because of the full employment, labor in the marginal export industry is assumed to be able to exact their increased productivity in the form of wage increases. The economy as a whole is then faced with the initial impetus for a round of wage increases. Only if the productivity increase experienced by the marginal export industry is matched by the economy as a whole (i.e. by the increase in average per capita productivity) can all entrepreneurs taken together absorb the equivalent of an across-the-board wage increase without an increase in labor costs. However, even in this case, in those sectors where productivity gains lag the national average, entrepreneurs must raise prices or, at least in the short run, see their profit position narrowed. These industries, which presumably include a large proportion of services, cause the domestic price level to rise by passing on wage increases in the form of price increases. Thus, it is argued, some rise in prices is inevitable.

Related to this is the contention that the recent price and wage increases in the Netherlands were inevitable because there was a gap between Dutch wages and prices and those of other Western European countries that must sooner or later be closed. Given the fixed exchange ratio between the guilder and foreign currencies, Dutch wages and prices were indeed low in comparison with those of the Western European neighbors. The Netherlands Bank, however, does not agree that because of this gap Dutch prices must inevitably rise. The Bank argues that while goods in international trade tend toward a uniform price level, it is not necessary that national price and wage levels do the same, and that equilibrium can be obtained even though Dutch wages and prices measured in foreign currency values remain relatively lower than the wage and price levels in the country whose currency is used for the comparative evaluation.

In fact, according to the Bank, the only way to keep the accounts in balance, given a relatively constant money supply and fixed exchange parties, is to let labor productivity in the marginal export industry set the nominal wage rate. From this it follows that the lower the efficiency of the marginal export industry, the lower the nominal wage rate measured in terms of foreign currency. One might agree that while relative factor scarcities, coupled with a lack of international factor mobility, may in fact dictate lower labor resource costs in the Netherlands than abroad, one might also conclude that Dutch labor is sold at a discount in order to secure foreign exchange.

By way of explanation of its position, the Bank argues:

> The nominal wage level may be relatively high in countries where exports can remain limited to products of industries having high per capita productivity; and this will be more readily possible insofar as the exports are relatively small. In . . . the Netherlands exports of goods and services are relatively great, and must necessarily extend to include the products of industries in which no particular high per capita productivity can be expected. For this reason, on an international comparison with countries which are less dependent on exports but are otherwise in comparable circumstances, the nominal wage level in the Netherlands will always have to be on the low side. The same will apply to the price level.[9]

The relatively low wage and price levels that existed in the Netherlands, according to the Bank, did not necessarily indicate a state of disequilibrium in relation to foreign countries because, in a static context, a low price level simply reflects the fact that the level of domestic prices (and hence that of real income) is governed by average productivity and the overall level of nominal wages.

In a dynamic context, the Bank argues that the transmission of changes in per capita wages in the export sector

9. Ibid., *1962*, pp. 21–22.

throughout the rest of the economy tends to force prices up. In the words of the Bank,

> Insofar as changes in circumstances lead to a widening of the gap between per capita productivity on the average and that in the exporting industries (which will probably happen in every period of rapid technological progress), the necessary maintenance of international equilibrium requires that: (a) a constant domestic price-level, based *inter alia* on international limitation of the rise in wages to not more than that in average per capita productivity, shall be accompanied by falling export prices, and/or that (b) where the level of prices for exported goods remains the same, nothing can be done to prevent a rise from occurring in the internal price-level (as measured by the range of consumer expenditure, which includes many services), this rise being larger to the extent that the difference between the per capita productivity in the exporting industries and the lower average per capita productivity becomes greater. . . . This explains why it has proved impossible in the Netherlands to prevent the rapid advance in prosperity, which has actually been nothing else but a fast rise in per capita productivity [along with little or no decline in export prices], from being accompanied by a certain upward movement in the cost of living.[10]

The Bank's argument is admissible if one assumes that changes in marginal per capita productivity in the marginal export industry parallel changes in average per capita productivity in that industry. On the static side, however, a low nominal wage level is more the cause of a favorable exchange parity, from the point of view of export sales, than its effect. In fact, it is low nominal wage costs, when measured in terms of foreign currency, that allows the marginal export industry to sell resources at less than their

10. Ibid.

cost of production in the country doing the importing. In slightly different words, the low wage level measured in terms of foreign currency is a condition enabling the marginal export industry to remain competitive in the world market and earn foreign exchange in the face of a system of fixed exchange rates. In this regard the Bank's dynamic argument for wage and price increases in conjunction with changes in productivity in the marginal export industry is more convincing than its argument that average per capita productivity in the marginal export industry determines whether the domestic nominal wage level is high or low relative to foreign countries.

Although in the long run large price increases are clearly undesirable for the reasons pointed out by the Bank, in the short run some portion of the price increases that have taken place can be inferred to represent implicit policy choices on the part of the authorities. In effect, the authorities have at times chosen to prevent a decrease in the relative share of capital as a result of nominal wage increases in excess of productivity gains. Nevertheless, despite the relatively large price increases during the last five years, the share of labor has risen from 69.4 percent in 1961 to an estimated 75.0 percent in 1965.[11]

As mentioned earlier, the reduction in the share of capital has made investment funds relatively more difficult to obtain. Its direct impact has been to narrow the basis for self-financing. Another effect of the decrease has been to lower the savings ratio. In addition, a number of recent anticyclical measures (reduced investment allowances and in 1964, the suspension of accelerated depreciation allowances), presumably have decreased investment incentives. At the same time the disappearance of the balance-of-payments surplus has reduced the liquidity of the banking system and led to a tightening of the capital market. Thus borrowing in the capital market, the alternative to using

11. *Centraal Economisch Plan 1965*, p. 177.

internal sources for investment financing, has become more difficult.

The authorities have been faced with a dilemma: on the one hand they want to facilitate the more intensive use of capital so that in the longer run per capita productivity can be raised; on the other hand, their price control and other short-run anticyclical policies work at cross purposes with their long-run investment objectives.

FULL EMPLOYMENT AS AN OBJECT OF ECONOMIC POLICY

In the early postwar period, many people feared the emergence of structural unemployment in the Netherlands. Perhaps the main object of the government's industrialization policy was to provide employment for the already large population. Emigration was also promoted in order to relieve the population pressure. As unemployment statistics show, the objectives of the employment policy have been fulfilled. Perhaps this objective has been over-fulfilled inasmuch as the unemployment ratio has recently been below the 3 percent unofficially regarded as normal for frictional unemployment. In addition, foreign labor has been imported in an attempt to fill the large number of employers' applications for labor.

In an economic sense, the object of wage and employment policy should be to enhance the possibility that workers are distributed among sectors and enterprises so that the greatest possible national product is realized. Dutch wage and employment policy has not always satisfied this condition.

Four phases in the evolution of Dutch wage policy have been distinguished by Willem Hessel:[12] (1) controlled national wage rounds based on increases in the cost of living index; (2) controlled national wage rounds based on the

12. See Hessel, p. 176.

increase in national income; (3) controlled wage increases based on differential productivity increases; and (4) controlled wage increases based on a yearly target for the national average wage increase. Considering the situation of over-full employment that existed during most of the period covered by this study, each phase of the wage policy resulted in some loss of economic efficiency; that is, the results must be presumed to differ from those that would have been achieved as a result of a competitive labor market.

The first and second phases of wage policy supposedly represent a claim to "equal wages for equal work." The adoption of such a principle, however, resulted in wage increases that were often passed on wholly, or in part, in prices. The degree to which wage increases were passed on depended on the profit and demand situation of the particular enterprises and their markets. Across-the-board wage increases imposed the burden of higher wages on industries regardless of their ability to absorb them without price increases. Therefore, the across-the-board wage increases tended to be self-sustaining in that one such increase inevitably led to another.

The across-the-board wage increases ignored the possibility of shifting demand patterns, which require differential wages among industries in order that growing industries may attract additional labor. Such wage increases in the long run could also be expected to have caused some otherwise unjustified substitution of capital for labor in industries where shifts in the wage rate brought about by the wage policy and movements in the value of the marginal physical product of labor did not correspond. Additionally, from the standpoint of labor supply, one may expect that a policy which maintains a stable pattern of relative wages will not in the long run offer sufficient inducements to accommodate changes in labor skills necessitated by changing technology.

A final objection to the across-the-board wage policy is that it does not allow for the worker to share in the economic possibilities of the enterprises in which he worked. This latter objection was one of the main underlying causes behind the adoption of the differential productivity wage guidelines in 1958. From an economic standpoint, however, differential wages also created difficulties. One effect of the differential productivity guidelines was that wages remained relatively low in branches of activity where per capita productivity was rising less rapidly than elsewhere, but wages rose in enterprises with rapidly increasing productivity. Thus industries where technology improved were forced to pay higher wages for the same type of labor that received lower pay in industries where technology had not changed as much.

In addition, labor tended to move toward the industries paying higher wages (those with larger changes in productivity); however, this did not necessarily reflect the relative needs of different kinds of work. The latter are determined mostly by demand conditions, and it often happens that industries having a ready market for their product are not those with the larger productivity gains.

One might also note that even the simplest formulas used to calculate the productivity guidelines by which wage increases are to be justified are themselves inflationary whenever productivity is falling. This is because the formulas usually take into account average productivity changes over a number of years. For example, productivity calculated for use in the 1962 bargaining weighed the trend increase in productivity three times as heavily as the expected productivity gain in the year ahead.

Regardless of the economic objections to the differential wage policy, the main reason it was given up was that it proved too cumbersome. The necessary data for its implementation simply did not exist. In addition, there was pressure on the government to give a freer hand to business and labor in the matter of wage determination. These factors led to the adoption of the guidelines based on the so-called "available margin." Since 1963 these guidelines have been used to determine the average annual permissible national wage increase.[13]

Growth as an Object of Economic Policy

One measurement of growth is the increase in real national income. During the period covered by this study real national income more than doubled. The rate of increase between 1951 and 1960 averaged nearly 5 percent per year. Real national income per head, another measure of growth, based on a 1958 index, rose from 80 in 1950 to 132 in 1965.[14] As is well known, increases in real national income are keyed to increases in the stock of capital. Thus a high savings ratio is an important precondition for economic growth. In the Netherlands the savings ratio increased from something over 14 percent in 1951 to upward of 23 percent in 1960. During the next five years the savings ratio was maintained at an average rate of approximately 20 percent per year.

When compared with the expectations that prevailed when the *First Industrialization Memorandum* was published in 1949, the situation in 1963 was indeed remarkable. War damage had long since been repaired. The Dutch labor potential was more than adequately utilized, and Dutch products had found ready markets abroad.

In April 1963, the Minister of Economic Affairs published the *Eighth Industrialization Memorandum* in which he summarized the progress that had taken place prior to 1962 and forecast the future development of the Dutch economy through 1970. The Minister discussed the fact that industrial production more than doubled from 1948 to 1962 and that

13. A further examination of this policy is carried out in Chap. 4.

14. *Centraal Economisch Plan 1965*, pp. 176–77.

in 1962 capital expenditure by volume was about twice the 1948 level. He pointed out the rise in real national income and the rise in per capita income that had accompanied these increases. During the same period the volume of exports rose by a factor of five. While national income per capita increased by approximately 60 percent, consumption rose by only one third, a fact that accounts for the increase in the savings ratio.[15]

The Minister called attention to the fact that if growth was to continue, the possibilities for short-run real wage increases would be limited. He reviewed the two ways by which increases in real wages could be brought about: (1) by raising labor productivity, and (2) by shifting the relative share of the available income toward labor.[16] If, as some maintain, the latter was not acceptable because of its effect on the savings ratio and capital investment, then the annual increase in real income became a direct function of the estimated rise in productivity per worker. As computed by the Central Planning Bureau and published in the *Eighth Industrialization Memorandum*, productivity was forecast to increase by about 2.8 percent per year. Hence his con-conclusions regarding the possibilities for increases in real wages.

In view of the then current situation of over-full employment, investment was shifting toward capital-deepening with the goal of raising labor productivity. The Minister of Economic Affairs indicated that the authorities expect that Dutch industry will experience increasing international competition in the future, notably as a consequence of the growing

15. The above statistics are taken from the *Eighth Industrialization Memorandum* as cited in the *Economic Quarterly Review*, No. 141 (Sept. 1963), p. 16. Through No. 147, March 1965, the *Economic Quarterly Review* was published by the Amsterdam Bank N.V. In 1965 the Amsterdam Bank merged with the Rotterdam Bank and a new series was begun by the Amsterdam-Rotterdam Bank N.V. under the same title, No. 1 being the June 1965 issue.

16. This disregards windfall gains due to favorable shifts in the terms of trade and other nonrecurrent increases in the stock of available resources.

Common Market. In addition, he pointed out that it can be expected that the shortening of working hours will continue in the years ahead. Clearly then, even higher levels of investment in industrial capital equipment will be necessary in the future. In his view, by 1970 industrial capital expenditure must double its level in 1960. However, unless the savings ratio increases, capital investment will be restricted with a consequent slackening of growth.

Even if the relatively optimistic assumptions of this report concerning productivity increases are borne out in fact, the growth rate in national product is expected to slacken somewhat with the growth of real national income leveling off at about 4 percent per year, as contrasted to the 8 and 9 percent increases experienced in the early 1950s and again during the early 1960s.

In summary, the economic advance that took place during the years since World War II was conditioned in large measure by the economic policies of the government. The objectives of government economic policy have been described in this chapter mainly in terms of their economic implications. In the next chapter the discussion turns to political issues, and in particular to the political structure within which Dutch economic policy is formulated.

CHAPTER 3

The Political Process

Particular political conditions have brought the technical economic planning process to a position of unusual influence in Dutch economic policy-making. This is not to say that the technical process has taken over the political decision-making process, but the reliance on quantitative economic analysis as a guide to political decisions has reached significant proportions in the Netherlands.

There are several reasons for this situation. One reason is derived from the central importance of international trade to the economy of the Netherlands, a condition that forces all parties to recognize that the economic house must be kept in order for the country to survive as an industrialized nation. Thus in the Netherlands there appears to be a willingness to view economic issues from all sides and in light of the best information available.

The second reason the technical process is accorded a position of major influence is the lack of a political consensus that might resolve economic issues through the electoral process. Dutch party politics in large measure follow religious rather than economic dictates. Since there is no majority religion in the Netherlands, there is no majority party. The parliament as a body is therefore relatively weak. As a result, the government often turns to extra-parliamentary bodies for advice in the economic field. There are four main extra-parliamentary bodies involved including two non-governmental advisory councils, the Foundation of Labor and the Social and Economic Council, and two government bureaus, the Central Bureau of Statistics and the Central Planning Bureau. Over the years the importance of these groups has grown, while the economic power of parliament has declined. In addition, because these bodies are either non-political or quasi-political, economic issues have become more and more separated from the area of party politics and have been brought closer into the realm of quantitative economic analysis.

The way seems to have been opened for quantitative analysis not because the various political parties were able to agree on last principles, but rather because they were not able to agree. It was the endless negotiation that took place within what has been, until recently, a well described and understood code of conduct that opened the door, in fact even helped to create the demand, for analysis such as that provided by the Central Planning Bureau. Some have claimed that the Dutch haggle endlessly over substance but keep the system going via sacrosanct ways of procedure. This is in part true, and the nongovernmental organizations outlined in the latter part of this chapter, and the technical bureaus described in Chapter 5, are both vital links in this procedure and adjuncts to it. The first portion of this chapter attempts to explain why such a political system has developed; the second portion describes the institutions involved in the process.[1]

THE GOVERNMENT OF THE NETHERLANDS

A number of institutional aspects of the Dutch political process have a direct effect on the formulation and execution of economic policy. This is particularly true of the power of parliament to influence government policy. From a technical standpoint, the Netherlands is a constitutional monarchy, hereditary within the House of Orange-Nassau. There is a parliament and a cabinet. Cabinet ministers, however, are not members of parliament. The monarch is advised by a Council of State, of which he is the chairman, and by the

1. See Chapters 4 and 6 for a discussion of pressures on governmental wage policy that threaten to substantively alter the Dutch system for determining and effecting economic policy.

presidents of the two chambers of parliament. However, the responsibility for the conduct of the government, as well as the actual workings of the government, are completely in the hands of the ministers of the cabinet.

For many years no party has obtained a majority of the seats in parliament; thus coalition government has been a necessity. The chairman of the cabinet, or Council of Ministers, as it is called, in which one or more representatives of each of the political parties making up the coalition serve, has the title of Minister President or Prime Minister. Although the Prime Minister and the members of the cabinet cannot be members of the States-General, they may, and usually do, participate in its deliberations.

The parliament, known as the States-General, exercises legislative power. Of the two houses, the first in order of importance is the lower house or, as it is called, the Second Chamber, with 150 members elected by popular vote.The upper or First Chamber has 75 members elected by the Provincial Councils.[2] Regular elections for the Second Chamber are held every four years. In practice the political composition of the two chambers is approximately the same.

Specific rules govern the relationship between the cabinet and parliament. These have an important bearing on the government's ability to carry out its legislative program. When the cabinet and the States-General are at odds over a legislative measure and a no-confidence vote is impending, the cabinet may do one of three things. First, the cabinet may resign, in which case the Crown appoints an *informateur* whose duty it is to describe to the Crown the political situation in detail; the Crown then appoints a *formateur* who tries to form a new government. However, as explained in detail later, the formation of a new government is often

2. The members of the First Chamber of the States-General are elected by the Provincial Councils for terms of six years. Under normal circumstances, half of the members resign every three years. However, if the States-General is dissolved, all 75 members resign at once and new elections are held.

an extremely difficult task in the Netherlands. As a second alternative, the cabinet may dissolve parliament, forcing new elections. For a number of reasons, which will also be discussed shortly, in actual practice this alternative is seldom used. Between 1848, the first year of constitutional government, and 1965, there had been less than ten dissolutions of the States-General over legislative crises.

The third option is for the government simply to avoid legislative issues likely to result in votes of no confidence by withdrawing the proposed legislation from consideration by the parliament. This has an important and direct influence on the government's ability to carry out its legislative program. In effect, the government postpones the issue and waits for a more opportune time. This strategy is often used in cases when the States-General has added to, or amended a government bill to the extent that the responsible minister considers the changes "unacceptable." This procedure cannot be used to thwart a determined legislature since the States-General may initiate legislation. In practice, however, the States-General does not generally resort to this measure unless the issue is considered to be extremely important.[3] Therefore, when the government wants temporarily to delay action on a bill and to wait for a more opportune moment, it is usually successful.

PUBLIC ATTITUDES AND POLITICAL PARTIES

One reason that parliament is not anxious to force the government to resign or to dissolve parliament is because political activities and political parties reflect public attitudes that identify politics with religion rather than political issues. Religious influence is a fundamental characteristic of a rigid social pattern in the Netherlands. Although for

3. It might also be the case that the obligation for ministers to resign seats in parliament before accepting a ministerial portfolio acts as a curb on the ambitions of members for ministerial rank and thus on the initiating of no-confidence legislation.

many centuries the country has been noted for religious tolerance, many aspects of social life continue to be colored by religious loyalties. Membership in political parties as well as membership in labor unions and employers' associations, and even the programming of state-owned radio and television stations, is based on religious conviction. According to expressed affiliation, the population of the Netherlands is roughly 40 percent Catholic, 37 percent Protestant, with 23 percent giving no preference.[4]

Although there are a number of small parties, it can be said in general that the political party system has five main divisions that for the most part follow religious lines. There is a Roman Catholic party called the Catholic Peoples Party, and the two main Protestant parties are the Christian Historical Union supported by the Orthodox Calvinist members of the Dutch Reformed Church, and the Anti-Revolutionary Party supported by the majority of the remaining Protestants. The Labor Party and the Liberal Party round out the fivefold division and represent the secular concept of political loyalty. With regard to economic viewpoints, the Protestant and Liberal parties represent the right wing, Labor the left, with the Catholic party occupying the middle-of-the-road position.

The Catholic Peoples Party is generally the largest bloc in the Second Chamber. The Labor Party, the second largest bloc, represents a postwar amalgamation of the nonsectarian political parties that existed prior to World War II. When the Labor Party was formed, in addition to absorbing most of the older nonsectarian parties, it explicitly opened its ranks to both Catholics and Protestants in an attempt to break through the rigid political lines that divide the confessional and nonconfessional parties.[5] In this attempt it

4. C. A. Ravenswaaij, "The Changing Face of Dutch Politics," *The Scholars Magazine* (The Hague, Netherlands Institute of Social Studies, July 1963), p. 16.

5. Confessional, meaning religious, is a term commonly used in the Netherlands.

has been partially successful. The Labor Party usually polls about 30 percent of the national vote. From 1945 until 1958 the Catholic Peoples Party and the Labor Party, at times joined by several smaller parties, made up the coalition government of the Netherlands.

The composition of the Second Chamber of the States-General following the elections of 1956, 1959, and 1963 is shown in Table 7. In 1959 the Liberal Party gained six seats, an extremely rare occurence in Dutch politics. For reasons discussed later, elections usually do not produce changes of this order of magnitude. However, the Liberal trend was reversed in 1963 when the party lost three of the seats gained in 1959. In 1963 a splinter group of farmers, a Dutch version of Poujadism, succeeded in obtaining three seats in the Second Chamber, although they had never previously elected any members to parliament.

TABLE 7. Composition of the Second Chamber of the States-General

	1956		1959		1963	
Party	Number	%	Number	%	Number	%
Catholic	49	33	49	33	50	33
Labor	50	34	48	32	43	29
Anti-revolutionary	15	10	14	9	13	9
Christian Historical	13	9	12	8	13	9
Liberal	13	9	19	13	16	10
Communist	7	4	3	2	4	3
Other	3	2	5	3	11	7
TOTAL	150	100	150	100	150	100

Sources: For 1956 and 1959, Netherlands Central Bureau of Statistics, *Jaarcijfers voor Nederland 1959–1960* (Statistical Yearbook of the Netherlands); for 1963, *Het Patrool* (Amsterdam), May 16, 1963, Extra Editie, p. 1. Totals may not add because of rounding.

The Influence of Religion on Voting Patterns

About half of the voters faithfully cast their ballot for the party that represents their religious affiliation. For such persons the raison d'être of membership in a political party is religious rather than political conviction, and for this reason Dutch political parties have been called "parties of affection."[6] In Tables 8 and 9 there is a comparison of the voting pattern over the last six elections to the 1947 and 1960 census figures for religious affiliation. Table 8 shows votes cast for parties classified as Catholic, Protestant, neutral, or radical. The radical parties are those whose platforms place them either to the far left or far right. Table 9 shows religious affiliation according to the 1947 and 1960 census.

TABLE 8. Comparison of Religious and Nonreligious Vote, 1946–63 (in percentages of total number of votes)

	1946	1948	1952	1956	1959	1963
Religious Parties						
Catholic	30.8	31.0	31.4	31.7	31.6	31.9
Protestant	22.8	24.8	23.3	21.2	20.4	20.3
Total Religious	53.6	55.8	54.7	52.9	52.0	52.2
Non-Religious Parties						
Neutral	34.7	33.6	37.8	41.5	42.5	38.5
Radical	10.6	7.7	6.2	4.8	4.9	7.9
Total Nonreligious	45.3	41.3	44.0	46.3	47.4	46.4
TOTAL[a]	98.9	97.1	98.7	99.2	99.4	98.6

a. Votes cast for parties that did not elect at least one representative are not counted.

Source: C. A. Ravenswaaij, "The Changing Face of Dutch Politics," *The Scholars Magazine* (July 1963), p. 16.

TABLE 9. Religious Affiliation According to the 1947 and 1960 Census (in percentages)

	1947 Census	1960 Census
Catholic	38.5	40.0
Protestant	40.8	37.3
Total Religious	79.3	77.3

Source: Ibid.

6. Hans Daalder, "Parties and Politics in the Netherlands," mimeo. (The Hague, Netherlands Institute of Social Studies, 1960), p. 3.

The tables clearly show that the Catholic Party has been the most successful in maintaining its voting strength in line with its potential denominational strength. The Catholic Peoples Party polls over three quarters of its potential vote. On the other hand, the Protestant parties succeed in obtaining only about one half of their potential strength. In light of the strong religious feeling that exists in the Netherlands, it is safe to conclude that the amount of interreligious voting is negligible and that the "lost votes" from both religious parties are cast for the nondenominational parties.

In order to accommodate the economic and social viewpoints that exist among the nonmonolithic Catholic population of the Netherlands, and thus insure group solidarity at the polls, the Catholic Peoples Party tends to adopt a middle-of-the-road position, or slightly to the left of center, with regard to most issues. On the other hand, the six Protestant parties represent the conservative wing of Dutch politics. Of the two main Protestant parties, the Anti-Revolutionary Party is somewhat to the right of the Christian Historical Union. In the secular segment of Dutch politics the Liberal Party is solidly conservative while the Labor Party is, as might be expected, the left-wing socialist party. The radical fringe of Dutch politics consists of the Communist Party and the Pacifist-Socialists on the left and the Farmers' Party on the right.

Although to some extent all political parties find support in all occupational groups, the Liberal Party, which supports a program of individualism coupled with a minimum of government economic activity, naturally finds relatively greater support among self-employed and managers than do the other parties. The Labor Party, on the other hand, finds relatively greater support among manual workers than other parties, with the exception of the Communist Party. Although the Dutch Labor Party is affiliated with the Socialist International, it does not favor the nationalization of all industry. As the middle-of-the-road party, the Catholic Party attempts to appeal to a broad range of voters. With regard to economic matters, it is, if anything, somewhat to the left of center; the party favors the welfare state concept and economic planning as the latter is interpreted in the Netherlands.

Within the Catholic Party there is a large labor element representing the Catholic labor organizations. In fact, there are as many members of the Second Chamber from the Catholic Party who could be said to be labor oriented from their background as there are members with like backgrounds from the Labor Party. In the heavily urbanized and industrial areas of south and central Holland, the Protestant parties, by virtue of their conservative approach to most social and economic issues, have not been able to attract votes in proportion to their potential strength. Conversely, it is there that the Labor Party finds its greatest source of support.[7]

VOTING PROCEDURES

The national election law of the Netherlands has an important bearing on the attitudes of the parliament toward specific social and economic policy measures. Because Dutch election law is written in terms of political parties rather than individuals, it perpetuates party control and adherence to party principles. As is the case elsewhere, when a voter casts his ballot, it is for a particular candidate whose name appears on the ballot. In the Netherlands, however, each vote is counted first as a vote for the party and only second for the individual for whom the vote was actually cast; thus individuals have little prospect of political success unless they conform to party doctrine.

7. For a more extensive discussion of differences among the various political parties in the Netherlands in terms of their programs and the viewpoints of their supporters, see A. Hoogerwerf, "Latent Socio-political Issues in the Netherlands," *Sociologia Needandica, 2* (Summer 1965), pp. 161–77.

Seats in the Second Chamber are awarded to the party in proportion to the percentage of the vote each party receives, rather than directly to the individual candidates. The selection of those candidates who will occupy the seats obtained by the party is a matter decided internally within the party and is not necessarily determined on the basis of the number of votes received by the individuals.

Seats in the Second Chamber of the States-General are apportioned on the basis of what is called an electoral denominator. In national elections the country is regarded as a single constituency in order to obtain this denominator. The denominator is calculated by dividing the total number of votes cast in the election by 150—the number of seats in the Second Chamber. Thus one seat is awarded for each $\frac{1}{150}$ of the national vote. In 1963, although a total of 16 parties entered the election, only 10 obtained enough votes (approximately 42,000) to qualify for at least one seat in the Second Chamber. A small Protestant splinter party just exceeded the electoral denominator and received one seat, while the Catholic Peoples Party obtained fifty times the electoral denominator and thereby was awarded 50 seats.[8]

For the election proper, the country is divided into 18 electoral districts. Lists of candidates are drawn up for each district and each political party may present a list of as many as 30 candidates in each district. Parties place candidates on the lists in relation to the relative desirability of placing the candidates in parliament. Some individuals appear on more than one list, depending on the parties' assessment of the candidate's voter appeal. In one recent election, each of the

8. Before election day, every voter in the Netherlands receives a personal summons to appear at a certain polling station between the hours of 8 a.m. and 7 p.m. on election day. If he does not appear, he may be fined an amount not exceeding five guilders (approximately $1.50). Voting is not compulsory in the Netherlands, but attendance at the polling place is. Thus, although a voter is obliged to appear at the polls, he is not obliged to vote and may deposit a blank ballot in the ballot box. However, about 90 percent of the eligible voters actually mark a ballot.

major parties placed the same people in the first 10 places on each of the 18 lists.

A voter expresses his or her preference by marking *one* name only on the district list of the party of his or her choice. However, as pointed out above, this vote is not registered directly for the candidate for whom it was cast. The vote goes instead to the party, and the party generally credits all votes on a particular list to the first candidate on the list. This candidate becomes the party's choice for a seat in parliament if the list as a whole receives the vote equivalent of one electoral denominator. If the list receives more votes than one electoral denominator, the surplus votes are passed on to the second candidate. If those votes equal a second electoral denominator, the second candidate is elected. If there are still extra votes, they are passed on down the list from one candidate to the next until the remainder is less than the number required to qualify for a seat.

In addition to the party vote, preference ballots are also recorded. Even though a candidate might appear far down the list, generally a candidate who contributes the equivalent of an electoral denominator to the common cause is given a seat. Therefore the rigid ordering of candidates who receive seats in parliament as a result of an election is sometimes broken, although this seldom happens because most voters simply cast their ballots for the first name to appear on the list. In Holland it is considered to show a lack of faith in the party leadership, who arranged the order of the candidates, to do other than vote for the first listed candidate. Thus it is important to the candidate who expects to be elected to be placed first on a list by the party.

The national election board must reconcile the fractional parts of electoral denominators which often exist when the total votes cast for a particular district party list are tallied and divided by the national electoral denominator. The board resorts to a sort of lottery system to determine which list shall acquire the fractional votes of other lists and thus qualify for a seat. A party that does not poll at least 75 percent of an electoral denominator forfeits a bond posted with the government. The sum varies according to the number of districts for which the party submitted candidates.

The result of the Dutch electoral system, reinforced by the common voter habit of simply marking the first name to appear on his party's list is that the major political parties are able to ensure the election of some candidates regardless of their appeal to the voters as individuals. This has both advantages and disadvantages. On the one hand this system tends to make elections basically contests between the major parties rather than between individual candidates. On the other hand the electoral system can be used to elect certain types of specialists to parliament. In 1963, for example, 14 members of the Second Chamber had degrees in economics.

The need for specialists appears to be a logical consequence of the increasing complexity and number of the problems discussed in parliament. Specialists are elected by placing individuals with the desired qualifications in high positions on relatively "safe" lists. While the party itself and the leaders of each list must have as wide a voter appeal as possible, the places behind them can for a substantial part be filled for reasons other than political attractiveness.

This development has had a number of significant consequences. In the first place, some very able people have been members of parliament, and they might not have become candidates under the usual system of crediting each candidate with only the votes he receives in his own right. This is because a great number of them, as a result of their specialization, could not expect to appeal to a broad enough spectrum of the electorate to be elected under such a system.

Once elected to parliament, however, the specialist is often prone to forget party interest and unite with specialists from other parties in promoting the interests of sectors in which he is particularly competent. For example, financial relations between the state and local governments are mostly debated by burgomasters and aldermen, education by teachers, and subsidies to agriculture by farmers and agricultural engineers.

Speeches and debates reflect the technical backgrounds of the debaters, with the result that other members of parliament have come increasingly to rely on the lead of the specialist who acts as the spokesman for the party. They, in turn, expect to receive his support when matters in which they have a particular competence are being debated and voted upon. An apparent result is that it is relatively easy for the general point of view to be lost among the interests of the specialists and, as a consequence, special interests receive perhaps more attention than their cases merit.

COALITION GOVERNMENT

Since before World War I, no single political party has obtained a majority of seats in the Second Chamber. As a result, coalition government has become a necessity. It may be said that it is now an accepted mode of political life. The formation of a coalition, however, has always been an extremely difficult task. Since 1945 the total number of days of cabinet crisis in the Netherlands is second only to the French record. After the elections of 1956, it took 122 days to form a new government; in 1959, 90 days; in 1963, 70 days, and in 1965, 45 days. According to a recent Dutch joke, "In Holland, elections are held in order to make the formation of a government impossible."

Despite the problems of coalition, governments are relatively stable once they have taken office. Several reasons for this longevity have an important bearing on the functioning of the Dutch parliamentary system. One reason is that once a government has been formed, it represents the result of lengthy negotiations. During the negotiations, the platform of the government has usually been broadened to such an extent that it can survive a great deal of intra-coalition tension before a complete breakdown occurs.

Another reason for stability is that the States-General is reluctant to turn out a cabinet. Taking account of the consistent voting pattern that exists in the Netherlands, the parliament realizes that new elections are not likely to produce significant changes in the composition of the Second Chamber and thus in the alternatives for cabinet formation. In the Netherlands parliamentary issues—those matters on which the parliament may be tempted to bring down a cabinet—are very different from election issues. For example, the States-General may disagree with the government's conduct of foreign affairs, but this issue would have little if any effect on the outcome of a general election, should one be called.

Commenting on election issues, Daalder says, "Election planks have less to do with politics than with eternal verities."[9] Elections become great debates between the religious and the nonreligious parties. The religious parties accuse the Labor and Liberal Parties of being antireligious, while the nondenominational parties accuse the others of confusing political issues by introducing irrelevant religious considerations.

As mentioned earlier, a large proportion of the vote is based on the confessional–secular division between those who believe in a close tie between religion and politics and those who do not. Because this division is a cultural pattern that changes only slowly over time, the leaders of all parties know there is little hope that forcing a new election will result in much change as far as the composition of the States-General is concerned. Inasmuch as party representation in parliament influences the formation of the government, the composition of the cabinet is usually not materially affected by the result of elections.

9. Daalder, p. 6.

Past experience has shown that when a new coalition is formed, the new cabinet tends to look like the old one as far as the individuals who make up the cabinet are concerned. Even after the record negotiations of 1956, the membership of the new cabinet was almost identical to the outgoing one. Between 1918 and 1940, there were eight cabinets, but only three different prime ministers. More recently, from 1946 to 1959, there were five cabinets, but only two prime ministers, each of whom, when not prime minister, served in some position in the coalition cabinet of the other.

One reason for the similarity of old and new governments is that the nonconfessional parties do not command sufficient parliamentary support and therefore have never been able to unite to form a government. On the other hand, even when confessional coalitions are formed, they seldom have unanimous participation by all religious parties. This is only partly caused by differences in political thinking. The main stumbling block is a bitterness of religious feelings that exists, even in the Netherlands, among some Protestants and Roman Catholics.

The practical result of all this is that the Catholic Party, because it is the largest party, is in a commanding position when it comes to forming a government. As mentioned earlier, from 1946 to 1948, the Netherlands was governed by a straight Catholic-Labor coalition. In 1948, the Christian Historical Union and the Liberal Party joined the coalition. In 1952 a new government was formed, composed of the Catholic Party, the Labor Party, and the two main Protestant parties. Partially as a result of the Liberal Party's gains in the 1959 election, it replaced the Labor Party in the government. These same parties comprised the government formed as a result of the 1963 elections. In 1965, the Labor Party, after six years in opposition, returned to the government replacing the Liberal Party. Thus, in practice, there is a high degree of continuity in government and government policy, even though on the surface it might appear that the system would tend toward instability because of the frequent elections and large number of political parties.

POLICY FORMULATION

The Dutch political patterns combine to limit the power of parliament to effect any alternatives in government policy. Parliamentary reluctance to bring a government down has been an important factor in the formulation of government positions because it has made the cabinet significantly independent of the parliament.

This cabinet independence has fostered the development of extra-parliamentary procedures for dealing with proposed legislation, particularly in the fields of economic and social policy. Prior to parliamentary debates, consultation takes place between the government and the representatives of various interest groups likely to be affected by the matters with which a policy is concerned. Direct discussions are held between ministers or civil servants and the leaders of these groups, or meetings of statutory (or sometimes ad hoc) bodies are set up specifically for this purpose.

As a result, the control of social and economic policy has passed more and more from parliament as a political body to the government and leaders of the influence or pressure groups. In some cases the leaders of the interest groups have also been elected to parliament; this is particularly true in the case of representatives from the Labor Party. Nevertheless, parliamentary debates very seldom change anything. In practice, once legislation is introduced, the government is hesitant to accept parliamentary changes in its proposal for fear they might upset the results of the often long and arduous bargaining that has taken place in the extra-governmental bodies. Thus parliamentary discussions of most important measures in the social and economic fields tend to become either a formality or a sort of second round where the factions that are perhaps not fully satisfied with the results of the behind-the-scenes negotiations get a chance to air the issues in public. If the government insists on the legislation, it is almost certain to obtain it. For the reasons previously outlined, the alternatives of a cabinet crisis is very unlikely.

ADVISORY ORGANIZATIONS: EMPLOYERS ASSOCIATIONS AND LABOR UNIONS

The main extra-parliamentary bodies that advise the government on matters of social and economic policy are the Foundation of Labor and the Social and Economic Council. While both groups have considerable political significance and both are focal points for discussion of current issues of social and economic policy, their origins are different. The Foundation of Labor is a private group, the product of voluntary cooperation between employees and employers, while the Social and Economic Council is a public body that owes its existence to the statutory requirement of the Industrial Organization Act of 1950. Their membership is also different although in some cases the same individuals sit in both bodies. The Foundation of Labor is a bipartite group composed of representatives from labor and management, while the Social and Economic Council is tripartite, with members from labor, management, and Crown appointees from the general public. Before discussing these groups in more detail, it is instructive to take a brief look at the national federations (unions) of employers and employees, whose leaders generally sit as members of the Foundation of Labor and of the Social and Economic Council.

Economic life in the Netherlands is highly organized, not only in manufacturing, but also in wholesale trade, transport, banking, agriculture, and the small, self-employed tradesmen and professionals. In the Netherlands each of these sectors is divided not only according to the distinction between labor and management but also, as mentioned earlier, according to religious belief. In many industrial plants there are three unions, one Roman Catholic, one Protestant, and one nonsectarian. At the industry level there are also separate Catholic, Protestant, and nonsectarian employers' associations. Each local organization belongs in turn to a Catholic, a Protestant, or a neutral central federation of employers or employees association. Finally, at the top there is a Central Council of Trade Unions and a Central Council of Employers' Organizations which combines the denominational and nondenominational organizations.

Although membership in a union is not compulsory, about half of the working population belongs to one or the other of the major trade unions. The largest is the nondenominational Netherlands Federation of Trade Unions with about 509,000 members. The next largest is the Netherlands Catholic Workers Movement, with 414,000 members. These two are followed by the Protestant trade union, the National Christian Federation of Trade Unions, with 224,000 members.[10]

Employers' organizations have existed in the Netherlands since about the middle of the nineteenth century. In the industrial sector 85 to 90 percent of the employers belong to one or the other of the federations; in agriculture, 70 percent; and among the self-employed, 30 to 40 percent.[11] Thus on both the labor and management sides, when leaders of the central federations of employers and employees associations express their views on social and economic issues, they can claim to speak for the majority of workers and employers.

THE FOUNDATION OF LABOR[12]

The Foundation of Labor was organized immediately after the Second World War. The history of the Foundation

10. Netherlands Government Information Service, *Digest of the Kingdom*

starts, however, with the German occupation, at which time all labor unions and employer organizations were disbanded by the occupational authorities. Most of the leaders of the unions and employer associations joined the underground resistance movement. There, cooperation against the common enemy brought about close personal relations between the former labor and management leaders. The Foundation represented an attempt to carry this cooperation over into the postwar years so that reconstruction could be carried out as rapidly as possible.

During the occupation secret meetings were held among a number of people who, before the war, had responsible positions in politics as well as in industry and the trade unions. As a result of these meetings, a plan was formulated for the organization of a Foundation of Labor as a voluntary private association of the three main employers' and the three main employees' federations. The form of a foundation was chosen because in Dutch law it is the simplest method of obtaining legal status.

Within a few days of the liberation the leaders of the six main prewar central organizations of employers and employees published a proclamation that had been secretly printed and held in readiness. This document set forth the means by which the newly formed federation would attempt to maintain industrial peace and discipline and raise the living standard of the Dutch population. It stated that:

> The Foundation will endeavour to realize its aims by:
>
> a. promoting measures tending to raise the social and cultural level of Netherlands workers;

---

of the Netherlands, Social Aspects (The Hague, 1962), pp. 50–51.

11. Ibid., p. 47.

12. See P. Brands, "The Netherlands Labor Foundation" (The Hague, Netherlands Labor Foundation, 1955).

b. promoting permanent consultation between employers and workers and between their organizations in the interest of industrial peace;

c. offering counsel and advice to employers and workers within the framework of their organizations, and also to Government bodies;

d. promoting the adoption of regulations of importance . . . including: regulations on wages and other labour conditions; on settling labour disputes; on engaging and discharging personnel; on longer working hours and remuneration for overtime; on shorter working hours and part time; on holidays for workers; . . . workers' pensions, accident insurance, . . . [and] unemployment insurance;

e. making these and other regulations binding upon employers and workers whose organizations have joined the Foundation of Labour.[13]

The controlling body of the Foundation of Labor is a board of directors, consisting of 20 members representing the Central Council of Employers' Organizations and the Central Council of Trade Unions, the interdenominational central organizations of management and labor. Votes are allocated on the basis of parity between the employers' organizations and the trade unions, although there are now a greater number of employers' organizations represented than trade unions.

It became the practice of the government to consult with the Foundation of Labor before making a decision of general importance with regard to issues affecting the determination of wages and working conditions. The Foundation set up a

13. The above translation of article 4 of the statutes of the Foundation of Labor was taken from a mimeographed copy of a speech of Dr. D. V. Strikker, the first chairman of the Foundation of Labor. Dr. Strikker was, prior to the war, the Managing Director of Heinekins Brewery. He was later ambassador to the United Kingdom and Director General of NATO.

number of permanent committees to handle matters referred to it by the government, the most important being the Committee on Wages. There are also committees for social insurance, public health, health insurance, and technical training.

It is indicative of the decreasing importance of parliament that although the Foundation of Labor is a private organization, it has been recognized by the government as an official advisor in all matters of industrial policy. Until 1950 it was the principal government advisor in this area. However, in that year, the Social and Economic Council was instituted as part of what was originally envisioned as a complete corporative organization of Dutch industry.

THE SOCIAL AND ECONOMIC COUNCIL

The legal status of the Social and Economic Council is completely different from that of the Foundation of Labor. While the latter is a private body, the former owes its existence to the requirements of the Industrial Organization Act of 1950, which deals with labor-management relations. The intention of the law was to establish a comprehensive statutory organizational framework at all levels and in all branches of industry. The Social and Economic Council was intended to be the apex of this pyramid. In practice, very few industries or enterprises have organized under the provisions of this law. Most have retained their old collective bargaining arrangements.

As a result of the lack of industrial support for the intention of the 1950 Act, the function of the Social and Economic Council has shifted emphasis and scope from that initially contemplated by proponents of the law. It never became the top executive body of the industrial organization scheme; however, for many years the Council replaced the Foundation of Labor as the most influential official advisory board of the government in matters of social and economic policy.

In general, the Social and Economic Council responds to government requests for advice on specific matters although, in addition, the Council has a broad mandate to investigate and advise the government on any social and economic issues that members of the Council feel should be brought to the government's attention.

The Social and Economic Council consists of 45 members, one third appointed by the employers' associations, one third by the trade unions, and one third by the government. While in general the most influential union leaders belong, this is not the case on the employer's side; usually some company officials other than the presidents belong to the Social and Economic Council. The Crown appointees are not considered to be representatives of the government; rather, they are independent experts, most of them being professors of law or economics. Government representatives, such as cabinet ministers or their delegates, may attend the meetings of the Social and Economic Council, but they have no vote and serve only as a liaison between the government and the Council.

In theory, Council members are supposed to be independent of the appointing organizations in the sense that they are instructed to vote as individuals rather than as delegates of the organizations they represent. Although the members are not bound by law to the viewpoint of their parent organizations, it is safe to say that in most matters their views faithfully reflect the views of the groups from which they come.

The Council has established a number of committees to deal with recurring matters. At the committee level, nonmembers of the Council are often invited to assist in developing position papers for consideration by the full Council. In addition, the Central Planning Bureau, a government agency, acts as a staff research group for the committees and for the Social and Economic Council as a whole. There have been several instances in which the government consulted directly with the committees rather than going to the Council.

THE INDUSTRIAL ORGANIZATION ACT

The reasons behind the passage of the 1950 Industrial Organization Act illustrate the philosophical tenets of the various political parties in the economic and social sphere.[14] As mentioned previously, the Act provides the framework for a limited reorganization of industry, stressing the formation of employers' and workers' organizations that are to regulate various aspects of production and distribution. The law offers a means for cooperative self-regulation as a venture between management, labor, and government, with the government's role limited to that of veto power over the actions of the various boards.

In addition to the Social and Economic Council, the law made provisions for vertical organizations (or commodity boards) and horizontal organizations (or industrial boards), on each of which employers and employees are represented. The industrial boards are instituted for enterprises performing similar or related economic functions (i.e. branches of industry), without regard to the actual end product. The commodity boards, on the other hand, are to cover the production and distribution of specific commodities and, consequently, can be extended over several branches of industry.

Although the Act did not directly institute any of these boards, it set forth the conditions under which they might be organized. It left to the Social and Economic Council the task of determining how, when, and where such boards would be implemented.

14. For a detailed analysis of the Industrial Organization Act, see B. M. Teldersstichting, *The Public Industrial Organization in the Netherlands* (The Hague, Martinus Nijhoff, 1957). Copies of the Act are available from the Public Relations Office of the Ministry of Economic Affairs, The Hague.

However, the initiative for creating the boards was expected to come from the industries concerned; the establishment of the boards and the definition of their powers were to be accomplished by separate acts or royal decrees. It was intended that the boards, once constituted, should have broad powers to regulate many aspects of production, competition, labor conditions, and training requirements. The law sets forth a list of items the boards could attempt to regulate, such as: the production, sale, and use of goods; the rendering of services; competition; wages and other working conditions; employment services, vocational training, the provision of new employment, and the prevention of unemployment.

The act or decree that establishes a particular board sets forth the areas in which it may issue regulations. These are carefully delineated and may or may not include all of the items mentioned above. However, even after these powers have been outlined by law, the government still must review each regulation. If it is in conflict with other laws or if, in the government's opinion, the proposed regulation is contrary to the common interest, the government can veto it. The government also may make the boards administrative organs for the implementation of other laws. However, the government cannot oblige individual boards to impose regulations unless the initiative for them has come from within the board itself. On the whole, the government can only guide the boards by virtue of the requirement for government approval of proposed regulations before they are put into effect.

Such legislation could have resulted in a major overhaul of the economic system, and this appears to have been the expectation of the Labor Party when it sponsored the measure. Most observers feel that the leaders of the Labor Party regarded the framework proposed by the Industrial Organization Act as a potential instrument of economic policy and a means by which the influence of labor could be effectively increased in areas that were generally regarded as the province of management.

In addition, the new organizational structure would increase the economic influence of the government, even though it represented a decentralization of the administrative apparatus. This increased influence was supposed to come about because the new bodies would operate closer to the source of economic activity, i.e. at the industry and plant level rather than at the level of the central government. In effect, labor regarded the act as a potential increase in the influence of the workers and the government through the functional decentralization of governmental responsibilities in the economic sphere.

Interestingly enough, the Industrial Organization Act was also supported by the religious parties and the Liberal Party, whose members regarded public industrial organization as a means of strengthening the foundations of the existing economic system. The reason for the differences in interpretation lay in the supposed application of the provisions of the law.

The religious parties and the liberals expected the formation of public boards to facilitate decentralization by enabling powers already invested in the central government to be transferred to the newly formed boards. Even though enactment of the law meant compulsory rather than voluntary cooperation between employers and employees, this was apparently considered to be a lesser evil than actual state control. Thus the boards seemed to offer the means of reducing the areas of state interference in the economic sector.

In addition to the above reason, the Catholic Party based its support of the Industrial Organization Act on the concept of subsidiary associations set forth in the Papel Encyclical *Quadragesimo Anno* of 1931. This paper stated that all persons who practice the same profession or trade are, in effect, members of a corporation; it should be the responsibility of these corporations to promote the common interests of the members within the industry and, in turn, to make them subservient to the general welfare. Thus the idea of a public organization of industry was regarded as a natural outgrowth of the Papal Encyclical.

Progress in setting up the comprehensive statutory organization was slower than the Labor Party intended. Most branches of industry preferred to continue with the established forms of collective bargaining. Apparently, they felt little need for the regulatory powers available when and if they organized according to the provisions of the act. On the whole, only agriculture, fisheries, and the distribution trades associated with these industries have adopted the commodity boards, while various branches of wholesale trade in agricultural products, the crafts, and retail traders have established industrial boards. Industrial boards have also been formed for coal mining, agriculture, forestry, fisheries, and hotels, cafes, and restaurants. There are also two General Industrial Boards, one for the retail trade and another for crafts. In the agricultural sector, the industrial boards have concentrated on quality improvement, although at times they have taken steps to restrict the output of certain commodities that were in long supply. In the retail and wholesale trade, where there are many small shopkeepers and dealers, the boards have used their power to regulate sales, delivery, and payment conditions.

There are several reasons for the widespread opposition to the creation of the industrial and commodity boards. First, it seems that a great many people in the Netherlands are basically opposed to the idea of compulsory cooperation, which is required when the boards are established. Basically, the law gives legal status to labor and acknowledges, in principle, a state of equality between the entrepreneur and the worker. It appears that many persons, particularly those who support the Liberal Party, believe the responsibility of the entrepreneur in the production process is specific and essential and cannot be borne by entrepreneurs and workers together.

Another body of opinion regards the powers of the industrial boards as being too extensive. The point at issue is whether or not the industrial organizations controlling the new public bodies have developed a sufficient sense of public responsibility to warrant the powers given them under the Act. Clearly, these powers can, and generally have, limited competition in the fields where industrial and commodity boards have been formed. At issue also is the question of how broad a viewpoint the government should take in determining whether boards should be allowed. While the government rejects public industrial boards prejudicial to other industries, many believe boards prejudicial to the general interest should not be established. The latter interpretation parallels the Dutch government's cartel policy, in which cartel arrangements are allowed only if they are shown to be nonprejudicial to the general interest.

Another objection to the Act is that it increases the tendency for decisions concerning an industry to become concentrated in the hands of persons who are no longer working in that industry. That is, the act gives rise to a demand for more full-time people to sit on the newly created boards. These are usually not workers; rather, they tend to be representatives of the central employers' associations and labor unions. This concentration of the industrial decision-making function in the central federations is felt by some to present a serious danger to the proper functioning of a democratic society.

The Act officially recognizes, first, that a public organization of industry is desirable; second, that the participation of the worker in the organization of industry is a matter of great importance; and, third, that labor as well as management should share the responsibility for the affairs of industry. Nevertheless, many people are not convinced that these principles will be maintained in practice. As a result of these objections, the Industrial Organization Act has not been implemented to a great extent.

THE INFLUENCE OF THE EXTRA-PARLIAMENTARY ORGANIZATIONS ON GOVERNMENT POLICY

The aspect of the Industrial Organization Act that has been favorably received on all sides concerns the Social and Economic Council as an advisory organization. Because the Act stipulates that the government must seek the advice of the Social and Economic Council prior to the formulation of important legislative proposals in the social and economic field, the Council has become very influential. It has, in fact, become a battleground for the various interest groups, each of which seeks to have its views incorporated in the recommendations the Council makes to the government.

From the government's standpoint, the presence of independent experts in the Social and Economic Council is important particularly when the two major interest groups, labor and management, take opposite sides on an issue. Except in cases when the independent votes split exactly in half, the Social and Economic Council can obtain a majority vote and thus present the government with a positive recommendation. Even when it is impossible to reach agreement between the major interest groups, the independent experts can represent the deciding votes. In this respect the Council has a positive advantage over the Foundation of Labor, in which only labor and management are represented. Thus within the Council, the influence of the Crown appointees is considerable. Their participation makes the decisions of the Council something more than a mere voicing of the views of the interested groups.

In practice, the dividing line between the roles of the Social and Economic Council and the Foundation of Labor has not always been clear. Generally, the Foundation of

Labor handles special problems of wage policy, such as negotiating and arbitrating the annual collective bargaining agreements, while the Social and Economic Council advises the government on less specific problems of social and economic policy.

Beginning in 1950, the Committee on Wages and Prices of the Social and Economic Council prepared the Council's position in wage matters, and this appears to have been influential in determining the government's policy with regard to wages. In 1958 the Council established a Committee on the Development of the National Economy; since that time the scope of the problems of wage policy dealt with by the Council has been broadened to include more explicitly the relations between wages and other aspects of the national economy.

It is during the deliberations of this committee, and later in the meetings of the full Council, that the effects of proposed increases in the wage level are discussed in relation to a number of important economic variables, such as the growth of national income, the current account of the balance of payments, the terms of trade, and export and import expectations.

It should be noted that both the Foundation of Labor and the Social and Economic Council have dual purposes so far as the government is concerned. On the one hand, they serve as a means by which the problems of the government in these areas may become better understood by labor and management in their broader aspects. On the other hand, both the Council and the Foundation offer an opportunity for the exchange of views between labor and management regarding the prospects for the national economy as they affect the overall goals of national policy, and the preferred means to achieve these goals.

CHAPTER 4

Wage Policy

Like certain other European countries, Dutch economic planning, which includes wage policy, is directed toward achieving and maintaining an "income policy." The main emphasis of such a policy is the regulation of national cost levels with the objective of attaining a high level of employment and relative price stability. While European income policies vary, most rely on negotiations between business, labor, and government that, depending on the country, produce outlines for future economic policy. These outlines range from a simple set of wage–price guidelines to a detailed set of rules for determining how fast output, investment, wages, and profits shall rise in major sectors of the economy.

In the United Kingdom, for example, income policy has no formal legislative backing. It is little more than a desired economic pattern serving as the basis for tentative agreements among major groups. In France, the process has also been, on the surface, quite informal because the French government has no legal means of insuring compliance with the guidelines resulting from the annual consultations between business, labor, and the government. However, indirect means of exerting pressures on important segments of the economy (particularly through the control of investment) appear to be very effective.[1]

Dutch income policy, in contrast to that of Britain and France, is part of a formal national planning process with legislative backing. Working within the framework of its

1. See Pierre Bauchet, *Economic Planning, The French Experience*, (New York, Praeger, 1964); and S. Wickham, "French Planning: Retrospect and Prospect," *The Review of Economics and Statistics*, *45* (November 1963) pp. 335–47.

income policy, the Netherlands' government has engaged in extensive efforts to influence the process of wage formulation and, to some extent, price determination ever since the end of World War II.

One of the reasons that the Dutch have pursued an income policy is that an income policy is a method of correcting for the effects of international disequilibrium that in some measure allows for a reconciliation of international and domestic economic objectives. Because of its reliance on international trade the Dutch economy has many times felt the effects of changes in economic conditions abroad and the public authorities have had ample occasion to seek means to offset the problem caused by balance-of-payments surplus or deficits.

They could, of course, rely on the natural equilibrating mechanism discussed in Chapter 2, by which balance-of-payments surpluses produce greater liquidity, lower interest rates, credit expansion, demand inflation, rising costs, and hence cause the surplus on the balance of payments to disappear. By the same token, balance-of-payments deficits bring about liquidity shortages, rising interest rates, credit contractions, limitations of spending, falling costs, and hence remove the deficits.

The natural mechanism, however, depends on fluctuations in the volume of national spending to achieve equilibrium, and such a process is clearly incompatible with a policy objective of a continuous high level of employment. Moreover, even if temporary fluctuations were acceptable to establish equilibrium in the balance of payments, the equilibrium may occur at a level of employment too low to be acceptable to the policy-makers.

Outside of the classic cycle outlined above, three other ways for dealing with an international disequilibrium resulting in a deficit or surplus in the balance of payments should be mentioned: (1) through the use of trade or exchange controls, (2) through an adjustment of exchange parities, and (3) through internal price and wage changes while attempting to maintain full employment.

As pointed out previously, the use of tariffs to regulate the flow of goods and services is becoming less useful as an instrument of economic policy because overall traffic barriers have been greatly reduced as a result of unilateral trade agreements and the spread of customs unions. Adjusting exchange parities influences directly the international flow of goods and services through changes in relative prices. However, as also pointed out in Chapter 2, the principle of fixed exchange rates is widely accepted internationally as an objective of economic policy.

Therefore, if these objectives are admitted, the policies that remain available for use in restoring balance-of-payments equilibrium as between the deficit and surplus countries are wage and price policies such as are incorporated in the concept of an income policy. Wage and price policies aim at producing differential trends in national cost levels without necessarily incurring deflationary decreases or inflationary increases in aggregate demand. If cost and price levels exhibit a sufficient flexibility, it is possible for the deficit countries to adjust their national cost levels so as to improve their chances of selling abroad in comparison with the surplus countries. This means that prices must rise in the surplus countries while either falling or at least not rising in the deficit countries. Thus, the Netherlands' income policy is directed toward regulation of the movement of the Dutch national wage and price level relative to those of the countries with whom Holland competes in the world market.

In Holland, as in most countries ascribing to an income policy, the government participates in some degree in the wage negotiations between labor and management. In fact, it appears essential in order to achieve a working income policy that labor and management be highly organized, inasmuch as the government uses the officials of the central employer and employees' organizations as instruments of economic policy. During most of the period 1950–65 the Dutch government had the cooperation of the central employer and employee organizations and there was general support of the government's income policy. Nevertheless, there was conflict among labor, management, and the government. Due to the overall tightness of the labor market and the generally favorable sales position, this conflict took an unusual form: the government found itself the sole opposition to wage rate increases.

Labor's demands for wage increases in the Netherlands were generally not characterized by pressure for maximum wage increases but were usually considered in terms of what business and the national economy could bear. Although it cannot be proven, it appears that both labor and management were often less rigid in their demands than they might have been, given the favorable domestic market conditions. Both exhibited willingness to adjust to the overall economic situation, and the labor organizations even seemed to give strong weight to considerations of Dutch competitiveness in the world economy.

In the Netherlands, it might be noted, labor and management leaders have become accustomed to thinking in terms of real income as well as money income and to considering long-run trends as well as immediate objectives. Their concern is directed as much toward percentage increases in the national income as toward guilders per hour, with the important issue being the "margin" that, subject to the maintenance of balancc-of-payments equilibrium, can be regarded as being "available" for wage increases.

Since wage policy is one of the foundations of any income policy, it is useful to discuss the Dutch wage experience in some detail. The institutional arrangements developed in the early postwar years for dealing with matters of economic policy, particularly with wage policy, were described in the previous chapter. The role of the Board of Government

Mediators, a government body not mentioned previously, and recent changes in the rules and procedures for dealing with wages are discussed in the paragraphs below, followed by a chronological development of Dutch wage policy during 1950–65.

THE BOARD OF GOVERNMENT MEDIATORS

Within the government the interpretation and direction of wage policy was for many years officially in the hands of a body known as the Board of Government Mediators.[2] In the early postwar years, this Board was vested with near dictatorial powers. In fact, decisions of the Board were subject only to the requirement that it consult the Foundation of Labor before making decisions of "more general importance."[3] The Board, however, interpreted this provision broadly and consulted extensively with the Foundation on almost all matters affecting wage determination and, although the Board was not bound by law to follow the advice of the Foundation, in practice, the Foundation's advice was followed in a large majority of cases.

The Board, which continues to operate although with reduced authority, is appointed by the Minister of Social Affairs. The members do not have the status of civil servants and serve only part time except for the chairman whose job is full time. The members are appointed individually, presumably on the basis of their skill and experience in the area of wage negotiation. Over the years the number of members has varied from six to eight.

The 1945 act that established the Board of Mediators set forth its primary functions as follows:[4]

2. Also translated as Board of Arbitrators or Conciliators.

3. This power was derived from a law known as the 1945 Extraordinary Employment Relations Decree.

4. Netherlands Government Information Service, *Digest of the Kingdom of the Netherlands, Social Aspects*, pp. 41–42.

1. To give the force of law to wages and other conditions of employment, either at the request of the organizations of employers and employees or ex-officio.
2. To establish general principles for the guidance of parties engaged in collective wage negotiations.
3. To approve all collective labor agreements.
4. To make the provisions of collective labor agreements binding or not binding in an entire branch of industry.
5. To draw up directives with regard to the regulation of wages and other conditions of employment where no collective agreements exist.
6. If requested to do so by the interested parties, to grant exemption from binding wage agreements which previously had been made binding.

The Board's original charter illustrates the fact that the statutory authority of the government in the area of wages and working conditions was at that time extremely comprehensive. Under the 1945 Labor Decree employers and employees were required to adhere to wage agreements approved by the government; when the parties could not reach an agreement, the government could fix the wage rate for the industry. The government could also determine the forms of incentive systems to be applied, including a system of wage differences based on skill and geographical differentials. Even during the early postwar years, however, when the needs of the country were most pressing, the government emphasized the need for cooperation in matters of wage policy rather than resorting to the statutory powers available to it under the 1945 Labor Decree.

For example, the Board of Mediators, rather than simply making an arbitrary decision in regard to collective agreements and, in some cases, deadlocked negotiations submitted to it from various branches of industry, always forwarded these cases to the Wages Committee of the Foundation of Labor. The Wages Committee discussed the proposal agreement or tried to arrange a settlement between parties that had been unable to agree themselves. The Committee meetings dealing with collective agreements were attended by representatives of the employers' and workers' organizations from the industry whose proposed contract was under discussion. Also attending were representatives of the Board of Government Mediators, the latter presumably to insure that the government's viewpoint was taken into account before the agreement was returned to the Board for final decision.

The meetings of the Wages Committee of the Foundation of Labor provided an opportunity for the central organizations of employers and employees to exert an influence on the negotiations of their component associations. The main purpose at these meetings was to discuss whether or not the proposals originating within the various branches of industry were consistent with the government's overall wage policy.

RECENT HISTORY OF WAGE POLICY

Fearful of the consequences of rising price levels, the Netherlands tried, and for a period managed, to maintain the rate of increase in its average wage level below that prevailing in neighboring countries. However, since the Netherlands exports nearly half of its output and spends nearly half of its income abroad, its economy is exceptionally sensitive to price and wage increases in its principal trading partners. From about 1960 onward external wages and prices increased rather rapidly, particularly in the other European Economic Community countries. Holland thus became a low-cost producer in a world of high and rising costs.

As a consequence, the Dutch economy came under intense pressure. Export demand increased substantially, and exporters, attempting to increase production, exerted additional demands on a tight labor market. As a result, the Dutch wage policy, and the entire income policy, was put to its most severe test. The final results are not clear as yet. However, the situation illustrates the tendency for wages to rise under the pressure of a high level of demand for labor, despite what appears to be a well-designed and conscientiously applied income policy.

The early success of Dutch wage policy can be attributed to two factors: (1) the annual collective agreements between union and management were never tied formally to any cost-of-living provisions; and (2) all parties to these agreements, particularly labor, presumably recognized the necessity of holding costs down so as to maintain the Netherlands' competitive position. On two occasions, for instance, in March 1951 and January 1957, the leaders of the unions voluntarily accepted cuts in real wages as a means of averting a potential wage–price spiral. It must be noted, however, that there have always been mandatory wage increases designed to compensate, wholly or in part, for specific price increases or decreases in take-home pay. For example, there have been wage increases designed to compensate for reductions in milk or rent subsidies or for the introduction of new schemes of social security. Several of these are described in Chapter 6.

During the years covered by this study there were two periods in which the tendency of wages to rise during a tight labor market was exhibited. The first period of excess labor demand lasted from early 1955 to early 1956. During 1956 and 1957 the index of hourly wages rose 11 points.[5] Unemployment was 1.5 percent on average, while employers' inquiries for male personnel exceeded the registered labor reserve. The second period, culminating in the wage demands of 1965, really began in 1960, when unemployment dropped from 2.3 percent to 1.4 percent. Subsequently, unemploy-

5. Netherlands Bank, *1957*, p. 35.

ment continued at 1 percent or less, while the demand for labor, as indicated by the number of unfilled vacancies, was at an all-time high.[6]

During these two periods the government attempted to resist the joint pressure of unions and employers for large wage increases since it felt these would reinforce the existing inflationary conditions. Nevertheless, during 1960–64 the average annual rise in weekly wages earned in industry was 10 percent.[7]

In retrospect, it appears that the Netherlands government prevented wage and price increases from continuing after periods of excess demand had passed. This is indicated by the fact that from 1954 to the beginning of 1956, the first period during which inflationary tendencies were at their peak, the index of total wages rose by approximately 30 percent, while in the two-and-one-half years that followed, there was only one general wage increase of about 4 percent.[8]

It remains to be seen how well the wage policy has adjusted to the effects of the mid-1960s tight labor market. There were rather large price and wage increases during 1963–65, and, from all indications, it appeared that these would continue. In 1963 wage costs per person employed rose by approximately 10 percent, while the wholesale price index increased by 2 percent and the cost-of-living index by 4 percent; in 1964 wage costs increased by 15 percent, the wholesale price index increased by 6.5 percent, and the cost of living increased by 5.5 percent. In 1965 the increase in wage costs was estimated at 11.0 percent, wholesale prices by 7.5 percent, while the cost of living rose by 5 percent.[9]

Even at its best, the Dutch wage system was not perfect. Wages tended to drift upwards. A wage drift is said to occur

6. According to the *Centraal Economisch Plan 1964*, vacancies averaged approximately 120,000 during 1963, while the average number of registered unemployed was a mere 42,000.

7. Netherlands Bank, *1957*, p. 39.

8. Fellner et al., *The Problem of Rising Prices*, p. 369.

9. Netherlands Bank, *1965*, pp. 32, 36.

when the actual increase in wages tends to be greater than the increase agreed upon in the annual collective bargaining negotiations. One cause of drift is the incidental wage increases due to the introduction of new piecework rates, the upgrading of jobs, etc.[10] Another cause is the payment of "black wages," wages in excess of official rates; this has been a common practice during periods of excess labor demand, particularly in the construction and metalworking trades. Several times the government recognized the "black" rate as the legal rate rather than ignore a situation about which little could be done.

FOUR PHASES OF WAGE POLICY

Broadly speaking, income policy, as reflected in wage policy, has passed through four phases in the Netherlands. Prior to 1953, the government sought to prevent wages from rising above what was regarded as a social minimum wage level. In retrospect, it appears that the wage increases permitted during this period did not absorb the full increase in productivity that occurred; as a result, the index of labor costs (hourly earnings divided by productivity) fell from 108 in 1946 to 100 in 1953.[11] After 1953 and until 1959 the emphasis of wage policy shifted toward securing for labor an equitable share of the national income within the limits of increases in national productivity. However, as pointed out in an earlier chapter, equitable was never defined precisely.

During the first two phases the slogan guiding government wage policy was "equal pay for equal work."[12] Through the

10. About 40 or 45 percent of all workers are paid on a piece-rate basis. Fellner et al., p. 370.

11. The figures are calculated from data published in the "National Accounts" and in the *Monthly Bulletin of Social Statistics*, issued by the Central Bureau of Statistics.

12. This concept cannot be defined precisely. Roughly the idea of equal pay for equal work means that increases in the national product should be apportioned equally regardless of productivity differentials between different

Board of Mediators the government authorized, and even obligated, employers to grant wage increases at a given rate. Initially the attempt to keep wage increases within the overall productivity gain was not too successful, primarily because of the scarcity of labor. From 1953 to 1957 earnings increased by 45 percent while productivity only increased by 15 percent.[13] Prices then tended to rise as a result of the increased labor cost per unit of product.

Fortunately for the Netherlands during this period, other countries also experienced inflationary price increases. As a result, the competitive position of the Netherlands in the world market was not seriously affected. In fact, the volume of Netherlands exports increased faster than world trade as a whole. Unfortunately, the boom was accompanied by an increased demand for imports, which resulted in a deterioration of the balance-of-payments position. As a consequence, in 1956 the government was forced to apply restrictive measures over the whole range of fiscal, monetary, wage, and price controls. These restrictive practices (discussed in some detail in Chapter 6) were relaxed in 1958 and for the next few years the price level remained relatively stable.

In 1959 the system of wage determination was changed with hopes of giving individual industries greater control of their own wage levels. The result was the introduction of a system of differential wages based on productivity increases in the branch of industry or firm concerned. Under this plan wage demands were to be based upon statistical studies of the economic situation of the different branches of industry and of the total scope for wage increases which the

---

industries. Thus, the janitor in a department store should receive the same percentage increase in wages as the janitor in a chemical plant even though the chemical industry, taken as a whole, may have exhibited a higher productivity gain or, to express it differently, contributed more significantly to the increase in national product.

13. Calculated from data published in the "National Accounts" and the *Monthly Bulletin of Social Statistics*.

economy could be expected to support without inflation. In 1963 this third phase broke down under the pressures of excess domestic and foreign demand coupled with a severe labor shortage. It has been replaced with an ad hoc arrangement.

The Early Postwar Years

During the period covered by this study, the government had comprehensive authority over matters affecting wages. In the early years the government used this authority routinely, although only after consultation with the main employer and employee organizations. Under the prevailing rules, employers and employees were required to adhere to wage agreements approved by the government. When the parties could not reach an agreement on their own, the government fixed the wage rate for the industry in question. For the most part, the government had the last word, not only in the broad outlines of wage policy but also in most details.

Shortly after the liberation, the Board of Government Mediators established a series of minimum wage levels based on the cost of necessities required by a family of four, as determined by the Central Bureau of Statistics of the Netherlands government. The minimum rates depended upon the level of skill and upon location. Five geographical zones were recognized; they ranged from industrial and commercial regions to rural towns in agricultural provinces. Differentials in pay were allowed on the basis of the level of skill required of the job. At first there were three skill levels; unskilled, semi-skilled, and skilled, with a 10 percent pay differential between each level. Subsequently, more intricate systems of job classification were developed under the direction of the Netherlands High Commission for Standardization, and the Board of Mediators began to approve collective bargaining agreements based upon job classes.

Most labor leaders were concerned with obtaining at least the minimum standard of living as defined above for all of the wage-earning population. During reconstruction, it appears that little thought was given to improving the position of wage earners relative to other groups. Until about 1954, official wage policy, with the cooperation or organized labor, was designed to maintain real wages in the face of cost-of-living increases. During these early years labor apparently conceded that increases in national income should be used almost entirely for reconstruction rather than for increasing real wages. The government used subsidies to prevent increases in the cost of living, and it was only when these subsidies were reduced that wage increases were allowed.

As a result of this policy, there was little increase in real wages during the first years of the recovery. The government did try to adjust wages paid to agricultural employees because they were considered to be too low in relation to wages paid in industry. The government also encouraged new incentive wage systems in order to stimulate production without changing the basic wage rate.

One example of government wage policy may be taken from 1951, when import prices rose rapidly following the outbreak of the war in Korea. At the same time, the Netherlands was faced with a large increase in defense expenditures due to its NATO obligations. Foreign exchange reserves accordingly began to drop and balance-of-payments difficulties appeared. In February 1951, the Social and Economic Council, in response to the government's request for advice, reported that consumption expenditures would have to be cut by 5 percent and capital investment by 25 percent if balance-of-payments equilibrium were to be reestablished. The government quickly cut food subsidies by 50 percent and raised both direct and indirect taxes. To reduce investment expenditure, direct controls were imposed.

The reduction of subsidies, combined with the increase in

taxes, caused a 10 percent increase in the cost of living. In the collective wage negotiations of that year the government persuaded the unions to accept only a 5 percent increase in wages. At the same time, the government obtained the cooperation of industry to prevent the transfer of the wage increases in the form of higher prices. Agreement by leaders of the central organizations to such an arrangement is a good example of how national considerations have been of primary concern in times of difficulty in the balance of payments.

Wage rates remained almost stable during the next two years, partly because of a slight recession in 1952 that alleviated the upward pressure on the wage level. Over the so-called "consumption restriction" period from mid-1951 to January 1954, the balance of payments moved from a deficit of 80 million guilders to a surplus of 350 million guilders in 1953. Unemployment declined and production increased as well.

There were no wage increases in 1953, and during that year union leaders began to press for a reassessment of the government's wage policies. To this end they were assisted by employers, who were in favor of less government interference. The three parties began discussions concerning possible changes in the method by which the annual wage increases were determined. These continued for several years with no basic agreement being reached. The main issue was labor's contention that during reconstruction, wage income had not risen as fast as national income.[14] In January 1954, the government authorized an average increase of 9 percent. This was followed in October by a further permissible increase not to exceed 6 percent. The latter became known as the "prosperity wage round," and

14. The Social and Economic Council subscribed, at least in principle, to labor's viewpoint. In 1954 the Council issued a report stating that the workers' share of the increase in national income, rather than changes in the cost of living index, should be the criterion for wage decisions.

although not compulsory, fairly general use was made of the authorization. The full 6 percent was approved by the Board of Government Mediators whenever negotiation in individual industries led to such an agreement.

Prosperity brought increasing tightness in the labor market. Unemployment declined from 1.8 percent in 1954 to .9 percent in 1956, while job vacancies increased from 1.7 percent to 2.5 percent of the labor force. By April 1955, the number of registered vacancies exceeded the number of unemployed. National expenditures quickly exceeded domestic income, resulting in a deterioration in the balance of payments. Unfortunately, under the influence of a 780 million guilder surplus in the balance of payments in 1955,[15] the seriousness of the balance-of-payments deterioration was not recognized, and the government intensified inflationary pressures by approving wage rate increases totaling approximately 15 percent during 1954 and 1955, the early phases of expansion. By the end of 1956, the balance-of-payments account showed a deficit of 710 million guilders.[16]

Faced with a serious shortage of labor, employers pressed for greater differentiation of wages among branches of industry, so as to allow industries with greater than average productivity gains to pay higher wages. In September 1955, greater wage differentiation was recommended by the Social and Economic Council. The government declared itself willing, in principle, to accept greater differentiation between the rates of pay for different industries, if employment, productivity, and financial position justified it, but nothing was said about how this was to be accomplished.

The Social and Economic Council continued to study the problem, and in 1956 it issued its "margin report," which dealt with the so-called lag of per capita wages in industry behind national income per head of the working population. The report illustrates the difficulty of arriving at a consensus

15. *Centraal Economisch Plan, 1964*, p. 161.
16. Ibid.

when attempting to quantify the goals of economic policy. The Council members were unable to agree on a base date, i.e. a date at which the relationship between per capita wages and per capita national income was satisfactory. Whether the growth of per capita wages lagged behind the growth of per capita national income depends upon the base chosen. Since a suitable date could not be chosen, the Council did not make any specific recommendations. However, the Council members generally felt that wages were lagging, even though they could not agree on the size of the lag.[17]

The government referred the problem to the Foundation of Labor, but with little success. Finally, the government stepped into the negotiations of the Foundation of Labor to act as arbitrator. After further negotiation, an agreement allowing an increase in wages and some differentiation among industries was reached. The government approved wage increases not to exceed 6 percent, providing they did not lead to price increases. In case higher wages increased cost to a point where prices would have to be raised, the size of the allowable wage increase was limited to 3 percent. The resultant price increase had to receive specific government approval.

The wage increases permitted by this agreement were gradually incorporated in the collective agreements as their terms expired. Although this wage round was permissive rather than compulsory, a majority of employers, under pressure of the labor shortage, increased wage rates by the maximum percentage allowed.

In 1956 it became obvious that an adverse balance of payments was developing. During the first nine months private consumption increased 8 percent over the corresponding period in 1955. At the same time, imports of consumer goods were up 30 percent.[18] Responsible leaders

17. For a discussion of this point, see Netherlands Bank, *1955*, pp. 27–30.
18. Fellner et al., p. 377.

of labor, management, and the government became concerned. In the words of the Central Bank:

> [T]he country's economic position has changed, in a way that appears strongly to the imagination, as a result, in particular of the deficit that has appeared in the balance of payments. This has considerably sobered the country, which has been brought by lowering of taxation, by wage increases, by social advancement and by the unceasing abundance of money and capital into a state of optimistic expectation of prosperity. People have now become aware that nothing but a fairly drastic cut in spending can restore equilibrium.[19]

This situation was caused primarily by an increase in disposable wage income. The Netherlands Bank reported that in 1954 and 1955 Dutch wages rose more relative to productivity than in other countries. Referring to the recent wage increases, the Bank stated: "Even though it may be assumed that in 1953 labor costs in the Netherlands were to some extent lagging behind the international movement, there is ground for wondering whether in wiping out the lag we are not overshooting the mark."[20]

To combat the inflationary situation, the Social and Economic Council recommended that national expenditure be reduced by 700 million guilders in 1957, half of this cut to fall on capital expenditure and half on consumption.[21] The government accepted this report and cut public expenditures by approximately 200 million guilders. It increased taxes, including the corporation tax, and withdrew the current investment allowance. In addition, a new insurance

19. Netherlands Bank, *1956*, p. 15.

20. Ibid., p. 31.

21. The Council recommended that government expenditure be reduced by 200 million guilders, industrial investment by 4 percent, and private consumption by 1.5 percent. This recommendation is discussed in greater detail in Chap. 6.

premium in excess of the average wage increase was introduced. Rents were raised, as were the guaranteed prices of farm products.

As a result of these measures, the cost of living index rose 12 percent while wages rose by only 11 percent; thus real wages fell by 1 percent.[22] As expected, there was a rise in unemployment, and the registered labor reserve at the end of 1957 was more than twice as large as it had been a year before. The seasonally adjusted male labor reserve amounted to 76,000 or 2.3 percent of the male labor force,[23] and the rate continued to rise into 1958. Faced with higher levels of unemployment, labor leaders were unable to seek general wage increases. After August 1957, there was a period of almost two years during which no across-the-board wage increases were granted, and the only increases authorized were in certain special sectors of industry and agriculture.

Economic conditions began to improve in 1958, resulting in a balance-of-payments surplus of over 400 million guilders. With the upswing of activity, unemployment declined, and by mid-1959 labor was again in a position to press for more general wage increases.

1958 Through 1962

The resurgence of economic activity coincided with a change in government. In December 1958, the socialist ministers resigned, thereby ending the Labor-Catholic coalition that had existed since the war. Following general elections, a new government was formed by the Catholic, Protestant, and Liberal parties, and the principle of differential wage increases was adopted: increases were to be justified chiefly by the increase in labor productivity in individual industries rather than in the economy as a whole.

22. Netherlands Bank, *1957*, p. 35.
23. Ibid., p. 28.

Thus the main criterion for wage advances was economic progress in each individual industry.[24]

The new wage policy was fundamentally different from the previous policy of "equal pay for equal work." There were, however, no real modifications of the institutional framework as a result of the policy changes. Collective bargaining still originated at the level of the firm or branch of industry, and the Board of Mediators was retained to administer wage policy. Requests for wage advances were justified by the local organizations according to anticipated productivity increases. The local productivity calculations were sent to the Central Bureau of Statistics for verification, after which the Board made preliminary comments before forwarding the wage proposals to the Wages Committee of the Foundation of Labor for possible revision or reconciliation. Finally, the proposals were returned to the Board for final disposition. Essentially, with the exception of the verification of the productivity estimates by the Central Bureau of Statistics, this was the same procedure as used previously.

Difficulties quickly developed, particularly as regards the method of calculating productivity increases. No one was exactly sure how such calculations were to be made and justified. At the time of the introduction of the new wage policy, the technical difficulties of defining productivity and of compiling the time-series required were underestimated. Since in practice the computation of time-series of productivity is a complex task requiring the services of trained statisticians, the Central Bureau of Statistics was called upon for technical help. Thus, the Bureau was often involved in both the initial calculation and the review of the productivity figures.

It soon turned out that the system required a new step

24. It is interesting to note that, while the Catholic and Protestant labor unions favored the new criterion, the socialist trade union favored a continuation of the across-the-board national wage policy.

in the bargaining process: the government had to negotiate with the central organizations of employers and employees in order to determine complicated guidelines for measuring productivity changes. An example of the productivity guidelines that resulted is the formula decided upon by the government and the Foundation of Labor for the 1962 wage negotiations. It took into account the anticipated increase in overall national production in 1962 and the average increase in productivity over the previous nine years for the particular industry involved in the negotiations. These two factors were weighted in the ratio of one to three. For example, if the increase in national output in 1962 was expected to be 5 percent, while the average increase in productivity in the industry had been 7 percent over the past nine years, the permissible increase in wages would be 6.5 percent.

The government attempted to prevent the appearance of large differentials between different industries or occupations. In some industries, where productivity increases were substantially above the national average, the government refused to allow the entire margin of price over cost to be absorbed by increased wages and profits; rather it insisted that part of this margin be passed on to consumers in the form of reduced prices. By this means the government hoped to be able to approve both wage and price increases in the service industries, where productivity was not expected to increase substantially, while maintaining a stabilized overall price level. The Minister of Economic Affairs held so-called "price discussions" to which the leaders of industries with high productivity increases were invited, but it is difficult to measure the actual effect of the government's efforts to lower prices. No one has been able to show statistically that the government accomplished its aim.

The differential wage policy encountered other problems as well. For example, there were many cases in which productivity in the same industry differed from firm to firm.

The wage question was resolved by setting the same basic wage for all firms, with the margin of the more efficient producers being taken up in fringe benefits, such as profit sharing or saving schemes, to which the employer contributed. Where productivity gains were achieved in export industries, it was sometimes deemed desirable neither to reduce export prices nor to increase wages, the latter because of possible undesirable structural effects on the domestic labor market. In these cases the government also encouraged profit sharing schemes.

In addition to these difficulties, the system of differential wages did not live up to expectations as a device to reduce government interference in the process of wage determination. In practice, since the Central Bureau of Statistics had to verify the productivity estimates of the local industrial organizations, the effect was just the opposite. In a number of cases the Central Bureau of Statistics did not agree with the local estimates and lowered them considerably. There was a tendency for local trade unions and employers to overestimate anticipated productivity increases because of the high level of aggregate demand and the shortage of labor existing at the time.[25] Employers were generally willing to pay wages higher than those suggested by the productivity calculations of the Central Bureau of Statistics. In the opinion of some observers, employers and the local union leaders simply agreed upon a mutually acceptable wage increase and then determined what change in productivity would be needed to justify it. The latter was then forwarded to the Board of Mediators as the anticipated productivity increase.

From January 1959 until the end of 1962, hourly wages rose on average by 6.75 percent per year; during the same period, the work week fell from 48 to 45 hours.[26] Wage increases greatly exceeded the productivity standard set in

25. In the first quarter of 1960 vacancies again exceeded the registered labor reserves.

26. Netherlands Bank. *1962*, pp 36–37

the official wage policy. As a result, labor costs per unit of production rose 1.5 percent in 1960, an additional 5.5 percent in 1961, and a further 6.5 percent in 1962.[27]

In view of these wage movements and the continuing tight labor market, the government consulted the Foundation of Labor in regard to possible changes in general wage standards. These discussions began in July 1962. In September the government asked the Social and Economic Council the specific question of how the rise of wage costs would be limited in the coming year.

The Social and Economic Council recommended a departure from the then current institutional procedures for approving collective agreements. Surprisingly, in view of the economic conditions then prevailing, the Social and Economic Council suggested giving greater responsibility to the Foundation of Labor. Rather than using tighter controls to enforce the principle that wage changes should conform to changes in productivity, the Social and Economic Council recommended that the government relax its formal guidelines and adopt a more flexible wage policy. The government was willing to agree in principle to the proposals of the Social and Economic Council. The reasons for this recommendation and the government's willingness to "go along" grew out of a real threat to the concept and functioning of the national income policy.

1963 AND AFTER

The key feature of these proposals of the Social and Economic Council was that, in return for government relaxation of statutory control over collective bargaining, the Foundation of Labor would accept the major responsibility for insuring that the collective agreements were consistent with the national interest. To understand why the government agreed to this proposal, in view of the

27. Ibid.

existing inflationary conditions, one must first look at the position of the leaders of the central federations of employers and employees. With an important role in the government's income policy, they were faced with a situation in which individual employers were willing to grant wage increases beyond the productivity standard in order to protect their labor supply. As a result, the leaders of the central organizations had the difficult task of restraining the wage demands of the local organizations. Many members of the local branches of these organizations began to doubt the usefulness of the central organizations as instruments for improving their economic conditions.

In order to prevent the complete disintegration of its income policy and to maintain the institutional framework within which the income policy functioned, the government had to protect the position of the central organizations. Thus under the new system, the central federations were given much greater authority over individual wage bargains. In line with the recommendations of the Social and Economic Council, added responsibility for wage determination was given to the Foundation of Labor. Nonetheless, the government retained responsibility for general wage policy and also retained the power to veto any individual wage negotiations it found unacceptable.

Specifically, the power to approve the collective wage agreements was transferred from the Board of Government Mediators to the Foundation of Labor, subject only to veto power vested in the Minister of Social Affairs. The latter could declare certain provisions of an agreement nonbinding if he felt they were at odds with the public interest. He could do this, however, only on the advice of the Board of Government Mediators. The Board itself no longer retained the right of final approval of every labor contract; it was to function solely as a staff agency for the Minister of Social Affairs. For the purpose of recommending approval or disapproval to the Minister, the Board received copies of each contract forwarded from the local organizations to the Wage Committee of the Foundation of Labor. If the Board intended to make an unfavorable recommendation, it notified the Foundation of Labor within three weeks after receiving the text of the agreement. Indeed, it was only when the Minister accepted the Board's disapproval and then actually vetoed an agreement that it failed to go into effect, even after approval by the Foundation of Labor.

The new system outlined a method by which the Foundation of Labor was to obtain guidance on the approval of the collective agreements submitted to it. Under this system the government and the Foundation agreed to consult regularly about wage-cost developments considered possible in the near future. These discussions, in turn, are guided by two reports which the agreement required to be prepared by the Social and Economic Council. The first report contains an outline of the likely course of economic events in the near future, and is based on the preliminary economic forecasts regularly submitted by the Central Planning Bureau, in September of each year, in conjunction with the government's annual budget proposals. The second report, covering the same subject in more detail, is based on the final version of the Central Economic Plan, which usually appears in February. In these reports the Social and Economic Council indicates the average increase of wage costs they believe to be tolerable in the near future. Depending on the circumstances, this indication is given in actual percentage rates of increase or in minimum and maximum figures.

The object of the discussions between the government and the Foundation is to secure an agreement as to wage developments during the forthcoming year. The discussions, guided by the information contained in the two reports, cover the full range of wages and working conditions, such as reduction in the work week, extension of holiday time, profit sharing schemes, etc. Prior to these discussions the Foundation is expected to consult the local organizations in order to ascertain likely wage developments in the various branches of industry.

In addition, it is expected that within the Foundation of Labor, the central organizations of labor and management will agree on the principles that govern wage differentiation among sectors and occupations. The overall purpose of the conversations between the government and the Foundation is to draw up a set of guidelines for the Foundation to follow in deciding whether to approve the local wage agreements forwarded to it during the year to come. If a fundamental difference of opinion emerges, and if the Foundation is not prepared to adopt the government's view, control over wages can be reimposed: the government can announce a temporary wage freeze or a uniform statutory increase in wages, or it can restore the Board of Government Mediators' former powers, thus returning to the previous system of wage determination.

The new system relies mainly on internal coordination within the central organizations of employers and employees in order to keep wage increases within bounds. The Foundation of Labor must take into account the macroeconomic possibilities agreed upon in its discussion with the government; it must then determine the size of wage increases in separate branches of industry and in separate enterprises within an industry so as not to exceed the permissible total wage increase.

In the first year of operation the new system worked relatively well. In fact, the wage negotiations for 1963 resulted in a smaller nominal wage increase than took place in 1962. For the 1963 negotiations, the Social and Economic Council recommended that the average wage increase on renewal of contracts expiring in 1963 should not exceed 2.7 percent, not including compensation for new social measures and incidental wage increases expected to occur during the year. The figures show that this standard was exceeded only slightly. The Central Planning Bureau estimated the average increase of wages as a result of 1963 contract revision at 3.5 percent.

According to figures published by the Central Bureau of Statistics, the total increase in weekly wages for the year 1963 amounted to 6.5 percent. The increase included the effect produced by contracts revised in 1962, the compensation for higher rents, and increased old age insurance premiums. This represents a reduction of 1.0 percent from the overall wage increase of 7.5 percent reported for 1962.[28] The Central Planning Bureau estimated the 1963 increase in the total wage per employed person, including social changes, incidental wage increases, and "black wages," to be 8 percent. Since the cost of living, including social insurance premiums and wages tax, was 3 percent higher than in 1962, the net increase in real wages was only 5 percent. This was less than in 1962 when, as a result of only a 1 percent rise in the cost of living, there was an increase in real wages of slightly less than 7 percent.[29] From the standpoint of the government's income policy, the smaller increase in real income was helpful because it served as a check on the inflationary tendencies of the economy.

Unfortunately, in 1963, as in the two preceding years, the rise in total wages per employee exceeded the advance in per capita productivity. Moreover, in view of the continued expansion in aggregate demand, the inclination to pay "black wages" became stronger during the second half of 1963, and in some cases the wages laid down in the collective agreements were openly exceeded. Judging from the gap between registered unemployment and job vacancies, pressure on the Dutch labor market in 1963 was not much stronger than it had been at the peak of the 1957 boom. However, there was a difference. In 1957 the leaders of the central organizations were able and willing to go along with

28. Ibid., *1963*, p. 33.
29. Ibid.

calls for restraint. In 1963 they were not. The leaders of the central organizations were under pressure from the local organizations for large wage increases. The entire structure of Holland's income policy, even the ad hoc arrangements just introduced, was threatened as a result of a possible break in relations between the central organizations and their rank and file.

In 1964, several large industrial concerns threatened to withdraw from the central employers' federation. Faced with this threat, the negotiating committees for management and labor and the government hastily concluded an agreement that clearly reflected the extent of the strain. The unions received a 10 percent increase in wages in two stages: a 5 percent increase as of January 1, 1964, and a further 5 percent on the renewal of contracts, which was to take place not later than April 1. Included in the agreement were a number of fringe benefits, such as increased holidays and a minimum wage of 100 guilders per week for able-bodied male workers. In addition, certain enterprises were permitted to raise official wage rates by 4 percent, i.e. to legalize "black wages" already being paid.

In practice, it was found that the agreement, although intended as a standard, was generally regarded as a minimum by most local organizations. In February the Central Planning Bureau estimated that total wages per employed person would increase by about 15 percent in 1964, about twice as much as the increases in 1962 and 1963.

Although the 1964 agreement was clearly inflationary, the government agreed to it since there was no practicable alternative. At worst, the government did little more than recognize the inevitable; at best, it salvaged the machinery of its income policy. However, while the machinery was salvaged, it seems doubtful that the income policy can ever be restored to its former effectiveness.

In 1964 the labor market remained very tight, with the registered unemployed numbering only one fourth the registered vacancies. Although there was a small increase in unemployment, it was for the most part caused by an extremely cold winter and almost entirely concentrated in the building trades. In the wage negotiation of November 1964, the unions asked for a 7 percent average increase and the employers offered only 3 percent. Neither side would compromise, and it again appeared that the whole mechanism for wage negotiation would collapse.

The government, however, finally persuaded the two sides to settle for a 5 percent average increase in wages, coupled with a 10 percent increase in the minimum weekly wage. It also promised to introduce a 10 percent cut in income tax. In return, the government insisted that the unions abandon their plans for separate negotiations with individual industries outside the framework of the income policy. As a result of this wage bargain, together with some changes in pension payments that would have a net deflationary effect, the cost of labor was expected to rise by about 9 percent in 1965.[30]

Incorporated in the final agreement outlined above was a provision for a special payment for 1965 if the economic situation in the first half of the year turned out to be better than had been foreseen at the end of 1964. At first no agreement could be reached between the employers and the employees regarding this special payment. However, the government after consultation with the Social and Economic Council and the Foundation of Labor approved a 2 percent increase in wages. For the year 1965 taken as a whole, the Central Planning Bureau estimated the increase in the weekly wage rate at 9.5 percent and the increase in wage costs per person employed at 11 percent.[31]

In 1965 a new element, which foretold of possible difficulties should the boom end, was introduced into Netherlands wage policy: agreements running for as long as three

30. *Economic Quarterly Review*, No. 1 (June 1965), p. 22.
31. Netherlands Bank, *1965*, p. 32.

and a half years were negotiated, particularly in the metal-using industries. These agreements called for a yearly wage increase of 5 percent, with further possible compensation for a rise in the cost of living up to a maximum of 2 percent per year. This latter stipulation was received with alarm by the government and by the Social and Economic Council. After some discussion, a number of points for limiting automatic links between wages and living costs were agreed to. The Foundation of Labor ruled that a collective labor agreement with a cost-of-living index clause must run for at least one and a half years. Furthermore, the clause must not come into effect during the first year, and there must be an interval between the computation of the cost of living rise and the date of adjustment of the wage agreement. Finally, an upper limit must be set to the permissible wage adjustment.

The liberalization of wage policy continued during 1965 with an agreement that the prime responsibility for wage formation should be transferred in the near future from the Foundation of Labor to the branches of industry concerned. The Social and Economic Council also decided not to continue its practice of laying down actual percentages as its recommended "permissible" rise in wage costs in the year ahead. The role of the Foundation of Labor was also considerably changed. Rather than approve the actual wage increase agreed upon by the contracting parties, the Foundation decided only to test the terms of the agreements for those elements of wage policy about which there is agreement at a national level, such as automatic cost of living allowances.

While both the Social and Economic Council and the Foundation of Labor agreed on certain moves toward greater freedom in wage policy, they could not agree on any specific criteria to govern the 1966 negotations which were then approaching. On the basis of the Central Planning Bureau's economic forecast for 1966, the government expressed the view that the collective labor agreements should not call for more than a 6 to 7 percent increase.

If the 7 percent maximum increase was adhered to during 1966, the Central Planning Bureau estimated that total wages per person employed, including social charges, will rise during 1966 by about 9.5 percent. Since contracts take effect at different times during the year, between 5 and 6 percent of the total 9.5 percent increase would be due to the 1966 revision of contracts. The rest would be caused by carry overs from contract revisions of previous years, changes in employers' contributions to social insurance, and other incidental and nonrecurring payments.[32]

The changes in the process of setting wage policies from 1950 through 1965 demonstrate how the principle of an income policy, as approved by the parliament, has been implemented: a workable consensus on wage policy has been obtained through institutional arrangements established outside of formal parliamentary channels. Because economic policy has been removed, in part at least, from party politics, the way has been opened for more rational, and less emotional, analysis of major economic issues.

32. Ibid., p. 35.

CHAPTER 5

The Technical Process

Most observers will agree that no other Western country started as early or has gone as far as the Netherlands in trying to forecast economic developments and in trying to evaluate the economic consequences of government decisions. The shift of economic policy initiative from parliamentary to extra-parliamentary bodies, a result of the Dutch mixture of religion and politics which impedes electoral consensus, has led to an increased reliance on quantitative economic analysis, because the experts of the Social and Economic Council and the Foundation of Labor have strongly encouraged the development of a whole range of economic data and analysis on which to base their recommendations to the government.

The two main institutions contributing to this analysis are government agencies: the Central Bureau of Statistics and the Central Planning Bureau. In general, the Central Bureau of Statistics collects the raw data used by the Central Planning Bureau in its analyses. Clearly, economic planning must be supported by are liable statistical base, and a relatively detailed description of the operation of the Central Bureau of Statistics indicates the extent to which the Dutch have gone in the development of a government statistics program. The work of the Central Planning Bureau itself takes two main forms: the first is the formal preparation of an annual Central Economic Plan; the second consists of nonrecurring, often ad hoc, studies prepared either at the initiative of the Bureau itself, at the request of some government department, or on behalf of the Social and Economic Council for which the Bureau operates as a staff agency.

THE CENTRAL BUREAU OF STATISTICS

The development of a government statistical program in the Netherlands began in the early 1800s. The name Central Bureau of Statistics dates from 1899 when the Bureau was established by the government to take over the actual completion of data from an organization known as the Central Commission of Statistics. Until 1932 the Central Bureau of Statistics was attached to the Ministry of Home Affairs, at which time it was transferred to the Ministry of Economic Affairs. In recent years, the Central Bureau of Statistics has operated with a staff of over 1,100 employees and an annual budget of approximately three million dollars.

The Central Bureau of Statistics is responsible for practically all statistical activities in which the government engages. Its mandate, the Royal Decree of January 9, 1899, states that:

> Within the limits imposed by available financial means, the Central Bureau of Statistics collects, processes, and publishes all statistical information which the Director considers useful for practical or scientific purposes . . . .
>
> The Bureau cannot undertake any new statistical enquiries, issue new publications, or discontinue existing enquiries and publications without the consent of the Central Commission of Statistics.
>
> On its own initiative or on the instruction of the Minister of Economic Affairs, the Central Commission of Statistics may instruct the Director of the Central Bureau of Statistics to collect, to process, and to publish certain statistical data.[1]

The 1899 Royal Decree was supplemented in 1936 by the passage of a law that formally stated the position of the Bureau vis-à-vis the persons or organizations from whom it desires

1. Netherlands Central Bureau of Statistics, *The Netherlands Central Bureau of Statistics* (The Hague, 1960), p. 10; hereafter cited as *Central Bureau.*

to obtain information of a statistical nature. The law concerns "the compilation of reliable economic statistics according to which all citizens and other persons residing within the Kingdom in Europe, with the exception of heads of government departments, are obliged to supply the desired data and information."[2] According to the wording of the law, however, this obligation is not automatic for every statistical inquiry. Each new inquiry is judged separately by the Minister of Economic Affairs. Once an inquiry is approved, The Minister of Economic Affairs may authorize the Bureau, in cases of doubtful information, to ask for access to the substantiating records. The law also deals with the obligation of the Central Bureau of Statistics to limit the use of the material to legitimate statistical purposes. Individual returns are considered confidential. They may not be published or divulged unless the respondent concerned authorizes such disclosure.

A great many of the economic statistics collected by the Bureau have been made compulsory by action of the Minister of Economic Affairs. Some of these include annual production statistics, short-term industrial statistics, and statistics concerning profits, investments, and installment credit. Such important statistics as those on wages and wholesale and retail prices are still, however, a matter of voluntary response. Other references to statistics are scattered throughout the Dutch legal code. There are special laws for the census of population and occupation, the housing census, and the census of industries. Special laws also pertain to agricultural statistics and statistics of foreign trade and transport.

Before turning to the detailed organization of the Central Bureau of Statistics, it is well to give a short description of the function of the Central Commission of Statistics. When, in 1899, the compilation of statistics was turned over to the newly created Central Bureau of Statistics, the role of the Commission became primarily supervisory and advisory. From a technical point of view, however, the Central Bureau

2. Art. 1, para. 3, quoted in ibid., p. 14.

is still under the control of the Commission. Statistical work is generally instituted or suspended on the initiative or authorization of the Commission, and all important changes in the statistical program have to be submitted to the Commission for approval.

The Commission is composed of 50 representatives from the government and from scientific and socio-economic groups. Thirty of the members, called ordinary members, representatives of both employer and employee organizations, representatives from other interest groups, and private citizens. They are joined on the Commission by representatives of the various ministries. The latter serve not as individuals but by virtue of their official capacity. The Director of the Central Bureau of Statistics is an ex-officio member, while another official of the Bureau acts as Secretary of the Commission. In general, the objective of the Commission is to preserve the impartiality of the Central Bureau of Statistics and to emphasize the professional nature of the work it does.

The Commission meets twice a year: in January when the working program of the Central Bureau of Statistics for the following year is outlined, and in May when a tentative Bureau budget is discussed. Once this budget is approved by the Commission, it is transmitted to the Minister of Economic Affairs, who exercises financial and administrative control over the Bureau.

There are twenty subcommittees of the Commission, each dealing with a particular field of statistics. In the subcommittees, questions concerning proposed statistical surveys are considered from a technical point of view. Nonmembers of the Commission are often invited to attend certain meetings of the subcommittees in the capacity of experts in the subject area being considered. Additional representatives of employers' organizations may be invited as a means of enlisting the aid of prospective respondents in the preparation of a particular inquiry.

The Commission is also the overall coordinator of the government statistics program. By law, no other department of government or government agency may undertake a statistical inquiry of its own without first consulting the Central Commission of Statistics. Although there are still statistical activities existing outside the Central Bureau of Statistics, those pertaining to national data are slowly being consolidated into the Bureau. This centralization pertains only to the collection of statistics and excludes statistical analyses, and many government departments have sections for the analysis of statistical data supplied by the Central Bureau. With the exception of banking statistics (still collected by the national bank), most other national statistics now come under the jurisdiction of the Central Bureau of Statistics.

ORGANIZATION OF THE CENTRAL BUREAU OF STATISTICS

The Director of the Central Bureau of Statistics has the official title of Director-General of Statistics and is responsible for all of the activities of the Bureau. To assist him in the coordination of the work of the statistical departments, whose employees do the actual collection and compilation of statistics, there is a deputy director and an advisor who specializes in mathematical analysis. The advisor is also the general coordinator of the international work of the Bureau.

There are eight departments, each of which is in charge of statistics pertaining to a particular subject area: General Censuses and Population Statistics, Socio-Economic Statistics, Statistics of Manufacturing and Construction, Judicial and Criminal Statistics, Financial Statistics, Foreign Trade and Transport Statistics, Cultural and Educational Statistics and Agricultural Statistics. In addition, there is a Department of National Accounts that is responsible for the construction of the national accounts of the Netherlands. This department does not collect statistical data but makes use of the data already gathered by the other departments. The Bureau also has a Section for Statistical Analysis, which is a research unit employing experts in sampling, mathematical statistics, and econometric analysis.

General Census and Population Statistics. The first decennial population census in the Netherlands was taken in 1829. Regular censuses were conducted during the latter part of the nineteenth century and the early twentieth century until interrupted in 1940 by World War II. Census-taking was resumed after the war, the first census being taken in 1947. The 1947 census was supplemented in 1956 by a partial census primarily concerned with housing statistics.[3]

The Department of General Censuses and Population Statistics also conducts a census of industries. The census of industries covers manufacturing, mining, construction, public utilities, distribution, and transportation. "Data are collected on the number of establishments, their type of economic activity, their geographical location, the number of personnel employed, and the amount of power equipment."[4] The plant is the main unit of industrial activity used in these surveys although, whenever possible, data are also taken for enterprises and technical units. The 1950 census distinguished 593 branches of industry. Since that date, the results of the 1950 census have been regrouped and published according to the United Nations International Standard Industrial Classification.[5]

The Department of General Census and Population Statistics in particular, and the entire Central Bureau of Statistics in general, maintains a close relationship with another group

3. In the Netherlands, the general census is not the sole source of population statistics. Each municipality, of which there are approximately one thousand, maintains a population register that is constantly kept up to date.

4. *Central Bureau*, p. 36.

5. "Indexes to International Standard Industrial Classification of all Economic Activities," *Statistical Papers*, Series M, No. 4 (New York, Statistical Office of the United Nations, 1958).

of statistical organizations, the statistical bureaus of the larger municipalities. Although there has been a great deal of centralization of statistical work within the central government, there are still many statistics that are collected at the municipal level because they are needed for proper administration of local government units. In order to avoid duplication, the Central Bureau of Statistics makes use of these data whenever possible.

The Central Bureau of Statistics operates entirely out of its Hague office, having neither branches nor agencies outside of that city. It might be said that the municipal bureaus are, in effect, the field agencies of the Central Bureau. The interchange of statistics between the Central Bureau and the municipal bureaus is for the most part voluntary, since, with the exception of certain statistics concerning births, deaths, and population movements, the Central Bureau lacks the power to force the municipal bureaus to supply it with data.

To illustrate the cooperation between the Central Bureau of Statistics and the municipal bureaus, an example concerned with the collection of data on schools, teachers, and students in Amsterdam may be cited.[6] The request for data originated with the Central Bureau. The forms requesting the desired information were sent to the various educational institutions in Amsterdam directly from the Hague office of the Central Bureau of Statistics. However, the respondents were instructed to return the completed questionnaires to the Amsterdam Municipal Bureau, where they were to be checked for accuracy and subsequently compiled, classified, and analyzed. A follow-up, if deemed necessary, was made at the local level before the completed forms, along with the totals, were forwarded to the Central Bureau.

The Department of Socio-Economic Statistics. This department collects data covering a wide range of subject matter, in-

6. This example is taken from a mimeographed paper on the Central Bureau of Statistics by Messrs. Amir Saleki, Cano, El Falaki, and Smaka of the Institute of Social Studies, The Hague, Netherlands, 1961.

cluding, for example, statistics pertaining to the service and handicraft industry, wholesale prices, retail prices, and consumer data. In the first category are index numbers of retail sales (about 140 indices covering different lines of retailing), installment selling, and a series of index numbers dealing with wholesale prices.

The Department of Socio-Economic Statistics makes extensive use of family budget surveys. The first such survey in the Netherlands was taken during 1935 and 1936. Included in this survey were 598 volunteer households representing various income and sociological groups. In 1951 a larger survey of 3,000 households was made. During recent years, a continuous survey of 200 selected households has been maintained in order to ascertain possible shifts in the pattern of consumption. In addition, a special inquiry was conducted during 1959–60 among lower-income families. The Department plans to extend this type of study to other social groups in the near future.

Another important function of this department is the publication of monthly retail price statistics, including over 300 goods and services. The survey makes use of over 2,000 respondents covering about 19,000 quotations.

In the area of labor statistics, the Department publishes a wide range of data, including figures on unemployment, absenteeism, industrial disputes, annual earnings, and a monthly series of index numbers on wage rates in manufacturing, transport, agriculture, and certain other groups.

The Department of Manufacturing and Construction Statistics. This department collects statistics of production for the various branches of the manufacturing industry, along with statistical information concerning the building industry. Also collected are certain financial statistics pertaining to the two industries. Recently the Department conducted surveys in several branches of manufacturing and in the wholesale trades to determine costs of production and distribution.

As this type of survey is made only upon the request of the employers' organization for the industry concerned, generally these organizations must pay a part of the cost of the survey. The value of such a survey is that it permits comparisons of the cost of production of different enterprises in the industry, the information for each enterprise being released under the guise of a code number. The unit of measurement usually used is labor time or machine time per unit of product. In some cases a detailed breakdown is given for separate divisions of each enterprise and occasionally even for separate operations.

The Department of Manufacturing and Construction Statistics also prepares statistics of production that cover about 40 branches of industry. The publication is based on a questionnaire sent to each enterprise, requesting data on the value of purchases, stocks of new materials, inventory of finished products, and annual sales figures.[7] Information is also obtained on the labor force. From the data obtained, the Department computes the value added by each branch of industry, as well as the proportion of value being paid to employees as wages and salaries. Although this information is available on an annual basis, it usually takes about a year for the data to be processed and published.

This department also produces a number of monthly and quarterly series dealing with production, consumption, and stocks. Familiar to 11,000 Dutch manufacturers is a regular quarterly questionnaire called "General Industrial Statistics," which requests information on labor turnover, labor shortage, and backlog of unfilled orders. After processing, the information is available in three different breakdowns; branch of industry, size of establishment, and geographical area.

In general, the statistics on the construction industry follow those of the manufacturing industry. Special categories deal with building permits, work-in-progress, the labor force

7. About 12,000 questionnaires are used in this survey.

at the building sites, and statistics on the types of buildings under construction.

The financial statistics prepared by the Department are those that concern the enterprise directly, such as those on profits, dividends, retained earnings, and depreciation allowances.

Foreign Trade and Transport Statistics. Because the economic prosperity of the Netherlands is so vitally linked to its foreign trade, approximately one fourth of the budget of the Central Bureau of Statistics is allocated to the Foreign Trade Department. Most of the data are collected by the customs administration in a continuous operation, resulting in a daily flow of over 15,000 forms to the Central Bureau.

For certain selected imports and exports, the Department publishes statistics within two weeks after the date of the final transaction included in the publication. A broader sample of imports, segregated by commodities, is published after a four-week lag. These data pertain to the previous month's international transactions and are followed two weeks later by a compilation of the same imports and exports listed by place of origin and final destination. If, for private purposes, more specific information is desired, it can be obtained from the Bureau upon payment of the Bureau's cost of compilation.

Financial Statistics Department. This department deals with financial data of enterprises operating primarily in the financial field. The statistics cover public finance, income and property data, and money and capital markets. Also compiled and published are data on income distribution by traditional socio-economic groups as well as by geographical areas. In addition, data on the profit position of certain corporations are collected and published. These data cover 38 percent of the corporative enterprises in the Netherlands, and in terms of corporate profits this is sufficient to account for over 90 percent of total profits. Much of the data for the published financial statistics is supplied by the government Revenue Service in connection with personal income tax and corporate profit tax returns.

For the collection of statistics dealing with money and capital markets, the Central Bureau of Statistics also relies on agencies not under its direct cognizance. These include the Netherlands Bank and the Insurance Chamber. The Bank supplies data on the commercial banking system and on the status of the balance of payments; the Insurance Chamber reports figures on the supply side of the capital market as it concerns the insurance companies.

National Accounts Department. The estimation of national income totals for the Netherlands began (on an official basis) in 1938. Prior to that time, there were several pioneer studies by private scholars whose work has since been incorporated in the historical series published by the Central Bureau of Statistics.

One task of the National Accounts Department is to make certain that the statistical work done by the other departments is of a form usable in the National Accounts. Frequently this department is consulted by other departments when a new inquiry is being made, in an attempt to make certain that the data collected will be suitable for national accounting purposes. On occasion, the National Accounts Department makes suggestions for new inquiries, frequently conducting the pilot studies involved.

The national accounts of the Netherlands distinguish seven sectors of the economy: (1) enterprise; (2) government: the central government and other public authorities; (3) government: social insurance; (4) household; (5) financial institutions: banks and postal clearing institutions; (6) financial institutions: life insurance companies and pension funds; and (7) that which falls into no other category.

In the Netherlands the government's budget, both the receipt and expenditure sides, is classified in accordance with economic categories of the national income accounts. Government expenditures, for example, are listed as consumption, subsidies, transfer payments, etc. The budget in this form is presented as an appendix to the traditional functional budget format. To arrive at the accounting totals, the government disbursing agency identifies each expenditure item by a special code number indicating its national income category at the time of the expenditure. A manual is provided to indicate which code number is to be assigned for each type of expenditure.[8]

A few words on items 3, 5, and 7 above seem to be in order, since these accounts represent a departure from the normal format used for national income accounts. The financial section includes banks, postal clearing services, life insurance companies, and pension funds. The accounts are confined to real and imputed interest transactions and to the specific insurance transactions of life insurance companies and pension funds. The latter include premiums received, benefits paid out, income from investment, and subsidies. Transactions on the money and capital markets do not appear, nor does the commercial activity of such organizations. These are included in the enterprise section.

The account dealing with social insurance follows the United Nations system.[9] According to the U.N. methodology, this section includes those "schemes imposed by the government which involve compulsory contributions by employees and/or employers and in which the whole community is included." Other types of insurance are included even when they do not meet all of the above conditions if "by way of public regulation and supervision or by virtue of a system of government grants, the scheme clearly forms part of the social policy of the government."[10]

8. An attempt is now being made to extend this system to the budgets and accounts of the local authorities.

9. "A System of National Accounts and Supporting Table," *Studies in Methods*, No. 2, Rev. 1 (New York, United Nations, 1960).

10. *Central Bureau*, p. 9.

The system of national accounts currently in use in the Netherlands distinguishes about eighty different types of transactions. Transactions are divided according to sectors, depending upon the economic significance of the persons or institutions involved in the transactions, and then subdivided within the sectors by accounts designed to distinguish the principal economic aspects of the transaction.[11]

The accounts cover: (1) transactions in goods and services; (2) (a) primary distribution of income and (b) secondary distribution of income; (3) consumption and saving; (4) real capital transactions; and (5) financial capital transactions. The accounts contain all the information needed to compute for each sector the value added, primary income, disposable income, consumption, savings, and so forth.

In addition to the national accounts, the Bureau publishes a number of monthly and quarterly economic indicators in the form of quantity, price, and value index numbers. Included are gross domestic product at market prices, imports and exports of goods and services, private consumption expenditures, general government consumption expenditures, gross domestic capital formation, and inventory changes. National wealth estimates are also published on a yearly basis.

Statistical Analysis Section. The Statistical Analysis Section deals with problems of a mathematical and statistical nature. It does not collect data but assists in the planning of surveys being contemplated by the other departments. This is particularly true when the data are to be collected on a sampling basis. The Section also aids in ascertaining the accuracy of the results of the various inquiries conducted by the Bureau.

11. For a more detailed explanation of the national income accounts of the Netherlands, see "National Accounts, 1960," and J. G. Kleve, "The National Income and Product Accounts of the U.S. in the Netherlands Arrangements," *Review of Economics and Statistics, 40* (November 1958), pp. 375–83.

In addition, the Statistical Analysis Section engages in some work of an econometric nature. In this field it cooperates closely with the Central Planning Bureau by supplying certain of the parameters necessary for the macroeconomic models used by the Central Planning Bureau. One of the reasons the Section is involved in the determination of these statistics is because of the confidential nature of much of the information in the files of the Central Bureau of Statistics. Since this information cannot be given directly to the Central Planning Bureau, a division of labor has been established between the Central Bureau of Statistics, Statistical Analysis Section, and the Central Planning Bureau.

THE CENTRAL PLANNING BUREAU

The Central Planning Bureau was established in 1945, although it did not acquire a statutory status until 1947. However, the roots of the Central Planning Bureau and the Central Economic Plan are found in the prewar era when the Netherlands, like most countries, pursued a rather haphazard economic policy in which the issues were not approached as a coherent entity. Even though the Netherlands was hard hit by the depression, the government did not adopt a coordinated economic policy. There was little or no uniformality among whatever policies were established in the areas of trade, wages, agriculture, credit, and prices. Individual decisions on policy matters were made in relative isolation by the ministries or agencies concerned and no effective action was taken to coordinate the policies of the various ministries and agencies beyond normal intra-cabinet cooperation.

In the early 1930s the Labor Party, the main opposition party, called for a program to organize production and investment in various industries, as well as a program of public works in order to reduce unemployment. In 1935 the Party published a plan that contained the basic outline for these programs. In the summer of 1939 the Labor Party entered the government, but no progress was made in implementing the plans before the war started that September, forcing evacuation of the government to London a few months later.

After the war the Labor Party was again part of the coalition government. The party leaders initiated legislation designed to provide a means of directing budgetary policy toward the attainment of labor goals, particularly full employment. Labor also felt that industry should be reorganized to facilitate the attainment of certain production targets and to avoid overproduction and incorrect investments, and sufficient aid was enlisted from the other major parties to pass the Industrial Organization Act in 1950.

Labor's efforts were also rewarded with the establishment of the Central Planning Bureau which had the primary duty of coordinating the economic planning of the government. When officially established the Central Planning Bureau was designated as an advisory body, with no executive duties. To quote from the 1947 law:

> The task of the Central Planning Bureau is to carry out all activities relating to the preparation of a Central Economic Plan, which at regular times shall be laid down by the government for the benefit of the coordination of the government's policy in the economic, social, and financial fields, as well as the submission of recommendations on general questions which may arise with respect to the realization of the plan.[12]

At the outset there was a question as to the way in which the new planning organization would develop. Certainly there was expectation on the part of some members of the Labor Party that the Central Planning Bureau would in time function as an executive body supervising the economy,

12. Netherlands Central Planning Bureau, *Scope and Methods of the Central Planning Bureau* (The Hague, 1956), p. 65.

but events have clearly not borne this out. The 1947 law set forth a requirement for an economic plan, describing it as a "balanced compendium of estimates and directives, relating to the Netherlands economy, which contains in particular those data which are important for the proper coordination of economic, social, and financial policy."[13] This plan might perhaps have become a centralized development scheme committing the government to the realization of a set of specific development goals, but it did not turn out this way. From the start the plan has consisted mainly of forecasts of the short-term economic situation, forecasts which exist only as an information aid and a coordination device.

Organization of the Central Planning Bureau

The act of 1947, which gave legal status to the Central Planning Bureau, also provided for a Central Planning Committee to act as a board of management for the Central Planning Bureau and to advise the Minister of Economic Affairs with regard to the activities of the Bureau. The Committee is comprised of 30 members, of whom 11 are representatives of different ministries and other government agencies, and 16 are from the central employers' and workers' organization or from other types of business not represented by the central organizations. The final three members are economic experts. The main function of this Committee is to review the annual economic plan prior to its transmission to the Council of Economic Affairs, a subcommittee of the cabinet.

The Bureau is supervised by a managing board headed by a director and two deputy directors. They are appointed by the Minister of Economic Affairs after consultation with

13. C. A. van der Beld, "The Procedures Followed by the Central Planning Bureau in Drawing up the Central Economic Plan," *Economic Quarterly Review*, No. 128 (First Quarter, 1960), p. 3.

the ministers of the other economic departments. There are also two senior advisors who have no direct organizational responsibilities. One advisor is for social problems and the other for statistical problems; they serve as full-time consultants on matters within their special fields. The professional composition of the staff of the Bureau reflects the analytical and scientific nature of the work of the Bureau. 40 of the 90 staff members are trained economists.

The Central Planning Bureau is divided into three scientific divisions, each with its particular area of competence. The First Division is primarily concerned with research dealing with long-range economic problems; the Second Division deals with short-term problems; and the Third Division is concerned with inter-industry (input-output) relations.

The First Division. The First Division is divided into five sections; (1) general structural problems, (2) market analysis and trade cycles, (3) socio-cultural problems, (4) international trade, and (5) income and property problems. The nature of the work undertaken by the First Division is such that particular studies may take months, or even years, to complete.

Due to the dependence of the Netherlands export market on the relative prosperity of certain of its trading partners, the First Division devotes considerable time to research concerning the future prospects of the economies of these partners. It is interesting to note that in the 1961 Central Economic Plan, and in other recent editions of the plan, one finds a special section devoted to the economic picture of the United States complete with tables and charts showing changes in production and expenditures by quarters and depicting sales and new orders of the United States' manufacturing industry. West Germany and the United Kingdom also receive a detailed analysis. This is understandable considering that West Germany, the United Kingdom, and the United States account for over one third of the value of the Netherlands' export sales.[14]

In 1955 the First Division produced a long-term study covering the Netherlands' economy over a twenty-year period entitled *An Exploration of the Economic Potentialities of the Netherlands, 1950–1970*.[15]

The Second Division. This division deals with short-term problems and is essentially concerned with the day-to-day questions upon which the Bureau is asked to give advisory opinions. In addition, the Second Division is the "keeper of the model," a system of simultaneous equations representing the Dutch economy. The Bureau uses this as a tool for testing the results of alternative policy decisions in the macroeconomic sphere and for projecting the future time-paths of certain economic variables. This model has been in operation for a period of about 15 years, although the current version bears very little resemblance to its more distant predecessors.

The forecasts prepared by the Bureau provide the framework around which the Central Economic Plan is developed. Although these forecasts are only published yearly, they are made much more frequently. For example, quarterly reports, which are not published, are circulated among the policy-making agencies, the ministries, and the Central Bank. These reports deal with economic developments in the preceding three months and the Bureau's opinion of the outlook for the next quarter.

In these reports, policy recommendations are sometimes made if, in the opinion of the Planning Bureau, they are appropriate. The reports are discussed by the Council of

14. Netherlands Central Bureau of Statistics, *Jaarcijfers voor Nederland 1959–1960* (Statistical Yearbook of the Netherlands), (The Hague, 1961), p. 176.

15. An English summary of this report is available under the title *Complementarity and Long-Range Projections*, by P. J. Verdoorn (The Hague, Central Planning Bureau Report 50); it is also published under the same title in *Econometrica*, *24* (1956), 429–50.

Economic Affairs, that is, the cabinet ministers concerned with economic policy. The meetings of the Council of Economic Affairs, are attended by the president of the Central Bank and the director of the Central Planning Bureau. When recommendations are made and accepted by the Council of Economic Affairs, the appropriate minister takes the proposal to the full cabinet which makes the final decision.

In 1961 the Bureau began to publish a preliminary forecast timed to appear simultaneously with the government's budget.[16] The forecasts, which are prepared as a result of a parliamentary request, are called macroeconomic estimates. Although they refer only to the next year, they have to be completed well before the statistical material for the current year is available; thus, in effect, the forecast covers a period just short of two years. The macroeconomic estimate is also used by the Social and Economic Council as the starting point for the discussions required by the new system for determining wage policy (see Chapter 4).

Internally, the Second Division is divided into five sections: (1) a general section; (2) a section specializing in the national budget; (3) a section dealing with consumption and investment; (4) a section on prices and wages and the general state of the labor market; and (5) a section dealing with monetary issues.

The evolution of the econometric model, the refinement of its structure, and the improvement in the estimation of its parameters are primarily the responsibility of the staff of the third and fourth sections of the Second Division. Roughly speaking, the division between consumption and investment, on the one hand, and between labor, prices and wages, on the other, corresponds to the two major groups of equations that appear in the model. The section staffs are expected to keep abreast of any developments in their particular fields

16. The government's budget is submitted to the States-General in September.

that might affect the correspondence between the model and the real world the model is supposed to represent. As experts, they are often called upon to prepare briefs (requested by particular ministries or by the cabinet) in the areas in which they specialize. Among the responsibilities of the fifth section is the monetary survey published by the Bureau as part of the annual Economic Plan.

The Third Division. This division of the Bureau is concerned with "branch of industry" analysis. Its members specialize in the economic and technical problems related to inter-industry transfers of goods and services. In the Third Division, there are four sections: (1) the general section; (2) a section for manufacturing industry; (3) a section for agriculture; and (4) a section covering all other branches of industry. The division, in cooperation with the Central Bureau of Statistics, maintains an input-output model of the industrial sector of the Netherlands' economy.

THE CENTRAL ECONOMIC PLAN

The Central Planning Bureau is charged by law with the preparation of a Central Economic Plan. In the words of this law:

> [T]he Central Economic Plan contains *inter alia* collections of figures relating to the future size of production in the widest sense of the word, to the future size and development of the level of prices, of the national income and further quantities, which are of importance for a good coordination of the economic, social, and financial policy.[17]

Thus, contrary to what the term "plan" might suggest, in the Netherlands a "plan" is merely a collection of figures that, in the strictest sense, is only a review of past events and

17. The Act of April 21, 1947, Article 3, part 3. See Central Planning Bureau, *Scope and Methods*, p. 66.

a set of forecasts pertaining to future economic developments.

Each plan is a combination of three separate forecasts: (1) the Central Planning Bureau predicts the actions economic agents outside of the government will take, and the effect of these actions on the economic process; (2) the Bureau predicts the probable course of action on the part of the government, based on the economic conditions expected to exist during the plan period as revealed by the first forecast; and (3) the Bureau arrives at a final forecast of economic conditions for the plan period by estimating the results of policy measures it expects the government to take. This final forecast is the framework around which the Central Economic Plan is built.

Each plan generally starts with a short survey of current developments and probable future trends.[18] It then proceeds to a detailed assessment of economic developments abroad during the current year. This is followed by an appraisal of the prospects abroad for the plan year, i.e. the year for which the plan is being prepared. This survey is particularly detailed with respect to the major trading partners of the Netherlands. An attempt is made to estimate domestic price changes and price changes in the international transactions of the individual countries and whether or not these are likely to affect the competitive position of exports from the Netherlands.

The plan next turns to the Dutch domestic situation with a review of the current year. The basic framework upon which this analysis is developed is the Dutch system of national accounts. Movements in production and in consumption are described as are changes in wage and price levels. In particular, the effects of these movements on the

18. Beginning in 1964, the introductory chapter of the plan has been written in such a manner that it can be used as a summary of the entire document. Mimeographed copies of this chapter are published immediately after the plan has been approved by the government and while the remainder of the plan is awaiting printing. This summary is published in English and French as well as Dutch.

balance-of-payments account is thoroughly analyzed. The plan also discusses the level of foreign exchange holdings and movements in the money and capital markets.

Finally, one comes to what is really the core of the plan, the discussion of the prospects for the plan year. Likely developments in key macroeconomic variables are considered. Assessments of export opportunities are made, as well as the prices of Dutch imports, the supply of labor, the wage level, and the expected changes in government expenditure and revenue. From these data, conclusions are drawn as to the probable level of general economic activity and the development of the different categories of private expenditure. Where possible, the data are presented in both nominal and volume terms to aid in drawing inferences from the plan.

The estimates of future economic conditions are based on an analysis of past trends and on assumptions regarding government economic policy. In some plans the consequences of possible mistakes in the estimates and unanticipated or alternative government policies are discussed. For example, in the 1952 Plan a number of different forecasts were offered, each corresponding to a different set of policy actions on the part of the government. This format focused attention on the anticipated results of several different feasible policy measures that might be taken by the government in light of a decrease in Dutch export trade expected in the forthcoming year.

Another example occurred in 1961 when the Minister of Finance announced an income tax reduction effective July 1, 1962. However, the parliament approved a supplementary proposal from the Minister to postpone the introduction of the tax reduction if, in the opinion of the cabinet, the prevailing economic boom would be overly stimulated by the tax reduction. Consequently, the 1961 Plan contained two forecasts, one based on the assumed tax reduction and a second based on no change in tax rates. In the 1963 Plan, the consequences of an additional 1 percent increase in the wage level over that predicted, as well as the consequences of an extra 1 percent increase in capital expenditure, were presented.

The final section of most plans deals with individual branches of industry and assesses their probable performance in the year to come. This section of the plan represents a more detailed analysis of economic developments than the analysis conducted on macroeconomic lines appearing in earlier sections. The importance of the inter-industry forecasts is that they afford a more detailed estimate of the future trends than the macroeconomic forecasts. The branch of industry estimates are used as a check on the macro-economic forecasts and in some cases lead to revision of the macro figures if there is a discrepancy.

Work on the plan begins approximately one year prior to the publication date. Initially the Bureau works with very rough figures, frequently only estimates by the section experts employed in the Central Bureau of Statistics. As the plan develops, the figures become better. Because the plan is published in February of the plan year, the calculations are usually completed about December of the previous year, allowing a month for review and printing. Therefore, practically all the data for the last quarter of the current year have to be extrapolated. In areas where quarterly data are not collected, the entire year must be estimated.

In the first draft of the annual plan, an unchanged government policy is taken as a starting point. This draft contains variants corresponding to alternative government policies with respect to wages, taxes, credit, and so forth, which in turn correspond to variables in the model that are, at least to some degree, under the control of the government, i.e. variables that can be changed by the authorities responsible for the formulation and execution of government economic policy.

Once the first draft plan is drawn up, it is sent to the various ministries for criticism. In principle, there is supposed to be a specific officer for liaison with the Central Planning Bureau within each of the ministries concerned with the plan. In reality, however, contacts between the Bureau and the government departments responsible for economic policy are many and varied. It is mainly through informal contacts that the Bureau keeps itself informed on what is happening within the government. When the first draft of the plan arrives at a ministry, each official whose policy may be affected is given the opportunity to study the relevant parts of the plan and to make comments. In this manner the Bureau is able to ascertain the intended policy of the ministries, in particular those points that have not already been fixed in the government budget. In each ministry these comments are collected by a senior official, submitted to the minister for consideration, and the minister decides which comments should appear in the official report of the ministry. He then returns the first draft of the plan along with the comments to the Central Planning Bureau.

The Bureau then constructs a second draft plan, taking into account the ministerial comments. This draft is sent to the Central Planning Committee, whose advice is given during a special meeting attended by the directors of the Central Planning Bureau.

Finally, a third draft of the plan is prepared and submitted to the Council of Economic Affairs.[19] When the plan

19. Before the draft is finished, staff members of the Central Planning Bureau go into the field to discuss the economic situation with industry leaders. A number of large firms are asked for their investment plans, sales expectations, etc. The Bureau is mainly interested in obtaining a final check on the forecasts of the econometric model which were used in preparing the draft plans. The information obtained as a result of these meetings sometimes offers new insights into the prospects for the forthcoming year. No matter how intricate a model may be, there are specific factors that either cannot be introduced systematically into the model or are left out because in a normal year they would not be important. In these meetings the personnel from the Bureau attempt to discern changes in the attitudes of business executives which would offer evidence that factors not taken into account in the original forecasts would be at work during the plan year.

is approved by this cabinet subcommittee, it goes to the full cabinet. After receiving cabinet approval, usually about the end of the calendar year, the plan is published in February, under normal circumstances.

This description of the steps that lead to the publication of a Central Economic Plan clearly shows that the plans are based on government economic policy and not the other way around. The plan is, for the most part, formulated after the most important economic policy decisions, in particular those embodied in the budget, have already been made. A government agency or department has never been required to consult the Planning Bureau prior to a policy decision. Through its informal contacts and by virtue of the fact that the director of the Bureau attends meetings of the Council of Economic Affairs and is a member of the Social and Economic Council, the Bureau learns of impending policy measures and may offer advice. However, it is not officially an operating agency of the government.

OTHER FUNCTIONS OF THE CENTRAL PLANNING BUREAU

Although the main recurring function of the Central Planning Bureau is the preparation of annual economic plans, the Bureau engages in a great variety of other activities. For the most part these take the form of special studies or reports. In some cases they are closely linked to the preparation of the annual plan, being concerned, for example, with the development of better structural equations or with the improvement of the prediction of the exogenous variables used in the model. In other cases these studies pertain to some specific measures contemplated by the government and they may be prepared as the result of a request from a particular ministry, the Cabinet, or from the Social and Economic Council. In recent years there have also been a number of reports compiled at the request of various international agencies, such as the Organization for

European Cooperation and Development, and the European Economic Community.[20]

The reports prepared for the Social and Economic Council are particularly important because of the influence of this body on government policy. These reports cover subjects ranging from the consumption habits of the Dutch population, unemployment compensation, and the future development of wages to the effects of changes in the length of the working day and the probable consequences of the introduction of a number of different types of social insurance. For all practical purposes, it is in this way that the Central Planning Bureau functions as the staff arm of the Social and Economic Council.

The remainder of the work of the Central Planning Bureau can conveniently be grouped under three general categories:[21] (1) forecasting the "rest of the world"; (2) long-term plans; and (3) monetary statements.

Forecasting the "rest of the world." The percentage of the Netherlands' gross national product linked with world markets either as imports of raw materials for further processing, imports of finished products for sale on the domestic market, or through the export of Dutch goods for sale on foreign markets indicates the degree to which the Netherlands' economy is dependent on foreign trade. In 1962 imports plus exports was approximately 96 percent of gross national product.[22] As a consequence, the forecasting of external factors plays an important role in any quantitative appraisal of the future prospects of the Dutch economy.

In the formulation of the short-term forecasting model, which will be described in Chapter 7, external factors are

20. Some examples are estimates of the social return of a number of large public investments, and estimates of the future supply of and demand for academically trained personnel.

21. Inter-industry analysis, the work of the Third Division of the Central Planning Bureau, is not discussed in this study.

22. Computed from statistics published in the *Centraal Economisch Plan 1963*.

left exogenous to the working of the model. This is true for both the world import price level and the price level of Dutch competitors on the world market. This is realistic, inasmuch as neither Dutch exports nor Dutch imports weigh heavily in the world totals, and thus, with such small shares, Dutch influence on the world price level is small or negligible. This is not true, however, so far as the effect of changes in world prices on the Netherlands' economy is concerned. Therefore, it is essential that accurate assessments of world price movements be made.

The prediction of changes in the level of world prices is done by the First Division of the Central Planning Bureau. For the most part, the forecasts are a combination of a subjective evaluation of the component parts of the world price index combined with the Bureau's estimate of likely movements in the business cycle for the world as a whole. The main indices used are those for raw materials, food, and industrial products. During the last decade, there seems to have been a steadily decreasing relationship between the sum of the food and raw material indices and the index of individual products.[23] This trend has been of some aid in the prediction of Dutch import prices.

The Central Planning Bureau is interested in predicting possible growth in the volume of Dutch exports. Changes in the demand for foreign (Dutch, among others) products are mainly related to changes in domestic economic activity on the part of the country concerned. Hence, the Central Planning Bureau tries to predict the general level of economic activity in each of its most important markets. To this end, the Bureau has constructed a quarterly model of the United States that is used for this purpose. From all appearances, staff members of the Central Planning Bureau are well-versed on the economic indicators of the Netherlands'

23. See F. J. M. Meyer zu Schlochtern, "Grondstoffen Trekken de Aandacht and Naar een Trendwijziging Van Grondstoffenprijzen," in *Economisch-Statistische Berichten* July 24, 1963, p. 691; and July 31, 1963, p. 711.

most important customers; they routinely watch, for example for changes in disposable income, order to sales ratios, inventories, profits, and labor costs per unit of output.

Potential developments in the balance-of-payments positions of Holland's main trading partners are also closely watched because of the possibility of import restrictions in response to unfavorable changes in the balance of payments of these countries. In addition, the Bureau has conducted special studies concerned with the affect of the United States and the United Kingdom business cycles on the economic conditions in the rest of the world. It has been found that the United States cycle is a good indicator, leading the index of imports of the rest of the world by about half a year.

The Bureau makes use of econometric models developed by other economists in predicting the levels of economic activity of certain of the Dutch trading partners. For example, the Klein, Ball, Hazlewood, and Vandome model is used in its forecasts for the United Kingdom, and the Konig and Timmerman model for evaluating the anticipated changes in the main economic indicators of West Germany. The French medium-term plans have been used in forecasting developments within the French economy. Recently a regular European Economic Community questionnaire and a conference regarding member countries' expectations of exports and imports has begun. It is expected that the information obtained as a result of these surveys and the discussion meetings will aid in refining the external predictions of the Bureau. Several years ago the Central Planning Bureau made use of a world model in order to obtain a clearer picture of developments in world trade. This model became outdated and is now being replaced by a new long-term model of the world economy.

Long-term plans. The Central Planning Bureau does not approach long-term planning in as systematic a manner as it approaches short-term planning. As stated previously, the objective of the long-term plan is clearly indicated by the title of the first published long-term plan, *An Exploration of the Economic Potentialities of the Netherlands, 1950–1970.*[24]

The recent long-term forecasts of the Central Planning Bureau are based, for the most part, on input-output tables constructed for a base year and a series of reference years. Imports are distributed by destination and the flow of investment goods is shown both by origin and destination. Future years' estimates are obtained by starting with a framework of fixed export estimates and then simply shifting inputs and outputs until a number of the traditional relationships, such as input-output ratios, capital-output ratios, and the like, are satisfied. These relationships are assumed to vary over time in order to take into account observed trends. The input-output tables form the basis for a series of models. These models are used mainly to analyze the possible implications of variations around a set of provisional estimates for 1970, 1975, 1980, and 1985.

Monetary analysis. Each year the Central Planning Bureau prepares a monetary survey that is published as an appendix to the Central Economic Plan.[25] This survey contains data relating to a number of important money flows. The data are shown in two sets of tables: the first set of tables is entitled the monetary statement and the second is the monetary accounts. In essence the monetary accounts consist of a more detailed exposition of the summary data presented in the monetary statement.[26] For the purpose of

24. See J. Sandee, "Possible Economic Growth in the Netherlands," in R. C. Geary, ed., *Europe's Future in Figures* (Amsterdam, North-Holland Publishing Co., 1962), pp. 162–83; J. G. Van Beeck and H. Den Hartog, "Consumption Forecasts for the Netherlands," in J. Sandee, ed., *Europe's Future Consumption* (Amsterdam, North-Holland Publishing Co., 1964), pp. 83–130; and J. Sandee, "A Long-term, Phased Policy Model for the Netherlands," paper read at the Boston meeting of the Econometric Society, December 1963.

25. For a more complete discussion, see Central Planning Bureau, *Monetary Statement and Monetary Analysis*, Monograph No. 7 (The Hague, 1959).

26. In addition to the monetary survey published by the Central Planning

monetary analysis, the Bureau divides the Dutch economy into five sectors: (1) enterprises and households; (2) institutional investors; (3) central government; (4) local governments; and (5) foreign countries.

The monetary statement shows each sector's savings, net investment, capital transfers, government credits, increase in claims arising from the difference between cash and accrual accounting, borrowing in the capital market, and creation of liquidities. The monetary accounts record transactions between sectors as well as the summary totals that appear in the monetary statement.

The monetary analysis of the Bureau focuses on a series of sector surpluses (or deficits): the income surplus, the claims surplus, the liquidity surplus, and the financing surplus. The surpluses show which sectors have exercised purchasing power in excess or deficiency of the sector's current contribution to production. Excess expenditures are termed inflationary, while deficit expenditures are deflationary. Inflationary financing can be accomplished either by financing expenditure out of the creation of new money or by drawing on available liquid reserves, i.e. dishoarding. On the other hand, deflationary impulses are caused by hoarding money, i.e. by taking it out of circulation. In the analysis of the Netherlands' Central Planning Bureau, the concepts of hoarding and dishoarding and the cancellation and resort to the creation of money are extended to apply not only to money and primary liquidities but also to secondary liquidities.

Bureau, another statement with slightly different format and focus is published by the Netherlands Bank. In years past there has been a lively controversy between the two institutions and other observers regarding the relative merits and policy implications to be drawn from the monetary survey. The interested reader is referred to: M. W. Holtrop, "Method of Monetary Analysis Used by De Nederlandsche Bank," *International Monetary Fund Staff Papers*, *5* (February 1957), 303–16; and H. C. Bos, *A Discussion on Methods of Monetary Analysis and Norms for Monetary Policy* (Rotterdam, Netherlands Economic Institute, 1956).

The income surplus represents the difference between a sector's savings and investment, indicating the excess of income over expenditure. If the sum of these surpluses for all domestic sectors is positive, the national income is higher than the national expenditure for the time period being considered. Therefore, the balance of payments on the current account will show a surplus equal to the excess of savings over investment, and the foreign country sector will show an income deficit.

The claims surplus represents the sum of all changes in credit relations. It is determined either by the algebraic sum of the income surplus plus capital transfers received, or by the algebraic sum of government credits supplied, the entry representing the difference between transactions on a cash or accrual basis, borrowing in the capital market, and the net change in liquidities.

The financing surplus shows the net monetary resources of the sector after account has been taken of government credits supplied and the difference between cash and accrual accounting. Stated more simply, it is the difference between the claims surplus and the latter two entries.

The financing surplus can be absorbed by the cancellation of liquidities by redemption and by a decrease in liquidities (dishoarding). This sum net change in liquidities is called the liquidity surplus. The liquidity surplus indicates the extent to which a sector finances in a monetarily deflationary manner, while a liquidity deficit indicates the extent to which a sector finances in a monetarily inflationary manner. The difference between a sector's liquidity surplus and its financing surplus is taken up by the transactions on the capital market.

In classifying financial transactions by sector, the greater part of the savings of private households appear in the sector called institutional investors. This is because institutions, rather than the households, make financial investments with the savings of the householder. The activities of financial institutions that create liquidities and invest funds at their disposal are disaggregated. Only the non-money-creating parts appear directly in the monetary statement. The liquidities-creating parts of the central government, local government, banks, and clearing agencies appear indirectly in the monetary statement when resort is made to them by the various sectors.

Although the Central Planning Bureau and the Central Statistics Bureau do not have the formal power to make policy themselves, their work as staff to the policy-makers, both in the cabinet and in the extra-parliamentary advisory bodies, strongly influences the range, rationality, and direction of the economic decision-making process.

In the next chapter the discussion turns to some examples of how the data and analysis provided by these two Bureaus has been used by the Dutch authorities in coordinating the economic policy of the government.

CHAPTER 6

The Coordination of Economic Policy

One general defect in the planning process in many countries is the lack of coherence. Decisions are often taken individually. Isolated decisions are taken to change one policy at a time, often in the belief that a particular policy can directly achieve a particular aim. For example, a tax is changed because the budget is not balanced, while the effect of the tax on other economic variables, such as employment or prices, is not taken into account. Because economic policies are, for the most part, interdependent, few policy measures will work solely in the direction of a single objective. More often, policy measures have a number of effects.

In the Netherlands an attempt is made to quantify these effects. Although some consequences of policy action escape even the most careful consideration and analysis, the Dutch believe that the process of political decision in the area of economic policy is sharpened significantly by at least attempting to remove as many aspects of the problem as possible from the realm of unsupported opinion and emotive rhetoric. Even rough quantification often enables the authorities to recognize more clearly the policies that are compatible and those that work at cross purposes. This brings policymakers closer to obtaining coherent solutions to problems of economic policy and closer to the elusive goal of attaining a consistent overall economic policy.

The first step in the planning process is for the Central Planning Bureau to prepare a set of preliminary forecasts that, given no change in government economic policy, predict (1) the actions economic agents outside the government will take, and (2) the effects of these actions on the economic process. If these preliminary forecasts reveal unfavorable developments, the government determines what courses of action might, in their opinion, counteract these developments. Next the Bureau evaluates the effects of these alternative sets of policy actions before a course of action is agreed upon. In each of the steps described above, the Bureau uses the current version of its short-term macroeconomic model to prepare forecasts, which in turn are used to ascertain the compatibility of the various objectives of economic policy and the likely effects (in given circumstances) of the means that might be applied to achieve them.

Unfortunately, it is difficult to know the influence of a particular forecast on a particular policy action by Dutch authorities. Direct evidence linking particular policy actions to particular manipulations of the Planning Bureau models is simply not available. Given a knowledge of the Dutch institutional arrangements for formulating economic policy, however, one can infer the connection between the models and the final decisions of the policy-makers. In addition, there are occasions where it is possible to point out when incorrect forecasts of certain important policy variables indicated inappropriate policy actions and to show if these actions were indeed taken.

The years from 1950 through 1965 exhibited a general upward trend in almost all areas of economic activity. Some variation around the trend did occur when inflationary or deflationary tendencies were clearly visible. Fluctuations in the unemployment rate, for example, varied from 1 to 4.5 percent, and the current accounts of the balance of payments showed rather violent fluctuations. The decade and a half can be divided into a Korean War inflationary period (1950–52), a post-Korean War recession (1953–54), an inflationary period (1955–57), a moderate recession (1958–59), and a long period of inflationary tendencies beginning in 1959.

As pointed out in Chapter 4, official Dutch economic policy is directed toward achieving and maintaining an income policy with the objectives of a high level of employment and relative price stability. Therefore, the level of employment and variations in consumer, export, and industrial prices are the major variables. Because of the openness of the Dutch economy, fluctuations in the level of the balance-of-payments account are also important to the policy-makers, and most policy actions, including those dealing with wages and prices, were to a significant degree determined by the desire of the policy-makers to maintain a favorable balance-of-payments position.

The examples of Dutch economic policy that will be discussed include the deflationary programs of 1951 and 1957; a 1959 suggested program designed to shift the pattern of expenditures; a proposed tax decrease scheduled for 1961; and the revaluation of the guilder which took place in 1961. The final section of the chapter contains a discussion of economic conditions that have affected economic policy since 1962. Along with each specific example of economic policy is an analysis of the main issues facing the policy-makers at the time and an account of the use of Planning Bureau models and forecasts by Dutch authorities as they tried to evaluate possible courses of action.

THE 1951 PROGRAM OF ECONOMIC POLICY

Short -term economic policy actions are contra-cyclical in nature; that is, they are designed to offset either short-run inflationary or deflationary tendencies. The 1951 program was deflationary and represented a coordinated attempt by the authorities to protect the Dutch balance-of-payments position in the face of the worldwide inflation that followed the outbreak of the Korean War. In designing the program, the authorities asked the Central Planning Bureau for advice regarding the likely primary and secondary effects of the policy actions contemplated by the government.

One of the main economic effects of the war was a series

of increases in world commodity prices. The price indices of tin, rubber, and wool more than doubled in the first six months after the outbreak of the war.[1] These increases were attributed to inventory hoarding, speculation on the commodity exchanges, and the build-up of raw material stockpiles undertaken by the United States government.

In the Netherlands inventory stockpiling was delayed by post-World War II import controls. These controls expired in 1951, at a time when commodity prices were at their highest levels, a factor that tended to worsen the effects on the balance-of-payments of inventory increases by Dutch manufacturers. For the Netherlands as a whole, the terms of trade between manufactured goods and materials fell from 100 in 1950 to 95 in 1951,[2] a sharp turn against manufactured goods. In addition, domestic aggregate demand was on the rise, imports increased as a result, and the Dutch balance-of-payments position became worse.

In the Netherlands, increased domestic demand for goods and services has a significant effect on the demand for imports. When consumer demand leads an expansion, there is a greater effect on import demand than increased investment. The effect of increased real consumption on import demand is approximately three times that of a similar increase in the volume of investment. According to the 1961 econometric model, a 10 percent increase in consumption will lead to a 7 percent increase in imports, while a 10 percent increase in investment leads to a 2 percent rise in import demand.[3]

By mid-1951 the monthly balance-of-payments deficit was running at a rate that indicated an annual balance-of-payments deficit of over two billion guilders, twice the 1950

1. Organization for European Economic Cooperation, Statistical Bulletin, No. 6 (Paris, OEEC, 1955), pp. 86–89.

2. Measured as the ratio of the export price index to the import price index normalized to 1950. Source: International Monetary Fund, *International Financial Statistics Supplement to 1964/65 Issues* (Washington, D.C., 1965), p. 163.

3. *Centraal Economisch Plan 1965*, pp. 172–73.

deficit.[4] For the year 1951 as a whole, average gold and foreign exchange holdings were sufficient to cover only 2.5 months of imports. During the second quarter of 1951, foreign exchange reserves fell to a point where they represented only 1.1 months of imports.[5]

To compound the problems facing the policy-makers, the deficit in the balance of payments and the deterioration in the foreign exchange position were accompanied by a domestic price inflation that reflected the world-wide price increases. Wholesale prices rose 16 percent in 1950 and 20 percent during the first half of 1951,[6] and the cost of living index (exclusive of social insurance and wages tax) rose by 12 percent by the end of the year.[7]

The fall in the Netherlands' terms of trade was in itself inflationary since it reduced the amount of imported goods and services a given volume of exports would buy. Thus the unfavorable shift in the terms of trade caused the real income of the Netherlands to be reduced. Measured relative to the 1953 terms of trade, 1951 showed a loss of 70 million guilders in national income as a result of the terms of trade deterioration.[8]

During 1950 and the early part of 1951, the government undertook a series of policy actions designed to check the domestic inflation and the drain on foreign exchange reserves. When it was apparent that these efforts were not sufficient, the government, in March 1951, formulated a package of policy measures, the so-called Program of 1951. Among these measures were a restrictive credit policy, a decrease in government expenditures, a decrease in consumer subsidies, an increase in taxes on luxury goods, an increase in profits taxes, a decrease in fiscal investment

4. Netherlands Bank, *1954*, p. 43.

5. Hartog, "Economic Policy in the Netherlands," pp. 93–95.

6. United Nations Economic Commission for Europe, *Economic Survey of Europe 1951* (Geneva, 1952), p. 103.

7. *Economic Quarterly Review*, No. 147 (March 1965), p. 49.

8. "National Accounts, 1960," p. 51.

allowances, an increase in inheritance tax, an acceleration in tax collection, a decrease in the building program, the issuance of a government loan for the purpose of absorption of liquidities, and a restriction of profit margins. Coupled with these steps was an obligatory wage round that compensated for only one half of the anticipated 10 percent cost of living increase. As a result of this measure alone, it was expected that real wages would decline by 5 percent.

While the Program of 1951 was the result of consultation among the various ministries concerned with economic matters, the advice of the Social and Economic Council was sought during its formulative stages and the total effects of policy actions were calculated by the Central Planning Bureau. Not only were the direct effects computed but also the indirect effects of the deflationary impulses contained in the policy program. As worked out by the Planning Bureau, the targets expected to restore equilibrium in the balance of payments and to check the inflation were a 5 percent decrease in consumption accompanied by a 25 percent decrease in investment.

According to Jan Tinbergen, the economist who at that time was Director of the Central Planning Bureau, one of the most important features of the program was the fact that the trade unions agreed with it, even though a net loss in real income was called for. He attributed the cooperation of the trade unions to the atmosphere of confidence that existed between labor and government.[9] Tinbergen also pointed out that the forecasts of the Bureau, as well as the Bureau's work in quantifying the alternatives that were likely to achieve the policy objectives, played an important role in formulating the policy program. Without the forecasts, according to Tinbergen, action might not have been taken until the actual evidence of a continued worsening of the balance of payments had been compiled by the Central

9. Jan Tinbergen, *Central Planning* (New Haven and London, Yale University Press, 1964), pp. 53–54.

Bureau of Statistics. Instead, the program was based on the forecasts made in late 1950 for plan year 1951.

The general recovery from the economic difficulties resulting from the Korean War inflation began shortly after the policy program was put into effect, and probably little of the Dutch recovery can be attributed directly to the Program of 1951. The most important factor in restoring the balance-of-payments account to a more favorable position was that the world-wide inflation in commodity prices turned out to be largely due to psychological fears, which later proved unfounded. Within a year after hitting their peak, these prices returned to the levels that had prevailed at the beginning of the war.

The balance-of-payments situation improved to the extent that the figures for the year 1951 showed a deficit of only .269 billion guilders.[10] The balance-of-payments fluctuations show that national reserves can be held in a number of ways, not only gold and foreign exchange but also stocks of raw materials. The gold and foreign exchange position went from 1.486 billion guilders in 1950 to 1.668 billion in 1951, 3.660 billion in 1952, and 4.445 billion in 1953.[11] The figures for the value of the increase or decrease in stocks and work in progress show an increase of 1.199 billion guilders in 1950 and a 1.088 billion increase in 1951, with a decrease of .316 billion in 1952, and a further decrease of .196 billion in 1953.[12]

During this period there was a significant shift in domestic expenditure from the private to the public sector. One factor was an increase in military expenditures, which more than tripled (from .360 billion to 1.500 billion guilders annually).[13] The compensating decreases in other expenditures, i.e. the targets for the policy program, caused the volume of private

10. IMF, *International Financial Statistics Supplement, 1964/65*, p. 163.
11. *Economic Quarterly Review*, No. 147 (March 1965), p. 52.
12. "National Accounts, 1960," p. 51.
13. Hartog, p. 92.

consumption expenditure to drop from 14.160 billion guilders in 1950 to 13.87 billion guilders in 1951. Private consumption remained almost stable in 1952 before rising to 14.650 billion guilders in 1953. The volume of private investment also declined from 1.730 billion guilders in 1950 to 1.480 billion guilders in 1951, to 1.190 billion guilders in 1952, and then increased to 1.680 billion guilders in 1953. However, it was not until 1954 that the volume of investment again regained and finally surpassed the 1950 mark set prior to the policy program.[14]

As it turned out, the effects of the combination of the policy program and the external developments were greater than anticipated. Unemployment increased in 1952 to 4.6 percent of the labor force[15] and was concentrated in the consumption goods industries. When unemployment surpassed 3 percent, the Social and Economic Council, assisted by the Central Planning Bureau, again formulated a policy program, this time a deflationary program based on an increase in public investment. The government was preparing to put this program into effect in early 1953 when a series of disastrous floods created an emergency situation that required government investment far in excess of the proposed reflation policy.

Industrial production, stimulated by a general increase in Western European economic activity, had begun to climb as early as the third quarter of 1952. However, the early increases in production did not affect the unemployment figures which went on rising, presumably due to a lag in dismissals. The Netherlands export sector led the recovery. For the years 1952 and 1953 taken together, thc percentage of import sales covered by export sales was 92 percent, compared with an average figure of 84 percent over the years 1950–64.[16] Accompanying the increase in export sales was a

14. "National Accounts, 1960," p. 57. In 1954 the volume of investment was 2,300 billion guilders. All figures measured in 1953 prices.

15. *Central Economic Plan 1961*, p. 156. Dependent labor force excludes independent entrepreneurs; it includes only those who work as employees of others.

16. *Economic Quarterly Review*, No. 2 (Sept. 1965), p. 50.

marked increase in the balance-of-payments surplus, which by early 1952 was accumulating at a monthly rate of 200 million guilders.[17] This rate declined, however, as the figures for imports began to reflect the increase in aggregate demand, with the result that 1952 ended with a balance-of-payments surplus of 1.755 billion guilders, and 1953 with a surplus of 1.359 billion guilders.

By 1954 the demand for labor had caught up to the rise in industrial activity, for 1954 as a whole, demand exceeded the net increase in the labor force.[18] Along with the increased labor need went an increase in labor's bargaining power. In fact, the year 1954 began with a general rise in wages amounting to about 9 percent.

Increased wages led to an increase in private consumption, which was a significant factor in the recovery. Compared with 1953, when the national product (at market prices) increased by approximately 3 percent and private consumption accounted for only 28 percent of this rise, private consumption in 1954 accounted for 72 percent of the 9 percent increase in national product.[19] Thus the growth of private consumption expenditure was an important factor in the 1954 resurgence of economic activity.

Prices also moved upward. The cost of living increased by 6 percent in the first half of 1954, because of a 23 percent increase in rents, an increased social insurance premium, and the bad weather during the spring of 1954 which raised food prices. In addition, approximately 1.5 percent of the increase in the cost of living was attributable to the wage increases that took place early in 1954.[20]

A second wage round was authorized for October 1954, the

17. Netherlands Bank, *1954*, p. 43.

18. According to a special survey of the Central Bureau of Statistics, the shortage of male workers in industry was approximately 6.5 percent of the total number of male employees in the enterprises surveyed. Netherlands Bank, *1954*, p. 24.

19. "National Accounts, 1960," p. 33.

20. Netherlands Bank, *1954*, p. 24.

so-called "prosperity wage round" discussed in Chapter 4. Its main justification was an equity consideration based on the general feeling that increases in labor income had been lagging behind advances in the national income per head. Calculated with respect to 1949 as a base year, this divergence was estimated to be between 3.0 and 4.5 percent and on the basis of 1951, between 2.0 and 3.5 percent.[21] The wage increase authorized in October averaged 6 percent. However, real income per head rose in 1954 because prices did not immediately reflect this wage increase.

The economic boom continued, and the Netherlands passed through a period of continuing expansion. Although 1955 was marked by stability with regard to new wage increases, agreements reached in 1954 had the effect of increasing the 1955 average wage covered by the collective bargaining contracts by about 7 percent over the 1954 figure. The growing prosperity was reflected in further increases in private consumption, particularly in durable consumer goods, and in capital investment. Imports also increased, reflecting in part the increased demand and in part a shortage of production capability in the Netherlands. This shortage affected the supply capability of the export industries, with the result that the increase in imports was not accompanied by a like increase in exports, and 1954 and 1955 export sales covered only 84 percent of import purchases.[22] As a result of the decrease in the percentage of import purchases covered by export sales, the surplus in the balance-of-payments fell to 250 million guilders in 1954.[23]

On the surface, 1955 appeared to be a year of unprecedented economic prosperity, although there was some evidence that the comfortable feeling of financial abundance that accompanied the economic boom might not in fact be

21. Ibid., p. 25.
22. IMF, *International Financial Statistics Supplement, 1964/65*, p. 163.
23. Ibid.

justified. One indication was the extent to which the boom was reflected in investment activity. The growth of gross investment in fixed assets by industry between 1953 and 1954 was 24.3 percent, as compared with a provisional estimate of 4.8 percent forecast at the beginning of 1954.[24] While increased investment is usually considered desirable, some feared that an increase as rapid as this would lead to the production of more capital goods than it would later be found profitable to use.

In September the government, which had been running a budgetary surplus, found itself obliged to give way under pressure to reduce taxes. The lower taxation rate increased the disposable income of consumers by roughly 500 million guilders and that of enterprises by 100 to 200 million guilders.[25]

The terms of trade also deteriorated between 1954 and 1955 as a result of a 2 percent rise in average import prices. Since this increase was greater than the increase in the price of exports (1 percent), it tended to reinforce the inflation. In addition, local public authorities expanded their capital expenditure for housing and other purposes. Unfortunately,

24. P. de Wolff and C. A. van den Beld, "Ten Years of Forecasts and Realizations" (an inquiry into the quality of the predictions by the Central Planning Bureau, 1953–62), paper presented to the American Statistical Institute Conference in Ottawa, Aug. 1963 (cited hereafter as "Ten Years"). Among earlier works are: Central Planning Bureau, *Comparison Between the Central Planning Bureau's Forecasts and Actual Economic Developments, 1949–1953*, Monograph No. 4 (The Hague, 1955); J. Lips and D. B. J. Schouten, "The Reliability of the Policy Model Used by the Central Planning Bureau," *Income and Wealth*, Series VI (London. Bowes and Bowes, 1957), pp. 24–51; C. van de Panne, "De voorspellingskwaliteit van de Centrale Economische Plannen" (The Predictive Quality of the Central Economic Plans 1949–56), *De Economist*, No. 107 (1959), pp. 91–123; Henri Theil, "Who Forecasts Best?" *International Economic Papers*, *5* (1955), 194–99 (original article in Dutch was published in *De Economist*, February 1954, under the title, "Wie Voorspelt Het Best?"); Henri Theil, *Economic Forecasts and Policy*, (Amsterdam, North-Holland Publishing Co., 1958), pp. 1–95; and P. J. Verdoorn and C. J. van Eijk, "Experimental Short-term Forecasting Models," mimeo. (The Hague, Central Planning Bureau, 1958), pp. 59–87.

25. Netherlands Bank, *1956*, p. 15.

financing for these expenditures was largely obtained from the money-creating institutions rather than from the capital market, with the effect of further increasing the inflationary tendencies by increasing the demand for current resources.

During the summer of 1955 there were new demands for higher wages, and the government approved an increase in the so-called secondary conditions of labor. The increase, which was to take effect in 1956, was equivalent to 3 percent of the prevailing wages. But this was not enough to reduce the strain on the labor market, and the pressure for further wage increases continued. According to the calculations of the Central Planning Bureau, however, there was little room for further increase within the bounds of increased labor productivity, which was forecast for 1956 as 4 to 5 percent, approximately the same as the estimate for 1955. Thus it appeared that wage increases in excess of 4 to 5 percent would lead to decreases in the entrepreneurs' share in national income.

During 1956 the cyclical upswing in economic activity continued without slackening. National income increased by 7 percent and, as expected, there was a considerable shift in the distribution of income, labor's share increasing from 66.7 percent to 68.0 percent.[26] Total wages paid by enterprises increased by about 12 percent,[27] and the equilibrium between national expenditures and national resources that had existed in 1954 and 1955 was greatly disturbed. This was shown by a deficit of 750 million guilders in the current account of the balance of payments.[28]

The events of 1956, characterized by a general overspending, are aptly summed up by the Netherlands Bank:

> [While in 1956] total nominal income rose by 7 percent, however, private consumption did so by 10 percent; public authorities' disbursements by 12.5 percent; and net investment in fixed assets, including house-building,

26. *Centraal Economisch Plan 1965*, p. 177.
27. Netherlands Bank, *1956*, p. 9.
28. *Economic Quarterly Review*, No. 2, p. 52.

by 25 percent. Since the increase of investment in stocks of goods is also provisionally put at more than 20 percent, it is not surprising that the national surplus—still quite substantial in 1955—changed to a deficit.[29]

THE 1957 POLICY PROGRAM

In the second half of 1956, the economic developments described above forced the government to intervene. The preliminary forecasts for 1957 showed that the deficit in the balance-of-payments and the deficit in the government budget would become worse if no changes occurred in economic policy. Since productive capacity was already stretched to the limit, any increase in demand as a result of an increase in wages, which for political reasons it appeared could not be avoided in 1956, would likely cause prices to rise, leading to a further loss of competitive position and a further increase in the deficit of the balance of payments.

The 1957 policy program again illustrates how economic policy in the Netherlands is largely shaped by committee action. The government first sought the advice of the Social and Economic Council as to how the adverse effects on prices and the balance of payments might be limited. In its report, which appeared at the end of 1956, the Council recommended that the 1957 national expenditure be reduced by 700 million guilders. Of this, about 200 million guilders was expected to come from a reduction in government expenditure, the remainder from the private sector. As intermediate targets, the Social and Economic Council stated that industrial investment be decreased by 40 percent and private consumption by 1.5 percent. The Council also recommended that full compensation not be granted for the old-age insurance program that was introduced in 1957.

The instruments recommended by the Council were, however, mostly fiscal. The suggested program consisted of the

29. Netherlands Bank, *1956*, p. 9.

following measures:[30] (1) a decrease in the subsidy on sugar (12 million guilders); (2) an increase in the prices charged by the public utilities, other state enterprises, and railways (300 million guilders); (3) an increase in indirect taxes (75 million guilders); (4) a decrease in government expenditure (235 million guilders); (5) a decrease in government investments in government enterprises (40 million guilders); (6) the suspension of a portion of the investment allowance (25 million guilders); and (7) an increase in corporation tax (100 million guilders).

The recommendations of the Social and Economic Council were put into effect by the government with only slight alterations. This is worth noting because during the period when the government was considering the report, the balance of payments position worsened considerably and the forecasts of 1957 had to be revised to show a higher deficit. Apparently, however, more stringent measures were not considered politically feasible. In line with the advice of the Council regarding wages, the government only partially offset the introduction of an insurance premium deduction calculated as equivalent to 6.7 percent of the prevailing wage bill. All in all, the government allowed wage increases that were expected to increase the overall wage level by approximately 4.5 percent.

There were actually two wage rounds in 1957. The first of these represented the partial compensation for the new old-age insurance scheme mentioned above. The second was designed to compensate for a 25 percent increase in rents permitted in August of 1957, which represented approximately a 2 percent increase in the cost of living index. This compensatory wage round was designed, in principle, to increase money wages by an offsetting 2 percent. In view of the position of unskilled workers, however, a minimum amount (varying according to the class of municipality) was

30. The amounts involved are shown in parentheses.

established, the result being that for all manual workers the average increase amounted to 4 percent.

During the latter half of 1957 and the beginning of early 1958, the foreign position improved rapidly. The labor market also loosened considerably, with unemployment (seasonally adjusted) increasing from 28,000 in the first quarter of 1957 to 92,000 in the second quarter of 1958. The registered male labor reserve at the end of 1957 (after the elimination of seasonal influence) amounted to 2.3 percent of the male labor force, which was more than twice that of the preceding year.[31]

The 1956 Netherlands Bank Report described the recommendations of the Social and Economic Council as "courageous." The proposals were particularly noteworthy in that the representatives of employers and employees again not only *accepted* but, in fact, actually *recommended* actions that were expected to result in lower profits on the one hand and lower real incomes and higher unemployment on the other.[32]

As with the earlier programs, the anticipated consequences of the 1957 program, reproduced in Table 10, were calculated by the Central Planning Bureau. It should be noted that the reduction in national expenditure necessary to obtain a restoration of equilibrium in the balance of payments was apportioned equally over private consumption, private investment, and government expenditure. The

31. Netherlands Bank, *1957*, p. 28.

32. Ibid., *1956*, p. 17. The 1957 economic policy program has been investigated extensively with the objective of inferring, from the discussions of the Social and Economic Council, the relative preferences held by the different groups for the various policy measures considered. See, for example: C. J. van Eijk and J. Sandee, "Quantitative Determination of an Optimum Economic Policy," *Econometrica*, *27* (1959), pp. 1–13; P. J. M. van den Bogaard and J. Versluis, "The Design of Optimal Committee Decisions," *Statistica Neerlandica*, *16* (1962), pp. 271–89, P. J. M. van den Bogaard and A. P. Barten, "Optimal Macroeconomic Decision Rules for the Netherlands," Report of the 5915 Econometric Institute of The Netherlands School of Econometrics, mimeo. (Rotterdam, 1959). Henri Theil, *Optimal Decision Rules for Government and Industry* (Amsterdam, North Holland Publishing Co., 1964), pp. 256–321.

TABLE 10. Estimated Consequence of the 1957 Program

Variable	Units	Initial situation	No change in policy forecast	Anticipated effects of program	Revised forecast
National income at factor cost	Millions of guilders	25,520	27,630	−230	27,400
Wage income	Millions of guilders	14,300	15,660	−170	15,490
Volume of private consumption	Millions of guilders	18,620	19,200	−260	18,940
Volume of investment in fixed assets	Millions of guilders	6,660	7,110	−210	6,900
Surplus on the current account, balance of payments	Millions of guilders	−590	−210	+300	+90
Consumption price level	1956 = 100	100	104.4	+0.1	104.5
Volume of industrial production	1956 = 100	100	102.2	−1.1	101.0
Unemployment	%	1.2	1.5	+0.4	1.9

Source: van den Beld, "Short-term Planning Experience in the Netherlands," p. 155.

Central Planning Bureau also computed the anticipated loss of real wage and nonwage income, estimated as 125 million guilders and 100 million guilders respectively. Thus the burden of the loss in real income expected to result from the program was almost equally apportioned, in absolute terms, between the two sources of income.

The wage round compensating for the rent increase was the twelfth and last wage round in a 13-year period from 1945 to 1957. Although the cost of living rose by 12 percent during 1957,[33] there was no further wage round as additional compensation would have been contrary to the government's program of restricting expenditure. The labor leaders, including those who, as members of the Social and Economic Council, had approved the advice to restrict expenditure, did not press for a further cost of living wage round. In fact, as pointed out earlier, the year 1957 marked the end of the philosophy of across-the-board wage increases.

As could be expected, the rise of wages that took place during the period when wage policy was directed to across-the-board wage rounds produced certain effects on the price level. However, across-the-board wage increases had different effects on various trades and industries, depending on their ability to earn profits. In cases where the profit margin was relatively low or where productivity increases had been moderate, it was impossible to prevent higher wages from being passed on in higher prices; and since these price rises were not always offset by price falls elsewhere, a general increase in wages was almost always followed by a general increase in prices. This occurred even though the authorities tried to stabilize prices through voluntary agreements between the employers' associations and the Minister of Economic Affairs. At times these agreements became more mandatory than voluntary, and the Minister required employers to submit intended price increases for his approval prior to putting them into effect.

33. Netherlands Bank, *1957*, p. 32.

In the Netherlands some measure of demand pressure is diverted to foreign countries through imports. Thus the policy of price stabilization is assisted by the possibility of importing freely. However, while increasing imports lessens the strain on prices, it also leads to a loss of foreign exchange—another example of the interdependence of economic goals. It was such a situation that precipitated the balance-of-payments crises which culminated in the deflationary program of 1957.

In summarizing the 1957 economy, the Netherlands Bank opened its annual report with the following statement: "Following an almost classical pattern the year 1957 brought the Netherlands to the end of a cyclical upswing which had lasted without interruption for nearly four years." The report then continued: "The previous inflationary trend had to end; it was threatening the exchange reserves and currency stability. It led people to expect continuous price and cost increases, which falsified costing calculations and caused over-readiness to invest; it cloaked weak management, threatened efficiency, and impaired good labor relations."[34]

Partially as a result of the restrictive measures, the growth of national expenditure slackened somewhat in 1958 and an equilibrium of sorts was attained. During 1958 the balance of payments again showed a surplus. However, the restoration of equilibrium could not be expected to remove all the difficulties mentioned above and yet preserve the exceptionally high level of activity and employment that existed during the peak of the boom.

In 1957 the increase in the national product was 1.5 percent, appreciably short of the 3.5 percent achieved in 1956 and the average from 1953 to 1955 of 7 percent per year. Real income per head did not increase at all because the 1957 increase in production barely exceeded the increase

34. Ibid.. pp. 9, 19, 20.

in the gainfully employed population. Hence, there was little rise in per capita productivity.[35]

As mentioned previously a sudden and rapid rise in unemployment took place during the latter half of 1957 and 1958, and there was some official concern because the regional distribution of unemployment was rather uneven. For the country as a whole, however, the unemployment rate of 3 percent—the generally accepted danger point, according to the Central Bank, beyond which measures for counteracting unemployment need be considered—was exceeded only briefly in the second and third quarters of 1958.

During 1958 the balance-of-payments position improved markedly. From July 1956 to June 1957, roughly the peak period of overspending, the deficit on the current account was 955 million guilders.[36] On a cash basis, the current account deficit for 1957 amounted to 419 million guilders, compared with a deficit of 627 million guilders in 1956. This favorable trend continued with the first quarter of 1958 showing a surplus of 932 million guilders, and the year as a whole a surplus of 1,694 million guilders.[37] All in all, the period during which the balance-of-payments account fell short of the policy target lasted from the beginning of 1956 up to and including the third quarter of 1957.

As 1958 progressed, it became clear that the restoration of the balance-of-payments situation made it desirable to relax some of the retrenchment measures taken in 1957. Because of the unemployment level there was little pressure for wage increases, even though it was now apparent that they could probably be granted without affecting, in any great measure, the competitive position of the Netherlands in its foreign markets.

The question at issue was how best to utilize the margin

35. Ibid., p. 24.
36. Ibid., pp. 47–48.
37. Ibid., *1958*, p. 51.

in the national income that had resulted from the restoration of a foreign payments equilibrium and the de facto wage pause of 1958. Differences of opinion over the answer to this question were partially responsible for the fall of the government in 1958. Some members of the cabinet, which was as usual a coalition, desired a reduction in consumer subsidies. As this is in effect a loss in real wages, the main burden of such a reduction would fall on wage earners. Therefore, it was not surprising that the Labor Party resisted such a move, and broke up the coalition by its withdrawal. Presumably, Labor was not willing to trade tax reductions, which were promised by the other parties in the coalition, for reductions in subsidies, but rather favored the continued use of subsidies as instruments for the redistribution of income.

ADVICE OF THE SOCIAL AND ECONOMIC COUNCIL: 1959–60

In September 1958, several ministries asked the Social and Economic Council for advice with regard to a possible reduction of consumer subsidies in milk, subsidies in house building, farmers' subsidies, and rent subsidies. The Council was instructed to keep such reductions within the framework of an "acceptable development of wages and prices." The advice of the Council, prepared with the assistance of the Central Planning Bureau, was transmitted to the government in April 1959, again illustrating the committee approach that is followed in formulating Dutch economic policy.

The 1959 advice was based to a large extent on data supplied by the Central Planning Bureau, and for the first time, explicit use was made of first and second year effects of contemplated policy measures. In Table 11 the type of information supplied by the Bureau for the quantitative assessment of the probable impact of selected policy measures is shown. The targets are (1) the government budget, (2) the balance of payments, (3) the price level of

TABLE 11. Effects of Policy Measures on Central Government Budget Surplus, Balance-of-Payments Surplus, Consumers' Prices, Investment, and Employment in the Netherlands[a]

Measures taken	Years	Effect on: Government[b] budget surplus (millions of guilders)	Balance-of-payments[c] surplus (millions of guilders)	Price level of consumers' goods (percentage)	Investment[d] in private fixed assets (millions of guilders)	Employment (persons)
100 million guilder increase in government expenditure on goods and services	1st	−70	−80	0	+10	+3,500
	2nd	−70	−60	0	+20	+3,900
100 million guilder reduction in direct taxes on wage income	1st	−65	−70	+0.2	+10	+2,200
	2nd	−65	−50	+0.2	+20	+3,700
100 million guilder reduction in direct taxes on nonwage income	1st	−100	−10	0	0	+300
	2nd	−85	−40	+0.1	+30	+2,300
100 million guilder reduction in indirect taxes on consumers' goods	1st	−75	−30	+0.5	+10	+4,400
	2nd	−65	−50	−0.5	+20	+6,000
1 percent general wage increase (175 million guilders)	1st	−15	−100	+0.4	−10	+100
	2nd	−35	−60	+0.4	−20	−1,000
100 million guilder increase in private construction activity	1st	+30	−80	0	+110	+3,500
	2nd	+30	−60	0	+120	+3,900

a. Computed on the basis of the Dutch model.
b. Net change in government financial assets.
c. Current account.
d. Volume figures.

Source: U.N. Economic Commission for Europe, *Economic Survey of Europe, 1959*, Chap. 6, p. 7. See also Netherlands Social and Economic Council, *Advies inzake bestedingen in 1959 and 1960*, p. V-19.

consumer's goods, (4) investment in private fixed assets, and (5) employment.

The table shows that a 100 million guilder increase in government expenditure on goods and services was expected to create 3,500 new jobs in 1959, while costing the budget balance 70 million guilders. Similarly, a 100 million guilder decrease in direct taxes on wages was estimated to be capable of creating 2,200 jobs, while reducing the budget balance by 65 million guilders. The difference between the first and second year employment effects with regard to changes in taxes, particularly between wage and nonwage income, should be noted: the ratio between first and second year effects is 1.7 in the case of tax reduction on wage income and 7.6 in the case of a similar reduction in taxes on nonwage income.

According to Pieter de Wolff, then Director of the Central Planning Bureau, and Jan Sandee, also of the Central Planning Bureau, the instrument variables actually considered by the Council were: government expenditures, wages, indirect taxes, wage taxes, profit taxes, and rents.[38] The targets considered were the balance of payments, government consumer prices, and the surplus or deficit in the budget.

This policy program was constrained by the fact that an increase in the cost of living because of reduction in the milk or rent subsidy programs was apparently not acceptable to the members of the council. Therefore any decrease in milk subsidies or in subsidies pertaining to rents would have to be fully compensated by increased wages. The Central Planning Bureau calculated that a 1.1 percent increase in wages would completely offset, in terms of the cost of living index, a 100 million guilder decrease in milk subsidies and a 2.3 percent increase in wages would be necessary to offset a rent increase of 25 percent.

38. P. de Wolff and J. Sandee, "Recent Experiences in the Application of Econometric Policy Models in the Netherlands," paper read at the 21st meeting of the European Econometric Society, Amsterdam, Sept. 1959.

The effects of changes in the policy variables on the targets are given in Table 12. One unit of rent increase is the equivalent of a 25 percent increase in the prevailing average rental. Wages, taxes, and consumer prices are in percentages; all other variables are expressed in millions of guilders. Milk subsidies are treated as negative indirect taxes.

TABLE 12. Effects of Unit Changes in the Policy Variables on the Targets

	Targets		
	Balance-of-payments surplus (millions of guilders)	Consumer prices (%)	Government budget surplus (millions of guilders)
Government expenditures	−83	+.02	−70
Wage rate	−100	+.39	−12
Indirect tax	+31	+.52	+75
Wage tax	+69	−.22	+66
Nonwage tax	+7	−.03	+97
Rents	+203	+1.52	+145

Source: De Wolff and Sandee, "Recent Experiences in the Application of Econometric Policy Models in the Netherlands," p. 4.

De Wolff and Sandee shed some light on how the Social and Economic Council arrived at their recommendations. One tenet of the argument is that because drastic changes in the instruments are virtually impossible, except in times of dire national emergency, there are relatively narrow limits to the magnitude of changes that can be effected in the instruments. Thus one might begin an evaluation of policy alternatives by attempting to estimate the limits that Sandee and de Wolff maintain are caused by psychological or political considerations. For example, most persons agree that nominal wage decreases are unacceptable; therefore the lower limit or boundary on this instrument is zero. Tax increases are also influenced by psychological feelings. According to de Wolff and Sandee, "the saying 'an old tax is no tax' shows that it is tax increases rather than tax levels that are felt, and resisted."[39]

Table 13 gives the de Wolff-Sandee estimates of the traditional or customary boundaries, i.e. the upper and lower limits of the six instruments considered by the Social and Economic Council. In addition, the table shows the boundaries for these same instruments according to the particular circumstances that existed at the time of the Council's discussions. Hence, the favorable balance-of-payments position existing in 1958 made an increase in taxes politically infeasible. According to de Wolff and Sandee, "reductions in government expenditure, difficult to realize even at the worst of times, were likewise excluded."[40] There was, however, a desire for a decrease in subsidies, even though the effect is, in fact, identical to an increase in indirect taxes. A subsidy decrease was apparently acceptable as a "structural improvement" since by 1958 most policy-makers, as well as the majority of the public, were aware of the discrepancy that existed between the subsidized rents for old dwellings and the rents charged for newly built houses. Moreover, in 1958 the house rent-reducing subsidies (including the premiums paid on new privately built houses) cost the government over 300 million guilders.

TABLE 13. Boundaries on the Instruments

Instruments	Customary Boundaries		1958 Boundaries	
	Upper	Lower	Upper	Lower
Government expenditure	+3.0	−2.0	+3.0	0
Wage rate	+5.0	0	+5.0	0
Indirect tax rate	+2.0	−2.0	+1.0	−2.0
Wage tax rate	+2.0	−2.0	0	−2.0
Nonwage tax rate	+2.0	−2.0	0	−2.0
Rents	+1.0	0	+1.0	0

Source: De Wolff and Sandee, pp. 5–6.

39. Ibid., p. 4.
40. Ibid., p. 6.

While a cutback in the rent subsidy was generally considered acceptable, labor was willing to agree to such a decrease only if wage earners were fully compensated for the rise in the cost of living incident to the shift in this portion of housing costs from the government to those renting the previously subsidized houses. Thus in Table 13, the zero lower limit on wage increases for 1958 is acceptable *only* if there is no increase in the overall price level. If a price increase occurred, labor would expect wages to rise in an amount sufficient to compensate for it.

The advice actually forwarded to the government by the Social and Economic Council contained not one but three sets of combinations of the proposed measures because the Council could not agree on the extent to which the measures should be implemented. While a rent increase of 25 percent was unanimously agreed upon, beyond that the position of the proponents of the three sets of policy measures differed considerably. This was particularly true with regard to wages, one group calling for a wage increase of 4 percent plus compensation for the rent increase, a second group against a wage increase except as compensation, and a third group that used the report as an opportunity to promote the differential wage increase mentioned previously. No mention was made in the report of government expenditures or changes in taxes.

Sandee and de Wolff developed their analysis graphically as shown in Figure 1. Using the macroeconomic model of the Central Planning Bureau, they first computed the target space, A, corresponding to the 64 combinations of what they called the "traditional limits" on the instruments. The target space is constructed so that any set of contemplated instrument values lies on or inside the limits of A in the figure. Then they plotted the specific constraints, B, that they believed to apply to 1958. Next they located the position of the three recommended programs plotted within the target space.

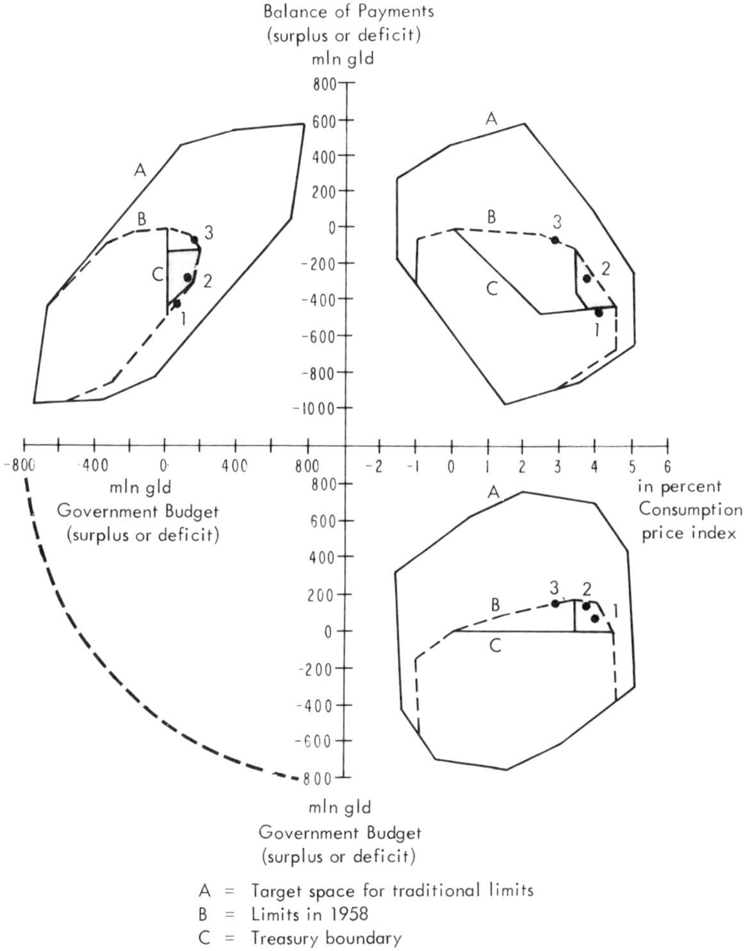

FIGURE 1. An Illustration of the Constraints Imposed on the Policy-Makers by the Interrelationship Among Instruments and Targets

Source: De Wolff and Sandee, p. 10.

In 1958, however, only a part of the space labeled B in the figure had practical meaning because the Treasury stressed the point that the relatively high rate of interest to be paid on new loans made any further increase in the deficit in the government budget extremely undesirable. Taking the Treasury preference into account, de Wolff and Sandee added a "Treasury boundary," labeled C in Figure 1. Moreover, if it is agreed that rents should be allowed to increase by only one unit (25 percent) and indirect taxes by only 1 percent (as a result of a decrease in the milk subsidy), the target space becomes even smaller, corresponding to the shaded area on Figure 1.

Finally, the three alternative programs are shown by the points labeled 1, 2, and 3. Point 1 represents wage increases somewhat greater than 5 percent. Point 2 indicates the results of a policy of no wage increases, and point 3 shows the effects of a differential wage policy averaging about 2.25 percent plus a 3.75 percent compensatory wage increase for rent and milk price increases.[41] It should be mentioned that the members of the Council favoring the latter policy (about half) did not want even to mention an average wage increase as they felt that such an average would act as a norm or magnet and hamper the flexibility of their approach.

As discussed in Chapter 4 the cabinet taking office in 1959 sought a greater differentiation in wages among different branches of industry. The new government adopted the position that wage increases should be based on the movement of per capita productivity as found for each branch of activity. Even in cases where a wage increase appeared justified, the government required the employers to give assurance that they would not pass on the wage increase in the form of a price increase. Partly as a result of this policy, it was estimated

41. The points on the figure disregard any effects of the careful step-by-step timing that was recommended by the Social and Economic Council's report. The Actual program put into effect in April 1960 called for a rent increase of 20 percent, and a 2/7 reduction in the government's contribution to rent and building subsidies. According to the Netherlands Bank, *1959*, p. 23, the reduction in housing subsidies would save the government about 120 million guilders a year; the annual saving through abolition of milk subsidies would amount to about 75 million guilders a year. As of the same date an obligatory 2.5 percent wage increase was to be effected in order to compensate for the rise in rents and in milk prices.

that only 15 to 20 percent of the wage and salary earning labor force (most of them industrial workers) received wage increases in 1959.

For the next two years prices were relatively stable. At the end of 1959 the wholesale price index was the same as it was at the end of both 1958 and 1957.[42] The average cost of living was only 1 percent higher in 1959 than in 1958.[43] Wholesale prices actually fell in 1960, while the cost of living index rose by 2.5 percent, mainly as a result of the rent increase and the rise in the price of consumer milk.[44]

Economic conditions continued to improve in 1960, and at the end of that year it was found that the average level of collectively negotiated wages for adult employed persons was 8.5 percent higher than at the end of 1959.[45] However, inasmuch as the cost of living increased by 2.5 percent in 1960, real wages increased by only 6 percent.

In previous years any increase in real wages was usually followed by a corresponding increase in consumption expenditure. However, in 1960 the rise in consumption was not as great as was anticipated, mainly because of contra-cyclical policy on the part of the government. This included the adoption of measures to limit the financing of sales by installment credit (consisting of raising the initial payment and shortening the maximum period of installment payment agreements) and a sterilization of liquidity brought about by government borrowing in excess of that needed to cover current expenditures. As a result of these policies, which in effect caused a lag in consumption behind national income, the savings ratio rose to 23.5 percent, representing an increase of 1 percent over 1959. The 23.5 percent figure was a proportion never previously attained by the Netherlands.[46]

42. Netherlands Bank, *1959*, p. 29.
43. Ibid., p. 31.
44. Ibid., *1960*, p. 34.
45. Ibid., p. 30.
46. Ibid., p. 39.

Because of the high level of investment and the rapid cyclical expansion within the country, the government reduced the fiscal incentives to invest, namely, the accelerated depreciation allowance and the investment allowance. The accelerated depreciation provision for industrial equipment was reduced from 16.66 percent per year to 8.33 percent, and the special tax allowances for investment, which amounted to 8 percent per year for two years, was lowered to 5 percent per year for two years.[47]

The expansion in the Netherlands was more than matched by its principal trading partners. In these countries wholesale prices and cost of living indices rose about the same amount or in some cases more than they did in the Netherlands, and for the third year in succession the Dutch balance-of-payments account showed a substantial surplus.[48]

REVALUATION

According to classical business cycle theory, one would not expect a balance-of-payments surplus to occur in the phase of the business cycle exhibited by the Netherlands in 1959–60, particularly in 1960. This year represented the third year of the upswing, and by the third year of the previous boom cyclical strain had led to a balance-of-payments deficit, which, as theory would have predicted, brought forth a liquidity shortage, rising interest rates, credit contraction, limitation of credit, tightening of costs, and finally the reversal of the deficit. However, in 1960 the continuing balance-of-payments surplus increased domestic liquidity to the extent that it was feared that any further increases in aggregate demand might cause domestic wages and prices to get out of hand.

47. For a further discussion of these changes, see *Economic Quarterly Review*, No. 128 (First Quarter, 1960), pp. 24–26, and No. 133 (Second Quarter, 1960), pp. 50–69. See also the article by Dr. M. J. H. Smeets, "The Influence of Taxes on the Capital Market," ibid., No. 133, pp. 3–15.

48. See Organization for Economic Cooperation and Development, *Policies for Price Stability* (Paris, 1962), pp. 12–14.

Thus for the first time the Netherlands was faced with imported inflation brought about by the continuing balance-of-payments surpluses. It was thought that one of the main causes of this situation was that a structural imbalance existed between the cost and price levels among the surplus countries and those countries whose balance-of-payments accounts were showing a deficit. By 1960 it was clearly evident that the differential trend in national cost levels had been running in favor of the Netherlands, as well as several of the Western European countries, particularly the Federal Republic of Germany.

In such a case, several courses of action are available to the policy-maker. On the one hand, the currency could be revalued. In the Netherlands, however, the adoption of such an alternative would violate the government's commitment to the International Monetary Fund's principle of fixed exchange rates. On the other hand, price stability can be sacrificed and the domestic price level (including export prices as well) allowed to inflate until domestic cost levels are brought in line with the cost levels of the main trading partners. Adoption of the second alternative, however sacrifices one of the objectives of Dutch economic policy, i.e. maintaining a stable price level.

The effects of the two courses of action, revaluation and inflation, are in some sense similar, since both tend to raise export prices relative to foreign price levels. For example, revaluation of the currency would increase Dutch export prices directly because it becomes more expensive, in terms of foreign currency, to purchase Dutch exports. On the other hand, a general increase in wages also increases costs that are eventually passed on in higher selling prices.[49] Thus both measures raise the prices of domestic goods relative to imported goods. These changes in relative price deter exports

49. It might also be noted that labor-intensive industries are affected relatively more by a wage increase than are industries that make less intensive use of labor.

while stimulating imports. As a result, imports increase, exports decrease, and the balance-of-payments surplus declines with, hopefully, the desired deflationary consequences.

There are, however, two main differences between using wage and price changes and changes in the rate of exchange for the purpose of equalizing domestic and foreign price levels. In the first case, increases in wages and prices cause a general rise in the price level. This brings about a fall in the real income of persons receiving fixed incomes, insofar as their incomes are not increased by compensatory measures. Revaluation, however, inasmuch as the fall in import prices is passed on to consumers, will lead to a general decrease in the price level.

The second major difference in the two methods of equalizing domestic and foreign prices pertains to the sector in which the equalization starts. In most countries the market can be characterized by three different groups of producers and sellers: one group selling on the home market without any foreign competition, a second group producing goods sold either on the world market or at home in competition with foreign sellers, and a third group that exports the main part of its product.

When wages are raised, it may be assumed that the wage–price spiral starts in the first group. These entrepreneurs, since they are not faced with foreign competition, can raise their prices and maintain the same profit margins. In export industries and industries in close competition with foreign producers, this is not fully possible. These latter groups will presumably be the last to be affected by the wage increase as they will, if possible, delay wage and price rises as long as possible. Revaluation starts the equalization of domestic and foreign price levels in the export industries, from which it spreads to industries producing import substitutes or producing export goods sold domestically.

In 1954, the Minister of Finance stated that in his view

> independent alteration of the rate of exchange was a course that could be adopted only in extreme circumstances. For a country such as the Netherlands, which derives so great a part of its prosperity from abroad, the maintenance of fixed exchange rates is a matter of outstanding importance. Any adjustments which may be necessary within the country, must not in principle be brought about by means of altering the rate of exchange.[50]

In a system of fixed international rates of exchange, alteration of the exchange rate is not intended to be a normal instrument of monetary policy. Nevertheless, there is an "escape clause." The articles of the International Monetary Fund agreement recognize that a "fundamental disequilibrium" can come about. In such a case the countries concerned are allowed to propose a change in the par value of their currency. If the proposed change, together with all previous changes, does not exceed 10 percent of the par value set for the currency in question at the time the agreements were signed, the Fund will raise no objection. If the proposed change does exceed 10 percent, objection can in principle be raised.

During 1960 the Dutch authorities were concerned about the possibility that the Federal Republic of Germany would revaluate the deutsche mark. In view of the large surplus in its balance-of-payments, the German economy showed even greater signs of a fundamental disequilibrium than the Dutch economy. Germany was also under strong political pressure from the members of the Organization for European Cooperation and Development, in particular the United States, to increase the external value of the deutsche mark.

A revaluation of the deutsche mark would have several effects. Because of the close commercial ties between West

50. As reported in Netherlands Bank, *1954*, p. 17.

Germany and the Netherlands, a West German revaluation would greatly increase the strain on the Dutch economy. Almost one quarter of Dutch trade is with West Germany; therefore any increase in the value of the deutsche mark vis-à-vis the guilder would be further expected to increase German demand for Dutch output and increase the Dutch balance-of-payments surplus. Put simply, since Dutch goods would be less expensive in Germany, export sales to Germany could be expected to increase. Second, Dutch exports could also be expected to increase in markets where Dutch products compete with German products because a revaluation of the mark would cause the price of German exports, expressed in foreign currency, to rise and the competitive position of Germany to deteriorate. The rise in German export prices would affect Holland in another way: the Netherlands is itself an important customer for German output which would, after a German revaluation, be more expensive.

During 1960 the Central Planning Bureau attempted to quantify the consequences of a possible German revaluation in light of the existing economic situation. One appraisal of the effects on Holland appeared in July 1960.[51] In this study the effects of a German revaluation of 10 percent were computed for the German and Dutch economies. In addition, the effects of a 10 percent German revaluation followed by a Dutch revaluation by a like amount were computed. The consequences of these actions were calculated with regard to the balance of payments, domestic price level, import and export price levels, volume of production, import and export volumes, and the volume of domestic expenditures.

The results of this study were hurriedly recomputed and updated when, on Saturday, March 4, 1961, the German

51. Netherlands Central Planning Bureau, "Revaluatie van Mark und Guilden," mimeo. (The Hague, July 1960).

mark was revalued by 5 percent.[52] In light of widespread speculation that Holland would follow the German example, it was important that the Dutch authorities decide whether to revaluate, and, if so, by what amount, before the opening of the money exchanges on the following Monday morning.

The Dutch cabinet was called into emergency session. After consulting the president of the Netherlands Bank and the Central Planning Bureau, the cabinet announced that the guilder would be revaluated by 5 percent. The revaluation, which was to take effect on March 7, 1961, represented an upward appreciation of 4.74 percent in relation to the old parity, or a reduction by 5 percent in the guilder value of foreign currencies other than the deutsche mark, its value relative to the guilder remaining the same.[53]

In explaining the government's decision to the Second Chamber, the Finance Minister stated that "after the devaluation of the guilder in 1949 tension in the Dutch economy and even excessive tensions on the labor market and in the production facilities had been growing steadily in Holland. The balance-of-payments current account generally showed considerable surpluses and only incidental deficits."[54]

52. The German announcement came as a surprise. In June 1960, the General Manager of the Deutsche Bank, Dr. Hermann Josef Abs, published an analysis entitled "Der Wechselkurs-Klein Feld fur Experimente," showing what the consequences would be if the mark were revaluated. The article led most observers to conclude that Abs opposed revaluation. *Frankfurter Allgemeine Zeitung*, Frankfurt a.m., June 11, 1960.

53. The revaluation represented a change in the official parity of 0.233861 grams of fine gold (corresponding to the rate of 3.80 guilders to the U.S. dollar) to 0.245489 grams of fine gold (or a price of 3.62 guilders per U.S. dollar). Over the years there have been very few changes in the gold parity of the guilder; it remained at the same gold parity from 1875 to 1936, when the Netherlands was one of the last countries to devaluate during the depression. A new parity was established in 1943, and in 1949 the guilder was devaluated by 30.2 percent following the example of the United Kingdom which devaluated by 30.5 percent in that year. No further changes in the parity of the guilder were made until the revaluation of 1961.

54. Netherlands Ministry of Economic Affairs, *Netherlands Economic Bulletin*, No. 319 (April 1961).

Thus the authorities saw a structural imbalance in the exchange rate for the guilder, an imbalance that would have been aggravated by the revaluation of the deutsche mark. The Finance Minister went on to explain that it was the government's viewpoint that "unless Holland followed Germany's example, the extra drain on the Dutch economy resulting from the large volume of trade between Holland and the Federal Republic would prove an intolerable strain on the [government's] policy which aims at internal and external equilibrium."[55]

Most observers feel that in the main the results of the revaluation were satisfactory.[56] A decrease in export demand was particularly noticeable in the revenue and profit positions of Dutch airlines and in the shipping companies which are probably in closer competition with foreign concerns than any other Dutch companies. According to the Central Bank's 1961 report, "Revaluation did affect the price level; this is shown by the fact that the Netherlands was the only country where the wholesale price index fell in 1961."[57] On the whole, there was a slackening in the rate

55. Ibid. The devaluation of 1949 had already exceeded the 10 percent initial change in the exchange rate agreed upon when the International Monetary Fund was first established. Therefore, the Netherlands was obliged to obtain the permission of the Fund for the 1961 revaluation. Since the Netherlands was voluntarily weakening its international economic position, however, it was not surprising that approval for the 5 percent revaluation was easily obtained.

56. De Wolff, "Central Economic Planning"; van den Beld, "Short-term Planning Experiences in the Netherlands"; Netherlands Bank, *1961*; and Netherlands Ministry of Finance, *Memorandum on the Condition of the Netherlands State's Finances, 1962*, p. 5. For other discussion of the revaluation, see H. J. Hofstra, "De revaluatie van de Gulden," *Economisch-Statistische Berichten* (March 15, 1961), pp. 272–74; and H. J. Wittersen, "Revaluatie, De Wisselkoers als instrument van structuurpolitick," in the same journal (March 22, 1961), pp. 300–04.

57. Netherlands Bank, *1961*, p. 11. The Bank also pointed out "that the passing of the lowered import prices [as a result of the increase in the international purchasing power of the guilder] on to consumers ran into resistances and that, so far as this happened, there was merely a switch of entrepreneur

of expansion. This was particularly pronounced in manufacturing industries, where production increased by only 2.5 percent as compared with 13 percent in 1960.[58]

One of the chief causes of the slowdown was a shortening of the work week. In the Netherlands, 1961 was the first year in which the 45-hour week was adopted on a large scale. For the economy as a whole, the shortening of the work week resulted in a loss of potential real production. For labor, the shorter work week meant a substitution of leisure for real income. However, it was the government's policy to give compensatory hourly wage increases to offset any actual reduction in total income, and it was expected that the introduction of fewer working hours would proceed gradually. Because of the productivity criterion for wage policy, it was also expected that these hourly wage increases would be met out of the available "margin," i.e. out of the expected rise in hourly per capita productivity and the anticipated decrease in the cost of raw materials. Otherwise, entrepreneural incomes would have to fall since the wage increases were not in principle to be passed on in prices. Elaborate rules were set up for the introduction of the shorter work week.[59] The Central Bank Report for 1961 describes what actually happened.

> In the strained labour market of 1961 however the good intention regarding gradual introduction of the free Saturday did not come to much, since this spread over the country like an epidemic. No employer who wished to retain his workers could afford to lag behind his com-

profit from exporters to importers." One result of this was a Price Order by the Minister of Economic Affairs concerning imported consumer goods. Issued in October 1961, its effect was to bind importers to observing the same absolute (money) margin as was charged at the end of 1958 on the purchase value of such goods.

58. Central Economic Plan 1961, p. 29, and *Centraal Economisch Plan 1962*, p. 35.

59. See *Economic Quarterly Review*, No. 131 (Fourth Quarter, 1960).

> petitors; and hence, in order to meet shortages of personnel occurring in a given enterprise or industry, the working hours were widely reduced . . . with the natural result that the shortage became acuter still . . . . [T]he introduction of shorter working hours was accomplished by a compensatory raising of the hourly wage. . . .
>
> In the existing cyclical condition the introduction of the abbreviated working week at such short notice produced serious consequences. Demand, still growing in conformity with the phase of the cycle, no longer found response in an expanding supply; on the contrary . . . industrial production abruptly declined . . . the great strain on the labor market was further increased, and . . . it became more and more difficult to keep the actual course of wages and labor costs within the limits set by the principles of wages policy.[60]

For the economy as a whole the Central Planning Bureau estimated that the reduction in the work week amounted to one-and-one-half hours, or approximately 3 percent of the average work week in 1960.[61] Productivity per man hour rose by about 4.5 percent in 1961.[62] Therefore, taking into account the decrease in man hours worked, the overall productivity of labor per man year probably increased by approximately 1 percent, in contrast to 1960 when production per employee rose by 9 percent.[63] Taken in conjunction with the total rise in overall wage per person employed, which amounted to 5.5 percent,[64] Dutch labor costs rose by about 4.5 percent.[65]

60. Netherlands Bank, *1961*, p. 12.
61. *Centraal Economisch Plan 1962*, p. 76.
62. Netherlands Bank, *1961*, p. 7.
63. Ibid., p. 29.
64. Ibid., p. 28.
65. According to ibid., p. 29, "the increase of labor costs in industry amounted to 6.5 percent. . . . As a result of the revaluation of the guilder, the rise of labor costs expressed in dollars was a good deal greater still; for all industries it amounted to about 11 percent."

OTHER POLICY MEASURES, 1960–61

During the years 1960–61 the government undertook a number of anticyclical policies, several of which centered on activities of the Central Bank. For example, after a rapid expansion in credit to the private sector in the early months of 1961, the Bank concluded an agreement with the commercial and agricultural banks which stated that if the banks exceeded a credit expansion of 1 percent per month, they would be required to pay into a special non-interest-bearing account at the Netherlands Bank an amount equal to a specific proportion of the surplus credit. Later the credit expansion was lowered to 0.5 percent per month. A number of banks exceeded the limit and were required to pay into the special accounts, with the result that by mid-1962 more than 100 million guilders were "frozen" in this manner.

There were a number of attempts to draw off excess domestic liquidity. Several times during 1961 the Netherlands Bank sold dollars at a price appreciably lower than the normal exchange rate, with the object of providing the banks with funds they could employ at interest abroad. The cost of the dollars bought by the banks represented a net reduction in domestic liquidity. Another attempt to drain off surplus liquidity worthy of note was the opening of the Dutch capital market to foreign borrowers. This was the first time since 1955 that foreign issues were authorized in Holland.

The Central Bank also changed the compulsory minimum reserve rate several times. During 1960–62 the reserve rate changed from 6 to 10 percent and back to 6 percent again. Reserve rate changes were frequently used to enhance the effectiveness of other policy instruments. For example, to offset a tightening of the money market due to a particularly high seasonal variation in tax payments and to facilitate the sale of a government bond issue, the government reduced the reserve rate from 10 percent to 6 percent from August to

October 1961. An important underlying reason for these reductions was to eliminate the temptation for banks to repatriate funds invested abroad.[66]

The Central Bank also raised the discount rate as a check to the expansion of credit. This rate was raised from 2.75 to 3.5 percent in November 1959; it remained at this level until April 1962, when it was raised to 4 percent, which still fell short of the previous peak of 5 percent that had been in effect in the latter half of 1957.[67]

During this period the Dutch government itself also endorsed a fiscal policy of tax reduction. In the *1962 Memorandum on the Condition of the Netherlands States' Finances*, the Finance Minister set forth the government position: "Structurally the aim of the [budgetary] policy is that the increase in state expenditure should relatively remain below that in the national income so as to leave room for an alleviation of the tax burden."[68] According to calculations of the Central Bank, the growth trend in national income is approximately 4 percent per year. As a consequence of the progressive tax rates, this growth results in a rise of 5.33 percent per year in government revenues. Therefore each year

66. On the whole, the reserve ratio is not an important instrument of economic policy in the Netherlands, where conditions are somewhat different than in other countries. Because of the fact that at least one third of the national expenditure goes outside the country, a credit expansion strongly affects the liquidity of the banks whose deposits are apt to rise far less than their loans. In order to counteract this effect, occasionally the Central Bank has decreased the reserve ratio (in times of credit expansion) and conversely increased the ratio (in times of recession).

67. *Economic Quarterly Review*, No. 147 (March 1965), pp. 66–67.

68. *Memorandum, Netherlands State's Finances, 1962*, p. 7. The tax burden is defined as the total proceeds of government taxes, including those of the local authorities in percent of the net national income at market prices. Data on the burden of taxation is given annually in the reports of the Netherlands Bank. During 1961 the burden again rose, this time to over 26 percent. Since 1957, when taxes were raised as a means of checking the inflationary situation then existing, the tax burden had risen by about .5 percent per year. In 1960 the burden of taxation amounted to 25 percent against 23.3 percent in 1955. See Netherlands Bank, *1961*, p. 87.

the government has a margin it can use for increased government expenditures or for lowering taxes.

In line with its declared policy, the government proposed a tax reduction to take effect in July 1961. The program consisted of (1) a decrease in the tax on wage and nonwage incomes, (2) a reduction in corporation taxes, and (3) miscellaneous decreases in property taxes and certain indirect taxes. The details of the tax reduction, however, were made contingent on the state of the business cycle.

In pointing out the objectives underlying the structural budgetary policy of the government, the Finance Minister emphasized that the government should not lose sight of the fact that budgetary policy is both structural and anticyclical. To quote again from the Finance Ministry's Memorandum on the budget, "Anticyclic considerations prompt the government to endeavor, via expenditure and tax policy . . . to exercise such influence on national spendings as will cause them to be in line with the real production possibilities."[69] In view of the existing inflationary situation, it was not surprising when the government announced that, on cyclical grounds, the reduction of wage and nonwage taxes would not be put into force.[70]

The effects of the proposed tax reductions were extensively discussed in the Central Economic Plan of 1961. In this Plan the Planning Bureau published its estimates of the consequences of an assumed 500 million guilders reduction in wage and income tax. Table 14, taken from the 1961 Plan, shows the anticipated effects of a joint reduction in wage and non-wage taxes with a total revenue loss to the government of about 500 million guilders. First and second year effects are given.

69. *Memorandum, 1962*, p. 7.

70. With some changes, this tax decrease was finally put into effect in July 1962. One change was that the decrease in the corporation tax was less than originally proposed. Added to the program was a tax reduction for employed married women, designed as an inducement to draw more women into the labor market.

TABLE 14. Short-run Consequences of a Reduction of 500 Million Guilders in Wage and Income Taxes

Effects of the tax decreases	First year (millions of guilders)	Second year (millions of guilders)
Export value	−100	−450
Import value	+120	+150
Surplus in the current account, balance-of-payments	−220	−600
Consumption price level	0	0
Value of private consumption	+1.0%	+1.5%
Investment volume	+1.0%	+3.5%

Source: Central Economic Plan 1961, p. 72.

It can be assumed that the predicted increases in expenditures were considered unacceptable in view of the shortage of productive capacity and the generally overstrained circumstances then existing in the Dutch economy. By 1962 unemployment had fallen to 1 percent, a level that could scarcely be reduced. In fact, since the summer of 1960, the number of employers' applications pending had exceeded the number of registered unemployed, even though the labor force had grown at about 1 to 1.5 percent per year. In 1962 the registered male labor reserve averaged only 1.1 percent of the wage- and salary-earning male labor force; the number of employers' outstanding inquiries for male workers was 3.1 percent; and the statistical deficit stood at 2 percent. In fact, fluctuations in the demand for labor have manifested themselves more in a decline in the number of unfilled vacancies than in increases in the number of unemployed. The effect of this situation on the annual wage negotiations was described in Chapter 4. Briefly, wages per person employed in enterprises rose by 6 percent in 1962, by 10 percent in 1963, by 15 percent in 1964, and by 11 percent in 1965.[71] During this period production by

71. Netherlands Bank, *1965*, p. 32.

enterprise rose by 3.3 percent in 1962, by 3.2 percent in 1963, and by 8.6 percent in 1964. The forecast for 1965 was for an increase of 4.3 percent,[72] the actual increase was closer to 6 percent.[73]

These nominal increases considerably exceeded the rise in real terms, which can be seen from the increases in the various price indices. In 1963, for example, the price index for the country's total spending rose in comparison with the previous year by 3.5 percent, the cost of living index was up by 4 percent, and the indices both for wholesale and for export prices were up by 2 percent.[74] For the years 1962–65 taken as a whole (including the 1965 estimates of the Central Planning Bureau), the cost of living rose on average by 4 percent per year.[75] Inasmuch as nominal wages rose on average by 10.6 percent per year, real wages increased approximately 6.6 percent per year.[76]

During 1961 and 1962 there was some fear that Dutch exports would face a period of noncompetitiveness in the world market as a result of the revaluation and the abrupt rise in labor costs that took place in those years. To some extent this did in fact occur. At the same time consumer demand was stimulated by the increase in real income of wage and salary earners. Since one third of total spending goes to imports, this increased demand was accompanied by an increase in imports which, as expected, resulted in a deficit in the current account of the balance of payments. The deficit appeared in 1964, but because of the favorable reserve position, it did not arouse the particular concern of government officials. By the third quarter of 1964 the overall account again showed a surplus, and the year ended with a surplus of about 200 million guilders mainly due to a

72. *Centraal Economisch Plan 1965*, p. 177.
73. Netherlands Bank, *1965*, p. 27.
74. Ibid., *1963*, p. 11.
75. *Centraal Economisch Plan 1965*, p. 177.
76. Ibid.

surplus in the capital account. Capital transactions reverted to their normal deficit position in 1965, and the overall balance-of-payments account showed a deficit of approximately 200 million guilders.

During 1963, 1964, and 1965 productivity increased by about 5 percent per year. The 1966 forecast was for a 4 percent increase in production per employed person. The threat of wage costs rising at a rate in excess of 10 percent per year has been a source of concern since the increases in labor costs which these imply have not been offset by productivity increases. Labor costs per unit of output did increase at between 6 and 7 percent per year from 1963 through 1965; this in turn affected prices, the cost of living rose by 17.5 percent in the space of three years. If the goal of price stability, vis-à-vis the principal trading partners, is not achieved, some observers feel that the trend toward a more liberal wage policy might be reversed, with the government once again imposing stricter standards and methods for wage formation.

1963 ECONOMIC PROGRAM

A final example of how the work of the technical bureaus has been used by Dutch policy makers occurred in 1963 when the economic program of the 1963 cabinet for the most part reflected the analysis presented in a paper of the Central Planning Bureau entitled *Increase and Spending of the National Income in the Coming Four Years*.[77] After calculating the expected growth of the national income, the Bureau computed the so-called "available surplus" in 1967 and compared this with the wishes of different groups of the population with regard to increased social benefits, shorter

77. Netherlands Central Planning Bureau, *Toeneming en besteding van het nationale inkomen in de komende vier jaren*, Monografie No. 9 (Den Haag, 1963). The discussion given here follows the review of this publication which appears in *Economic Quarterly Review*, No. 141 (September 1963), pp. 18–20.

working hours, additional investment, the expansion of housebuilding, and so forth.

The available surplus was calculated on the assumption of a 4 percent annual increase in real national income. Allowing for necessary investments and other fixed expenditures, the Bureau estimated that there would be available in 1967, as compared with 1963, a surplus of 5.9 billion guilders that could be used to affect some changes in the pattern of expenditure.

One possibility for absorbing the available surplus would be to increase consumption, and the Bureau calculated this increase in terms of no changes in spending habits and a larger absolute real income. Based on the assumption that wages rise at the same rate as labor productivity, this increase in consumption could, in itself, be expected to use up 3.5 billion of the available surplus.

In the Netherlands, one object of economic policy that commands wide support is the shortening of working hours. The effect of this would be to reduce the growth of the national income to less than the previously assumed 4 percent per year. The Bureau estimated that shortening working hours by one-half hour per day plus an additional two days of holidays per year would reduce the initial 5.9 billion guilder surplus to 3.05 billion guilders.

Another possibility of using up the expected surplus in national income is to increase housebuilding. The Bureau estimated that if the rate of housing starts were raised to the extent necessary to remove the housing shortage by 1967, the cost would be 1.25 billion guilders in the year 1967. However, it must be remembered that in view of the limited building capacity, an increase in housebuilding could most likely cause a decrease in industrial investment. The latter would tend to reduce the growth rate of the national income and thus the available surplus.

Another possibility for absorbing the available surplus is to increase government spending. Certain groups in the population would like to see an increase in expenditures for defense, eduction, culture, and recreation. Others demand increases in old-age pensions, compensatory allowances for increases in house rents, and so on.

The total of these various possibilities for utilizing the available surplus are summarized in Table 15. It is clear from the data that the total of the desired increases in spending greatly exceed the expected surplus in national income.

TABLE 15. Available Surplus and Claims on the National Income in 1967 (billions of guilders)

Available surplus based on a 4% growth of the national income	5.90
Claims on available surplus	
Shortening of working hours	2.85
Increasing construction of housing	1.25
Increase in private consumption	3.50
Increase in public expenditure	6.08
Total claims	13.68

Source: Economic Quarterly Review, No. 141 (1963), p. 18.

Although the government did not formally give a list of priorities encompassing all of the options described in the Bureau's paper, it did decide that first consideration would be given to expansion of the building industry, in particular in the area of housebuilding. The government also stated that increases in the burden of taxation due to the progressiveness of the tax scale and the increase in the nominal wage level would be prevented, and that a few social security benefits would be extended. Decisions as to relative priority in regard to the other claims on the national income and to lower taxation, wage increases, and so forth were postponed.

During the process it was emphasized by the Dutch government that the study by the Central Planning Bureau had not only clarified the necessity to choose between alternatives but also outlined the consequences of various possible actions.

As government economic decisions from 1950–65 involved such extensive use of data resulting from the application of the Central Planning Bureau econometric models, the next chapter deals with the 1955 and 1961 versions of the models themselves.

CHAPTER 7

Econometric Models of the Central Planning Bureau

Macroeconomic models such as those developed by the Central Planning Bureau are quantified representations of the interrelationships among certain economic variables. The magnitudes, and in some cases the fluctuations, of the variables chosen for a model are those which are significant in determining appropriate economic policy measures. For example, such models attempt to demonstrate the interrelation among the levels of consumption, investment, imports, exports, and employment. Thus the model approach offers a method of analyzing data in the context of explicit hypotheses about the workings of an economy.

To the extent that these hypothesized relationships are valid, they perform two functions for policy-makers. First, they provide short-term economic forecasts and thus presumably enlighten policy-makers as to future economic conditions. Second, they provide estimates of the consequences of possible changes in economic policy and thereby aid policy-makers in choosing desirable policy alternatives, i.e. in formulating a rational and consistent overall economic policy.

The Netherlands government holds the model approach in high regard; in fact, in recent years it has been said that the Netherlands government demands models and the Central Planning Bureau supplies them. Likewise, it has been said that the Central Planning Bureau's way of "thinking out things" is the "model way." As a result of this emphasis, construction of such models has come to represent the focus of effort at the Central Planning Bureau.

Over the years several types of models have been developed and used by the Central Planning Bureau, each consisting of a system of equations. For purposes of exposition, two variants, the 1955 model and the 1961 model, are discussed in this and the succeeding chapter.[1] Essentially, both the 1955 and 1961 sets of equations represent models of effective demand for an open economy. Both models have consumption and investment equations and a national income—national product accounting identity. Also included are technical equations showing import demand and employment demand. At the outset it should be noted that neither the 1955 nor the 1961 models contain classical production functions of the type that explain output as a function of labor, capital, and technological change.

The selection of these two models does not imply that the models used in other years were exact copies of either. The specifications of the equations are changed whenever a formulation is developed that appears to be better able to depict the actual workings of the economic system. The coefficients are also reestimated periodically as new and better statistical information becomes available.

The variables contained in the models are of two types: those known beforehand or predicted independently are called predetermined or exogenous variables; the variables that are not known beforehand, but are predicted on the basis of the models, are called jointly dependent or endogenous variables. Among the endogenous variables are the "target variables," those at which policy decisions are aimed. The jointly dependent variables and the predetermined variables are mutually exclusive. Variables that are dependent variables (jointly determined) in one sector of the economy may themselves be causal factors somewhere else in the system. This is one means by which the effect of a change

1. For the 1955 model see Netherlands Central Planning Bureau, *Scope and Methods*, and the Central Economic Plan 1955. The 1961 model is published in the Central Economic Plan 1961.

in any one predetermined variable is transmitted throughout the system, even though the predetermined variable itself may appear in only one equation.

To be useful for governmental planning, the variables chosen in specifying the structure of the model and the concepts employed in formulating the equations of the model must produce an operationally meaningful tool for dealing with economic problems. It is thus desirable for the model to be structured so that it has some "open ends" that may be closed in order to meet certain policy objectives.

Solving problems of economic policy on the basis of models of national economies such as those of the Central Planning Bureau has been the subject of a number of publications. Of these, Jan Tinbergen's *On the Theory of Economic Policy* and *Economic Policy: Principles and Design* were among the pioneering works in this area. Tinbergen was himself the first Director of the Central Planning Bureau.

Using models for determining the appropriateness of alternative economic policies implies that some of the variables included in the model must be under the control of the policy-makers. These enter the equations as predetermined variables. By establishing certain values for one or more of these variables the policy-makers affect the values of the remaining variables. Tinbergen distinguishes between those variables that are subject to the direct control of the policy-makers and those that are not. The former are called "instruments" and the latter, the predetermined variables not under the control of the policy-maker, are known as "data."

In summary, an instrument is a restriction placed upon the value a controlled variable shall have, and a target is a restriction placed upon the value that it is hoped a particular endogenous variable will assume during the policy period. Finally, it should be noted that a model is useful only to the extent that it can reliably describe the relationship between instrument variables, data variables, and target variables.

The 1955 Model

The first of the series of models, of which the 1955 model is representative, was constructed in the early fifties. These early models were based on what Theil has labeled "intuition, courage, and least squares,"[2] and were not used to forecast the absolute levels of the plan year's jointly determined variables; instead, the *annual changes* from the base year to the plan year in the endogenous variables were forecast, given certain assumptions about the exogenous variables.

Twenty-seven equations comprise the 1955 model. The system is complete in the sense that there are as many equations as there are endogenous variables. However, the model is essentially static since in the strictest sense there are no lagged variables. All relationships are expressed as linear equations.[3]

The equations of the 1955 model are shown in Table 16 and are numbered 1 through 27. There are nine behavioral equations consisting of two consumption equations (19, 20), one investment equation (21), one export equation (22), and five price equations (23 through 27). In addition, there are eleven definitional equations (1 through 11), several of which are used for the conversion of one set of definitions to another. For example, economic variables were measured in constant as well as current prices and eight of the definitional equations are simply means of transition from volume

2. Henri Theil, "Survey of Foreign Postwar Developments in Economic Thought," *American Economic Review* (Supplement), Vol. 54, No. 2, Part 2 (1964), p. 36.

3. Initially, some of the equations were not linear, but they were made so by dropping terms representing cross products of annual changes. The rationale for this is that the cross products have a negligible effect relative to the total magnitudes involved. For example, the equation, which corrects for the effect of changes in the price level of investment, appears in the model as $\Delta I = p_i \Delta i + i \Delta p_i$, whereas it should read $\Delta I = p_i \Delta i + i \Delta p_i + \Delta i \Delta p_i$. The variable p_i is the base year price index, always 1.00, i is the base year investment figure, Δi is the change in i between the base year and the plan year, and Δp_i is the change from the base year in the price index of investment goods p_i.

measurement to value measurement. Equation 11 shows the relationship between national output and its components on the input side: wages, taxes, imports, etc. Equation 12, a balance equation, shows the relationship between national output and its components on the output side: consumption, investment, exports, etc. There are also four institutional equations describing relationships between economic quantities that are tied to statutory provisions (13, 14, 15, and 16). One of these (13) is an equation for determining unemployment benefits; the remaining three are tax equations, two dealing with direct taxes (14 and 15) and the other with indirect taxes (16). Equations 17 and 18 are technical relationships, the first dealing with imports and the second with labor demand.

Two definitional equations (2 and 11) define the components of consumption and nonwage income. The latter is a residual quantity equal to total output minus the wage bill, indirect taxes, depreciation, and imports. The former adjusts total consumption for foreign purchases and government sales. Equation 1, also a definitional equation, shows that changes in the total wage bill in guilders are equal to the base year wage bill times the sum of the change in the index of average wages per worker and the change in the index of the number of workers employed.

TABLE 16. The System of Equations Used for the Central Economic Plan, 1955

DEFINITION EQUATIONS

1. $\Delta L = L\ (\Delta a + \Delta l)$
2. $\Delta C = \Delta X_L + \Delta X_{ZC} - \Delta C_F - \Delta C_O$
3. $\Delta C = \Delta c + c\Delta p_c$
4. $\Delta X_O = \Delta x_o + x_0 \Delta p_{xo}$
5. $\Delta I = \Delta i + i\Delta p_i$
6. $\Delta D = \Delta d + d\Delta p_i$
7. $\Delta N = \Delta n + n\Delta p_n$
8. $\Delta E = \Delta e_g + \Delta e_d + e_g \Delta p_{eg} + e_d \Delta p_{ed}$

9. $\Delta V = \Delta V + c\Delta p_c + x_o\Delta p_{xo} + i\Delta p_i + d\Delta p_i + n\Delta p_n + e_g\Delta p_{eg} + e_d\Delta p_{ed}$

10. $\Delta M = \Delta m + m_g\Delta p_{mg} + m_d\Delta p_{md}$

11. $\Delta Z = \Delta V - \Delta L - \Delta T_K - \Delta D - \Delta M$

BALANCE EQUATION

12. $\Delta V = \Delta C + \Delta X_O + \Delta I + \Delta D + \Delta N + \Delta E$

INSTITUTIONAL EQUATIONS

13. $\Delta W_L = .54\ BO_{LW}\ (\Delta b - \Delta a)$

14. $\Delta T_L = .09\ (\Delta L + \Delta W_L + \Delta L_O + \Delta L_F + \Delta O_L + \Delta U_L - \Delta P_L - \Delta P_W) + \Delta T_{Lau}$

15. $\Delta T_Z = .30\ (\Delta Z + \Delta Z_F + \Delta O_Z - \Delta P_Z) + \Delta T_{Zau}$

16. $\Delta T_K = .03\ \Delta L + .04\ \Delta M + .09\ (\Delta V - \Delta E) + \Delta T_{Kau}$

TECHNICAL EQUATIONS

17. $\Delta m = .38\ \Delta c + .63\ \Delta e_g + .28\ \Delta e_d + .71\ (\Delta i + \Delta d) + .79\ \Delta n + .39\ \Delta x_o + \Delta m_d$

18. $\Delta a = .40\ \dfrac{\Delta v - \Delta m}{v - m}$

BEHAVIORAL EQUATIONS

19. $\Delta X_L = .85\ (\Delta L + \Delta W_L - \Delta T_L + \Delta L_O + \Delta L_F + \Delta O_L + \Delta U_L - \Delta P_L - \Delta P_W)$

20. $\Delta X_{ZC} = .40\ (\Delta Z - \Delta T_Z + \Delta Z_F + \Delta O_Z - \Delta P_Z)$

21. $\Delta i = .25\ (\Delta v - \Delta n) - .10 i + \Delta i_v - \Delta d$

22. $\Delta e_g = -2.00\ (\Delta p_{eg} - \Delta p_w)\ e_g + \Delta e_{gau} + \Delta e_d$

23. $\Delta p_c = .35\ \Delta l + .20\ \Delta p_{mg} + \dfrac{\Delta T_{Kau,c}}{c}$

24. $\Delta p_{eg} = .50 \left(.35\ \Delta l + .30\ \Delta p_{mg} + \dfrac{\Delta T_{Kau,eg}}{e_g} \right) + .50\ \Delta p_w$

25. $\Delta p_{xo} = .30\ \Delta l + .50\ \Delta p_{mg} + \dfrac{\Delta T_{Kau,xo}}{x_o}$

26. $\Delta p_i = .25\ \Delta l + .50\ \Delta p_{mg} + \dfrac{\Delta T_{Kau,i}}{i}$

27. $\Delta p_n = .10\ \Delta l + .70\ \Delta p_{mg} + \dfrac{\Delta T_{Kau,n}}{n}$

SYMBOLS USED IN THE 1955 MODEL

Symbol	Description	Unit	Base value
e	Exports of goods and services by enterprises	guilder x 10^9	
e_g	Commodity exports by enterprises	,,	$e_g = 9.10$
e_{gau}	Autonomous commodity exports by enterprises	,,	
e_d	Exports of services by enterprises	,,	$e_d = 3.70$
m	Imports of goods and services by enterprises	,,	$m = 12.34$
m_d	Imports of services by enterprises	,,	$m_d = 1.71$
m_g	Commodity imports by enterprises	,,	$m_g = 10.63$
i	Net investments by enterprises	,,	$i = 2.29$
Z_F	Income from abroad of the group "other income"	,,	
O_L	Income transfers by government to the group "wages, salaries, and social benefits"	,,	
O_Z	Income transfers by government to the group "other income"	,,	
U_L	Social benefits from insurance funds to the group "wages, salaries, and social benefits"	,,	
P_L	Premiums to insurance funds from the group "wages, salaries, and social benefits"	,,	
P_Z	Premiums to insurance funds from the group "other income"	,,	
P_W	Premiums to the unemployment insurance fund	,,	
T_L	Direct taxes from the group "wages, salaries, and social benefits"	,,	
T_Z	Direct taxes from the group "other income"	,,	
T_{Lau}	Autonomous changes in T_L	,,	
T_{Zau}	Autonomous changes in T_Z	,,	
T_K	Indirect taxes net of subsidies	,,	

SYMBOLS USED IN THE 1955 MODEL—continued

Symbol	Description	Unit	Base value
$T_{Kau,c}$	Autonomous changes in T_K on private consumption	guilder x 10^9	
$T_{Kau,eg}$	Autonomous changes in T_K on commodity exports	,,	
$T_{Kau,xo}$	Autonomous changes in T_K on government expenditures	,,	
$T_{Kau,i}$	Autonomous changes in T_K on investments	,,	
i_v	Actual replacements by enterprises	,,	
d	Depreciation by enterprises	,,	$d = 2.21$
n	Increase in commodity stocks	,,	$n = 1.00$
x_o	Government expenditure on goods and services bought from enterprises	,,	$x_o = 2.33$
c	Private consumption bought from enterprises	,,	$c = 15.56$
v	Output of enterprises	,,	$v = 36.19$
X_L	Consumption out of wages, salaries, and social benefits	,,	
X_{ZC}	Consumption out of nonwage income, referred to as "other income"	,,	
C_O	Net government sales to households	,,	
C_F	Private consumption in foreign countries	,,	
L	Wage bill of enterprises, including contributions to social security systems	,,	$L = 9.51$
Z	Income of the group "other income"	,,	
W_L	Social benefits from the unemployment insurance fund	,,	
O_{LW}	Annual social benefits per unemployed paid by the unemployment insurance fund	guilder	$O_{LW} = 1{,}800$
L_O	Wages and salaries, paid by the government	guilder x 10^9	

SYMBOLS USED IN THE 1955 MODEL—continued

Symbol	Description	Unit	Base value
L_F	Income from abroad of the group "wages, salaries, and social benefits"	guilder x 10^9	
$T_{Kau,n}$	Autonomous changes in T_K on commodity stock building	,,	
T_{Kau}	Autonomous changes in T_K	,,	
B	Dependent working population in enterprises	number of persons	$B = 2{,}632{,}000$
p_{eg}	Price index of commodity exports by enterprises	1954 = 1	
p_w	Index of competing world market price level	,,	
p_{ed}	Price index of exports of services by enterprises	,,	
p_{mg}	Price index of commodity imports by enterprises	,,	
p_{md}	Price index of imports of services by enterprises	,,	
p_c	Price index of private consumption	,,	
p_{xo}	Price index of government expenditure on goods and services bought from enterprises	,,	
p_i	Price index of investments	,,	
p_n	Price index of commodity stock building	,,	
l	Wage rate in enterprises	,,	
a	Employment in enterprises	,,	
b	Dependent working population	,,	

Note: Capital letters represent values or number in 1954, or forecast values in 1955. Lowercase letters represent values in 1954, or forecast volumes in 1955. First differences in capital letters are changes in values from 1954-level, current prices. First differences in lowercase letters are changes in values from 1954-level in 1954 prices, and changes in indices from 1954-level, 1954 = 1.

The most complicated equations of the model are the behavioral equations, the others being relatively self-explanatory. The coefficients for the behavioral equations were not estimated statistically but were set a priori.

The two *consumption equations* are:

$$(19)\quad \Delta X_L = .85\ (\Delta L + \Delta W_L - \Delta T_L + \Delta L_O + \Delta L_F + \Delta U_L - \Delta P_L - \Delta P_W)$$

$$(20)\quad \Delta X_{ZC} = .40\ (\Delta Z - \Delta T_Z + \Delta Z_F + \Delta O_Z - \Delta P_Z).$$

The right-hand sides of the two equations represent disposable income, that is, disposable wage income and disposable "other income," (other than wage income). In each case disposable income represents the distribution of primary income plus income transfers minus taxes.

The coefficients are the marginal propensity to consume out of disposable wage and nonwage income, repectively. The relationship between the two marginal propensities is significant from a policy-making standpoint. It clearly shows that efforts to shift the distribution of income in favor of wage earners can be expected to increase the demand for consumption goods, given the same total of disposable income. The relative size of the coefficients also shows that tax measures taken to restrict consumption can be more effectively applied to wage income than to nonwage income.

The investment relation makes use of the concept of the flexible accelerator. Specifically, if the actual stock of capital deviates from that required for a given level of output, it is assumed that a certain portion of the gap is closed each year. The *investment equation* is

$$(21)\qquad \Delta i = .25\ (\Delta v = \Delta n) - .10i + \Delta i_v - \Delta d.$$

In this equation, i represents net investment, v is the output of enterprises, n is the increase in commodity stocks, i_v is the actual replacement of capital by enterprises, and d is the depreciation allowances of enterprises. Ignoring the last two terms, the first part of the equation may be written as

$$\Delta i_p = \beta\{\alpha(\Delta v - \Delta n) - i\}.$$

The term α, which represents the desired capital/output ratio, is assigned the value 2.5. Similarly, β, the percentage of the gap between actual and desired capital stock closed each year, is assigned the value .10. Like the capital/output ratio, β is based on the assumption that a definite volume of production necessitates a definite stock of capital goods. Both α and β are based on the results of statistical research by the Central Bureau of Statistics and Central Planning Bureau.

The quantity $(\Delta v - \Delta n)$ in the two preceding equations is the increase in output forecast for the plan year, netting out the expected change in the rate of inventory accumulation. Underlying these equations is the assumption that capital requirements are based on an expectation that there will be no change in inventory accumulation over that experienced in the base year period. The dependent variable Δi_p in the equation directly above can be interpreted as the induced net increase in productive capacity forecast for the plan year. The final variable, i, on the right-hand side of the above equation, represents net investment for the base year. In equation 21, the final two terms Δi_v and Δd make allowance for the fact that the induced net increase in productive capacity may not equal actual net investment, as there may be a discrepancy between the sum set aside for depreciation allowances and the amount used by businessmen to offset actual depreciation. This discrepancy may in turn cause net investment to be smaller or larger than the forecast Δi_p which did not take this consideration into account.

Each year the Central Planning Bureau calculates depreciation allowances and estimates the amount required from this source for the actual replacement of old equipment. Thus in specifying the investment relationship the Bureau starts with the following two equations:

$$i_g = i + d \text{ and } i_g = i_p + i_v.$$

In this instance i_g is gross investment, d is depreciation allowances, i_p is induced investment, and i_v is the actual replacement by enterprises. Solving for net investment yields:

$$i = i_p + i_v - d.$$

In terms of first differences,

$$\Delta i = \Delta i_p + \Delta i_v - \Delta d$$

is a simplified form of the equation as it appears in the model. Its economic meaning is that actual net investment is equal to gross investment, expressed as the sum of induced investment plus replacement due to depreciation minus the depreciation allowances.

The *export equation* is written as

$$(22) \quad \Delta e_g = -2.00\,(\Delta p_{eg} - \Delta p_w)\, e_g + \Delta e_{gau} + \Delta e_d$$

where e_g represents commodity exports by enterprises, p_{eg} is the price index of commodity exports, p_w is the index of competing world market prices, e_{gau} is autonomous commodity exports, and e_d is the export of services by enterprises. In constructing the equation it was assumed that fluctuations in the volume of Dutch exports are a function of the difference between the Netherlands' export price level and the price level of competitive foreign goods on the world market. Changes in $(p_{eg} - p_w)$ represent improvement or deterioration in the Dutch competitive position in the world market. The coefficient of $(\Delta p_{eg} - \Delta p_w)$ is derived from previous statistical studies. It can be interpreted as a price elasticity of demand by the world market for Dutch exports, and from the -2.00 value, export demand can be seen to be elastic. The policy implications are self-evident.

The term e_{gau} represents the estimated effects on Dutch exports of variations in the internal economic conditions of countries purchasing Dutch exports, in cases when such internal conditions are not caused by changes in the world price level. Estimated exogenously, this term is used to take into account the influence of such happenings as a domestic recession in the United States.

The remainder of the behavioral equations are price-determining relationships. They are based almost solely on the assumption that entrepreneurs fix prices on the basis of costs. Three cost components are considered: wages, the cost of imports, and taxes. In the export price equation, however, an addition variable, p_w, the world price level, was added on the assumption that competition on the world market (as well as internal costs) influences the export price level. None of the price equations makes allowances for cost reductions due to increased productivity or for economies of scale.

The final equation to be discussed is the *technical equation* used to forecast changes in the level of employment:

$$(18) \qquad \Delta a = .40 \frac{\Delta v - \Delta m}{v - m},$$

where a is the index of employment in enterprises and $v - m$ is the difference between total output of enterprises and imports of goods and services by enterprises. The coefficient .40 represents the elasticity of employment with respect to domestic production. This equation implies that the elasticity of demand for labor with respect to output is constant, and that a 10 percent increase in domestic production will result in a 4 percent increase in the demand for labor. Thus for a growing economy the labor content of output is presumed to fall, while the marginal output to labor ratio is assumed to rise; and labor productivity is assumed to vary, rising with increased output and falling when output declines.

In the 1955 model, it was assumed that production is adjusted to demand, so total output is equal to the sum of the various expenditure categories. Thus the system is closed by the accounting identity:

$$(12) \qquad \Delta V = \Delta C + \Delta X_o + \Delta I + \Delta D + \Delta N + \Delta E.$$

In this equation V represents total output, C is total private domestic consumption, X_o is total government expenditure in goods and services bought from enterprises, I is net investment of enterprises, D is depreciation of enterprises, N is the increase in commodity stocks, and E is the export of goods and services by enterprises.

Models the size of the ones used by the Central Planning

Bureau cannot, however, be used to solve problems of economic policy, to predict, or to evaluate policy proposals without further manipulation. This is because the model in its structural form, that is, as it is discussed in this chapter, is not directly suitable for policy analysis. The reason is that the specifications of the individual equations of the model contain some variables that are dependent in one equation but are considered to be causal factors in one or more other equations. In other words, some of the structural equations contain jointly dependent variables (current values of the endogenous variables) on their right-hand sides.

It is necessary, therefore, to solve the structural form of the model for what is called the reduced form, which expresses each jointly dependent variable in terms of the predetermined variables and the coefficients of both the jointly dependent and the predetermined variables. Every complete linear model, i.e. one in which there are sufficient equations to explain the variation of all the jointly dependent variables, has a reduced form.[4] Unlike the structural equations, which may or may not contain all of the predetermined variables, each reduced-form equation contains every predetermined variable in the system.[5]

Given the initial values and certain assumptions about the exogenous variables, the model in the reduced form is solved

4. Providing the matrix of the coefficients of the jointly dependent variables is nonsingular, i.e. that the equations are independent.

5. In matrix notation the structural equations can be written as $B(y) - \Gamma(x) = 0$. Here (y) and (x) are column vectors of the jointly dependent and predetermined variables respectively, and B and Γ are the coefficient matrices associated with the two sets of variables. To obtain the reduced form of the model one first transposes $\Gamma(x)$ and then premultiplies both sides by B^{-1} (the inverse of the matrix of the coefficients of the jointly dependent variables). Thus, $(y) = B^{-1}\Gamma(x)$. The product of $B^{-1}\Gamma$ represents the matrix of multipliers whose elements are the induced change in the ith dependent variable in response to a change of one unit in the jth predetermined variable. The total cumulative (the combined primary and secondary) effects on the vector of the dependent variables (y) caused by changes in the vector of predetermined variables (x), taking into account the interdependencies of the system, can be computed easily once the elements of $B^{-1}\Gamma$ are known.

for changes of the values of the endogenous variables and forecasts obtained by adding these changes to, or subtracting them from, the initial values. In this manner the Central Planning Bureau obtains the short-term forecasts it provides to the government policy-makers. By solving the model for various combinations of the instrument variables, such as the tax rates, the Bureau is also able to estimate the likely effects of changes in economic policy such as those described in the previous chapter.

THE 1961 MODEL

The 1961 model of the Central Planning Bureau was the outgrowth of a project begun in 1955 for the purpose of improving the short-term forecasting model.[6] The 1961 model contains 38 equations—11 behavioral equations and 27 technical and definitional equations.[7] The behavioral equations consist of a consumption relationship, an investment equation, an inventory equation, a demand-for-labor equation, an unemployment equation, an export equation, an import equation, and four equations describing the price indices of consumption, investment, exports, and autonomous (government) expenditures.

Unlike the 1955 model, whose coefficients were set a priori, the coefficients of the 1961 model were estimated statistically. In the preparatory stages, the method of ordinary least

6. Four groups participated in the project entitled "An Economic Analysis of the Netherlands Economy": the Central Planning Bureau, the Central Bureau of Statistics, the Mathematical Center in Amsterdam, and the Netherlands Economic Institute. The project was supervised by Dr. P. J. Verdoorn and the late Dr. L. M. Koyck.

7. The model under discussion was designated as 60.07 by the Central Planning Bureau. The analysis follows four sources: T. A. Klock, "A Comparative Survey of Two Econometric Models," mimeo. (Rotterdam, Netherlands School of Econometrics, 1962), 32 pp.; Central Economic Plan 1961 (Annex 1, August 1961), pp. 113–28; Netherlands Central Planning Bureau, "An Econometric Analysis of the Dutch Economy," Report A-10, mimeo. (The Hague, 1960), 32 pp.; and Verdoorn and van Eijk, "Experimental Short-term Forecasting Models."

squares was used to estimate each equation individually. When an acceptable formulation for each structural equation was decided upon, however, the coefficients of the complete system were reestimated simultaneously by the method of two-stage least squares.[8]

The sample period covered by the 1961 model extends from 1923 to 1958. The war years were discarded and the period split into two parts, 1923–38 and 1949–58. In addition to the fact that the available war years' statistics are generally considered to be unreliable, the war itself imposed numerous structural constraints not typical of the period as a whole.

The prewar years provide most of the fluctuations that occur in the sample period, as the postwar years have, for the most part, been devoid of cycles. However, since the principal aim of the model is to provide a basis for short-term projections in the present economic environment, the postwar years were given twice the weight of the prewar years in estimating the coefficients of the behavioral equations.

There are a number of differences between the 1955 and the 1961 model. One of these is the units in which the variables are expressed. The 1955 model used first differences, while the 1961 model used percent changes. The choice of percentage was conditioned, to some extent, by the facts that the coefficients of the behavioral equations of the 1961 model are estimated on the basis of time-series data and that relatively large changes had taken place in the magnitude of some of the variables during the time period covered by the observations. For example, the absolute levels of prices and of some other variables had doubled or even tripled. In many cases, most of the increases occurred during the break in the data, i.e. during the war years 1938–49. The use of percentage

8. The technique of two-stage least-square estimation was first proposed by Henri Theil, who was at the time a staff member of the Central Planning Bureau. See Theil, *Economic Forecasts and Policy*, pp. 334–55. The method was also suggested by R. L. Basmann in "A Generalized Classical Method of Linear Estimation of Coefficients in a Structural Equation," *Econometrica*, **25** (1957), pp. 77–83.

changes makes the two periods of the series more comparable.

Except for the equation defining capacity,[9] the model relationships imply an exponential equation of the form $y = ax^b e^{ct}$. An equation such as this is linearized by taking the logarithm of both sides: $\ln y = \ln a + b \ln x + ct$. After some manipulation, the linearized form may be written as:

$$100 \frac{\Delta y}{y_{-1}} = 100b \frac{\Delta x}{x_{-1}} + 100c,$$

or after introducing the notation $\dot{y}$ and $\dot{x}$ [where $\dot{y} = 100 (\Delta y/y_{-1})$ and $\dot{x} = 100(\Delta x/x_{-1})$] as

$$\dot{y} = b\dot{x} + 100c.$$

In the equations that follow, variables such as $\dot{y}$ and $\dot{x}$ represent percentage changes.[10] Consequently, the coefficient b is an elasticity and, in general, the constant c may be interrupted as a residual trend expressed in percent.[11] By definition, the trend represents the influence of factors that develop gradually over time and that are not accounted for by the explanatory variables in the equation.

Because the variables of the 1961 model are expressed as percentage changes, the model is constructed on the hypothesis that elasticities, ϵ, are structurally constant in the Dutch economy. Under this assumption, incremental relationships, $\Delta x/\Delta y$, vary from year to year, depending on the magnitudes of the base year figures involved. This can be seen from the following equation:

$$\frac{\Delta x}{\Delta y} = \epsilon_{xy} \frac{x_{-1}}{y_{-1}},$$

9. The 1961 model differs from the 1955 model in that a curvilinear capacity ceiling was introduced into the 1961 equation system.

10. The method of transition from $\ln y$ and $\ln x$ to $\dot{y}$ and $\dot{x}$ is explained in Appendix A.1.

11. In some equations, however, the standard interpretation of the constant as the rate of change in the basic trend component of the dependent variable is not permissible. These exceptions will be pointed out in the text.

where $\Delta x/\Delta y$ is the incremental change in x as a result of an incremental change in y, and x_{-1} and y_{-1} are the base year figures for x and y respectively.

The 1961 model contains variables expressed in both real (volume) and nominal (value) terms. As in the 1955 model, definitional equations are used to effect a transition from one metric to the other. For example, the definitional equation $C = cp_c$ appears in the model as

$$\dot{C} = \dot{c} + \dot{p}_c.$$

For the equation in question, $\dot{C}$ is the percentage change in the value of consumption, $\dot{c}$ is the percentage change in the volume of consumption, and $\dot{p}_c$ is the change in the price index of consumption from a base-year figure of 100.

The equations of the 1961 model can be divided into several categories. The behavioral equations contain three categories: (1) expenditure equations, (2) equations explaining factors of production and capacity, and (3) price equations. Definitional equations also can be divided into three categories: equations showing (1) the relationship between value and volume, (2) expenditure totals, and (3) costs and margins. The complete model appears in Table 17.[12] The equations of the model are followed by a list of the endogenous variables and a glossary of definitions.

TABLE 17. The Equation System Used for the 1961 Central Economic Plan

BEHAVIORAL EQUATIONS

Expenditure Equations

1. $\dot{C} = .64\,\dot{L}^{B}_{-\frac{1}{3}} + .17\,\dot{Z}^{B}_{-\frac{2}{3}} + .46\,\Delta\dot{p}_c - .16\,\Delta\dot{C}_{-1} + .05\,\dot{c}^{r}_{-1} - .63$

2. $\dot{I} = .82\,(\dot{Z}_{-1} - T''_z) + .46\,\dot{p}_i + .80\,\dot{c}^{r}_{-1} - 7.18\,\Delta w_{l_{-\frac{1}{2}}} - \psi_i + 29.62$

12. The model as it appears here is slightly different from the model published in the Central Economic Plan 1961. Several simplifications were made to the Bureau's model prior to its publication as part of the 1961 Plan.

TABLE 17—continued

$$3. \quad \dot{N} = .39\,\dot{v}' - 1.34\,\frac{N_{-1}}{V'_{-1}}(100) + .96\,\Delta K + .18\,\dot{p}_m + .41\,t^*$$

$$4. \quad \dot{b} = 1.46\,\dot{b}_c - 1.71\,(\dot{p}_b - \dot{p}'_b) - 1.11\,(\dot{p}_b - \dot{p}_b)_{-1} - 64\,\Delta\dot{p}' + 1.42\,w_l - 7.52$$

Factors of Productivity and Capacity

$$5. \quad \dot{m} = 1.24\,\dot{v}_m + .29\,\Delta\dot{v}_m + 2.50\,\dot{N} - .38\,\dot{p}_{m-v'} + .32\,\Delta\dot{p}''_v - .30\,k + .11\,k' - .08$$

$$6. \quad \dot{a} = .39\,\dot{v}_a + .76\,\Delta K + .07\,\dot{p}_{m-v'} + .12\,\psi_a + .66$$

$$7. \quad \Delta w = -.42\,\dot{a} + .39\,\frac{\Delta P - \Delta a_o}{P_{B_{-1}}} - .04\,\Delta T_c + \Pi_w - 4.49$$

Price Equations

$$8. \quad \dot{p}_c = .21\,\dot{H} + .20\,\dot{p}_{m_{-\frac{1}{2}}} - .42\,(\dot{v}' - \dot{m})_{-\frac{1}{2}} + .17\,\dot{T}'_{K_{-\frac{1}{3}}} + 1.82\,\Delta r_{k_{-\frac{1}{2}}} + \Lambda - 2.26$$

$$9. \quad \dot{p}_i = .41\,\dot{H} + .39\,\dot{p}_m + .33\,\dot{p}_{i_{-1}} + 1.03$$

$$10. \quad \dot{p}_b = .32\,\dot{H} + .43\,\dot{p}_m + .23\,\dot{p}''_b + .25\,\Delta\dot{p}'_b + .15\,\dot{p}_{b_{-1}} - .65$$

$$11. \quad \dot{p}_x = .69\,\dot{H} + .31\,\dot{p}_m + .27\,\dot{p}_{x_{-1}} + 1.22$$

DEFINITIONAL EQUATIONS

Relations Between Value and Volume Variables

$$12. \quad \dot{B} = \dot{b} + \dot{p}_b$$

$$13. \quad \dot{C} = \dot{c} + \dot{p}_c$$

$$14. \quad \dot{I} = \dot{i} + \dot{p}_i$$

$$15. \quad \dot{X} = \dot{x} + \dot{p}_x$$

$$16. \quad \dot{M} = \dot{m} + \dot{p}_m$$

$$17. \quad \dot{V}' = \dot{v}' + \dot{p}_{v'}$$

Expenditure Totals

$$18. \quad \dot{v}' = .59\,\dot{c} + .11\,\dot{x} + .08\,\dot{i} + .22\,\dot{b}$$

$$19. \quad \dot{v}_a = .46\,\dot{c} + .20\,\dot{x} + .16\,\dot{i} + .18\,\dot{b}$$

$$20. \quad \dot{v}_m = .45\,\dot{c} + .15\,\dot{x} + .11\,\dot{i} + .29\,\dot{b}$$

$$21. \quad \dot{p}_{v'} = .50\,\dot{p}_c + .12\,\dot{p}_x + .09\,\dot{p}_i + .29\,\dot{p}_b$$

$$22. \quad \dot{V} = .44\,\dot{C} + .13\,\dot{X} + .10\,\dot{I} + .92\,\dot{N} + .25\,\dot{B} + .06\,\dot{D}$$

$$23 \quad \dot{p}_v = .48\,\dot{p}_c + .13\,\dot{p}_x + .09\,\dot{p}_i + .30\,\dot{p}_b$$

Costs and Margins

$$24. \quad \dot{H} = \dot{l} - (\dot{v}' - \dot{a})_{-\frac{1}{2}}$$

$$25. \quad \dot{p}_{m-v'} = \dot{p}_m - \dot{p}_{v'_{-\frac{1}{2}}} + .06\,\dot{T}'_{K_{-\frac{1}{2}}}$$

$$26. \quad \Delta K = \dot{p}_{v'} - .27\,\dot{l} - .30\,\dot{p}_m - .06\,\dot{T}'_{K_{-\frac{1}{3}}}$$

* Period 1923–38.

TABLE 17—continued

Unemployment

27. $w_l = .434\,\dot{w}' - .30\,\Delta w + w_{l_{-1}}$

28. $\Pi_w = 1.68\left\{\dfrac{P_{-1}}{P_{B_{-1}}}\right\}^{*} + 2.18\left\{\dfrac{P_{-1}}{P_{B_{-1}}}\right\}^{\dagger}$

29. $\dot{w}' = 7.299\,\Delta w$

Income Equations

30. $\dot{L} = \dot{a} + \dot{l}$

31. $\dot{Z} = 3.77\,\dot{V} - 1.06\,\dot{L} - .24\,\dot{T}_K - 1.23\,\dot{M} - .24\,\dot{F}$

32. $\dot{L}^B = .87\,\dot{L} + .87\,\dot{O}'_L$

33. $\dot{Z}^B = 1.50\,\dot{Z} + 1.50\,\dot{O}'_Z$

Taxes

34. $\dot{T}_K = \dot{V}' + \dot{T}'_K$

35. $T''_Z = \Delta\dfrac{T_z}{Z_{-1}}(100)$

LAGGED INFLUENCES

36. $\psi_i = 2.30\,(100)\log I_{-1} - 1.06\,(100)\log p_{i_{-1}} + 7.18\,w_{l^r_{-1\frac{1}{2}}}$
$- 1.88\,(100)\log(Z_{-2} - T_{z_{-1}}) - 1.84\,(100)\log c^r_{-2}$

37. $\psi_a = (100)\log z_{-1} - 1.59\,(100)\log a_{-1}$

38. $\Lambda = -.35\,(100)\log\left\{\dfrac{v'}{m}\right\}_{-1\frac{1}{2}} + .56\,(100)\log H_{-1}$
$+ .17\,(100)\log p_{m_{-1\frac{1}{2}}} - .65\,\Delta r_{k_{-1\frac{1}{2}}} + .14\,(100)\log T'_{K_{-1\frac{1}{3}}}$
$- .83\,(100)\log p_{c_{-1}}$

ENDOGENOUS VARIABLES OF THE SYSTEM

Resources

$\dot{a}, \dot{L}, \dot{Z}, \dot{T}_K, \dot{m}, \dot{M}$

Expenditures

$\dot{c}, \dot{p}_c, \dot{C}, \dot{p}_x, \dot{X}, \dot{i}, \dot{p}_i, \dot{I}, \dot{N}, \dot{p}_b, \dot{b}, \dot{B}, \dot{v}', \dot{p}_{v'}, \dot{p}_v, \dot{V}', \dot{V}$

Unemployment

Δw

Secondary Incomes and Taxes

$\dot{L}^B, \dot{Z}^B, T''_z$

Composite Variables

$\dot{v}_a, \dot{v}_m, \dot{H}, p_{m-v'}, \Delta K, w_l, \Pi_w, \psi_i, \psi_a, \Lambda, \dot{w}'$

* Period 1923–38. † Period 1949–57.

GLOSSARY OF SYMBOLS USED

a		Number of persons employed in enterprises
a_o		Number of persons employed in the government sector
B	b	Exports of commodities
	b_c	Competing exports
C	c	Total private consumption
	c^r	Time and demand deposits at the end of the year
D		Net invisibles
F		Depreciation of enterprises
H		Labor costs per unit of total output
I	i	Gross investments of enterprises (excluding government enterprises and residential construction)
	k	Quantitative import restrictions (1932–37)
	k'	Rate of liberalization (1949–55)
K		Gross profits per unit of output
	l	Average gross wages per standard year of 300 days
L		Wage bill of enterprises
L^B		Disposable wage income
M	m	Imports of commodities
N		Stock formation (expressed as a percentage of total output less stock changes and net invisibles)
O'_L		Income transfers with regard to wage income, including government wages and direct taxes on cash basis (expressed as a percentage of wage bill of enterprises)
O'_Z		Income transfers with regard to nonwage income, including direct taxes on cash basis (expressed as a percentage of total nonwage income)
P		Population in the working ages (14–65 years)
P_B		Dependent working population (exclusive of the self-employed)
	p_b	Export prices
	p'_b	Prices of competing exports
	p_c	Consumption price
	p_i	Investment price
	p_m	Import price
	$p_{m-v'}$	Margin between import price adjusted for the incidence of indirect taxes and the price of total output (with a lag of half a year)
	p_v	Price of total output
	$p_{v'}$	Price of total output (less stock changes and net invisibles)
	p_x	Prices of autonomous expenditure

	r_k	Short-term rate of interest (discount rate of the Central Bank)
T_c		Minimum temperature below 0° centigrade (sum of monthly averages)
T_K		Indirect taxes minus subsidies
T'_K		Incidence of indirect taxes minus subsidies ($T'_K = T_K/V'$)
	t^*	Prewar decreasing trend (1923 = 15; 1938 = 0)
T_z		Direct taxes on nonwage income (on cash basis)
T''_z		Variation in the incidence of direct taxes on nonwage income
V		Total output
V'	v'	Total output less stock changes and net invisibles
	v_a	Total output less stock changes and net invisibles (reweighted with intensity of labor demand)
	v_m	Total output less stock changes and net invisibles (reweighted with import quota)
	w	Registered unemployment as a percentage of dependent working population
	w_l	Curvilinear indicator of available capacity
	w'	Composite variable related to changes in the level of unemployment
X	x	Autonomous expenditure (government expenditure, investment of government enterprises, and residential construction)
Z	z	Nonwage income
Z^B		Disposable nonwage income

Note: Capital letters represent variables expressed in value terms and lowercase letters represent variables expressed in volume terms. Letters with dots above represent percentage changes from the base year, 1960. All indices are based on 1960 = 100. Thus the initial values for all prices equal 100; and, for the initial period, the volume figure for each flow of goods or factors is equal to the corresponding value figure.

The Central Economic Plan of 1961 gives both the equation system on which the plan was based and a limited discussion of some of the more important relationships of the model. However, the description of the model given in the 1961 Plan is written primarily for the layman and avoids technical details wherever possible. This chapter presents a comprehensive description of the 1961 model, including several statistical measures, not available in the Plan itself, that show both the extent of the specification errors in the behavioral equations and the statistical reliability of the estimated coefficients of the causal variables.

The statistics given are: R (the multiple correlation coefficient), σ_y (the standard deviation of the dependent variable), and σ_u (the standard deviation of the residual). Also shown are the ratios of the standard error of each coefficient to the coefficient itself.[13] This ratio is found in parentheses directly below each coefficient. Below the ratio are a series of numbers showing the percentage of explained variation attributable to each causal variable.

These statistics show that there are a number of cases where coefficients are less than twice the standard errors. In such a case the statistical reliability of the coefficients is extremely low. At the same time there are a number of causal variables whose presence in the equations in question accounts for only a small amount of the explained variation in the dependent variable. One might question why causal variables fitting either of these categories were retained in the final specifications of the model. The validity of including these variables, however, is not discussed here

INSTRUMENTS AND TARGETS OF DUTCH ECONOMIC POLICY AS 1961 MODEL VARIABLES

The exogenous variables of the 1961 model of the Central Planning Bureau include the chief instruments of Dutch economic policy. As discussed previously, most of these are budgetary instruments and they include: the volume of government employment, the quantity of government commodity purchases, government transfer payments, direct taxes collected from wage income and nonwage income respectively, and indirect taxes. In addition to these fiscal items, the general wage rate and the interest rate, which are

13. Thus .50 indicates that the standard error is one half the coefficient. The larger the ratio, the less the likelihood that the coefficient is statistically significant.

also instruments of government policy, are expressed as exogenous variables in the model. Table 18 shows the instruments of government policy as they appear in the 1961 model of the Central Planning Bureau.

TABLE 18. Survey of Policy Instruments, 1961 Model

Symbol	Description	Units*
l	General wage rate	In % change with respect to the base year
x	Autonomous expenditure (government expenditure, investment of government enterprises, and residential construction)	In % change with respect to the base year
T'_K	Change in indirect taxes minus subsidies: $T'_K = \frac{\Delta T_K}{V'_{-1}}$	In annual changes with respect to the base year
T_L	(a) Autonomous changes in direct taxes on wages ($\dot{T}_L$ is a component of the variable $\dot{O}'_L$)	(a) In annual changes as a % of the wage bill of enterprises in the base year
	(b) Changes in government wages	(b) In annual changes as a % of the wage bill of enterprises in the base year
	(c) Changes in income transfers with regard to wage income	(c) In annual changes as a % of the wage bill of enterprises in the base year
T_Z	(a) Autonomous changes in direct taxes on nonwage income (T_Z is a component of the variable O'_Z)	(a) In annual changes as a % of the nonwage income in the base year
	(b) Changes in income transfers with regard to nonwage income	(b) In annual changes as a % of the nonwage income in the base year

* As the variables appear in the model.

TABLE 18. Survey of Instruments, 1961 Model—continued

Symbol	Description	Units*
T''_z	Autonomous changes in the incidence of direct taxes on nonwage income	In changes in rate with respect to the base year
$\Delta r_{k-\frac{1}{2}}$	Short-term rate of interest (discount rate of the Central Bank)	In changes in rate with respect to the base year
Δa_0	Changes in the number of persons employed in the government sector (man years)	In annual changes with respect to the base year

* As the variables appear in the model.

It should be noted that the instruments include—as they should—changes in autonomous expenditures in terms of quantities rather than in money value. The instruments also include autonomous changes in tax tariffs rather than actual changes in tax receipts. The latter is because total budget outlays and total tax receipts—and hence the budget balance—are only in part determined by autonomous budgetary measures taken; they also depend on the way in which commodity prices, incomes, and other endogenous variables react to the policy measures and to changes in other exogenous variables. That is to say, they depend in part on the model itself and must therefore be treated as endogenous variables.

The target variables consist of the component parts of total expenditures and total resources as these economic quantities are defined in the model. Total expenditure, V, is defined by the component variables of equation 22:

$$V = C + X + I + N + B + D.$$

The component parts of total resources are as shown by the variables in equation 31:

$$V = Z + L + T_k + M + F.$$

Also classified as target variables are those variables related to employment and wages, a, Δw, L^B, Z^B, and ΔK; and the price indices, p_v, p_c, and p_b.[14]

THE BEHAVIORAL EQUATIONS

There are three categories of behavioral relationships. The first category consists of four expenditure (demand) equations, each of which describes quantities bought and sold as determined by the buyers in the relevant market. The first three expenditure equations concern consumption (C), investment (I), and stock formation (N), expressed in the prices of the forecast year. The fourth equation is for the volume of exports (b) expressed in the prices of the base year. In the second category of behavioral equations are three relationships, each representing the demand, or the lack of demand, for certain factors of production. The three relationships are: imports (m), employment in enterprise (a), and changes in unemployment (Δw). Four price relationships comprise the last category of behavioral equations, each describing prices paid as determined by the sellers in that particular market.[15] These four relationships are the consumption price index (p_c), the investment price index (p_i), the exports price index (p_b), and the index of prices of autonomous expenditures (p_x). Autonomous expenditures are government expenditure, investment of government enterprises, and residential housing.

Expenditure Equations

Consumption equation.

(1)
$$\dot{C} = .64\,\dot{L}^{B}_{-\frac{1}{3}} + .17\,\dot{Z}^{B}_{-\frac{2}{3}} + .46\,\Delta\dot{p}_c$$
$$\qquad (.09) \qquad\qquad (.22) \qquad\qquad (.14)$$
$$\qquad .41 \qquad\qquad .29 \qquad\qquad .12$$

14. For a model such as the Central Planning Bureau's 1961 version in which variables are expressed in terms of link relatives, i.e. first differences divided by the level of the first year, $(x_t - x_{t-1})/x_{t-1}$, the coefficients of the structural equations are elasticities. The product of $B^{-1}\Gamma$ mentioned earlier, therefore, is a matrix whose elements should be interpreted as impact elasticities.

15. Two additional terms are added to the export price equation. They represent the export price level lagged one year and the price level of competing exports.

$$R = .992 \qquad \sigma_y = .67$$

$$- 16\,\Delta\dot{C}_{-1} + .05\,\dot{c}^{r}_{-1} - .63.$$
$$(.19) \qquad (.33) \qquad (.37)$$
$$.80 \qquad .10$$
$$\sigma_u = .008$$

The dependent variable in the consumption equation is $\dot{C}$, the percentage change in the value of total private consumption. It is determined as a function of five causal variables. The first two are wage and nonwage disposable income, $\dot{L}^B$ and $\dot{Z}^B$, lagged one third and two thirds of a year respectively;[16] the third, $\Delta\dot{p}_c$, is the second difference of the price level. The fourth causal variable, $\Delta\dot{C}_{-1}$, is the second difference of the percentage change in consumption lagged one year; the fifth, $\dot{c}^{r}_{-1}$, is the percentage change in the stock of liquid assets measured in terms of time and demand deposits of the commercial banks over the previous time period.[17]

The variables $\dot{L}^B$ and $\dot{Z}^B$ represent the influence of income on consumption. When base year figures are inserted in

16. Since the Dutch only collect annual data, lags of less than one year must be estimated. The procedure for this is relatively simple: see L. R. Klein, *A Textbook of Econometrics* (Evanston, Ill., Row, Peterson, 1953), p. 315. The variables that result may be called semi-endogenous. They are computed on the basis of the assumption that a variable with a lag of less than one year can be estimated by taking a weighted average of the variable for the current year and the variable lagged one year. For example: $L^B_{-\frac{1}{3}} = L^B_{-1} + \frac{2}{3}\,\Delta L^B$; $L^B_{-\frac{1}{3}} = L^B_{-1} + \frac{2}{3}\,(L^B - L^B_{-1})$; and $L^B_{-\frac{1}{3}} = L^B_{-1} + \frac{2}{3}\,L^B - \frac{2}{3}\,L^B_{-1}$. Thus, $L^B_{-\frac{1}{3}} = \frac{2}{3}\,L^B + \frac{1}{3}\,L^B_{-1}$, and $\frac{2}{3}\,L^B$ is the endogenous portion and $\frac{1}{3}\,L^B_{-1}$, the exogenous portion of the variable. When the Central Planning Bureau estimates the coefficients of the behavioral equations, they use the time series of the constructed variables (such as $L^B_{-\frac{1}{3}}$). However, due to the semi-endogenous nature of these variables, when the Central Planning Bureau uses the model for prediction, they do not use $L^B_{-\frac{1}{3}}$ but rather substitute $\frac{2}{3}\,L^B + \frac{1}{3}\,L^B_{-1}$. This occurs wherever $L^B_{-\frac{1}{3}}$ appears in the model. The same type of substitution is made for the other semi-endogenous variables.

17. The liquidity term c^{r}_{-1}, along with r_k, the discount rate at the Central Bank, which appears in the consumption price equation 2, are the only financial variables in the model. The liquidity term itself, c^{r}_{-1}, appears twice, once in the consumption equation and again in the investment equation.

Equation 1, the marginal propensities to consume from wage and nonwage income can be computed. On the basis of 1957 values, the marginal propensity to consume out of disposable wage income was .86 and for nonwage income it was .41. In the 1955 model discussed previously, these propensities were a priori set at .85 and .40.

The effects of the changes in taxes and income transfers on consumption are expressed through these same two causal variables, $\dot{L}^B$ and $\dot{Z}^B$. Equations 32 and 33 in the model define these variables.[18]

$$\dot{L}^B = .87\,\dot{L} + .87\,\dot{O}'_L. \tag{32}$$

$$\dot{Z}^B = 1.50\,\dot{Z} + 1.50\,\dot{O}'_Z. \tag{33}$$

$\dot{L}$ equals the percentage change in the wage bill of enterprises; and $\dot{O}'_L$ equals the ratio of the change in the government wage bill, plus transfer payments, less taxes on wage income, to the wage bill, lagged one year. $\dot{O}'_L$ is defined as:

$$\dot{O}'_L = 100\,\frac{\Delta O'_L}{L_{-1}}$$

where O'_L equals government wage bill (L_G) plus transfers of government (T_G), minus taxes on wages (T_L). After taking lags and subtracting,

$$\Delta O'_L = \Delta L_G + \Delta T_G - \Delta T_L.$$

In equation 33, $\dot{Z}$ equals the percentage change in nonwage income; and $\dot{O}'_Z$ the ratio of the change in nonwage income transfers, minus taxes, to nonwage income, lagged one year. As before:

$$\dot{O}'_Z = 100\,\frac{\Delta O'_Z}{Z_{-1}}.$$

The next two explanatory variables are $\Delta\dot{p}_c$, the difference in the percentage changes in the index of the consumption

18. For the method of calculating the coefficients of equations 32 and 33, see Appendix A.3.

price level, and $\Delta\dot{p}_{c-1}$, the difference in the percentage changes in consumption prices lagged one year. Essentially, these variables are second differences, i.e. they represent differences in percentage changes. For example:

$$\Delta\dot{p}_c = 100\left(\frac{p_c - p_{c-1}}{p_{c-1}} - \frac{p_{c-1} - p_{c-2}}{p_{c-2}}\right).$$

Variables of this type are called quasi-accelerators. The direct effect of $\Delta\dot{p}_c$ on the dependent variable is such that, should the price level of consumer goods increase at an increasing rate, consumption in money terms would also increase. However, whether consumers purchase more or whether they purchase less in real terms in the face of a continuing price increase cannot be determined from the equation as it appears in the model. To answer this question, T. A. Klock converted the entire consumption equation into volume terms.[19] As a result, he obtained $-.06$ for the elasticity of real consumption with respect to the current change in the price level, $-.29$ elasticity for the same effect lagged one year, and finally $+.16$ elasticity for the price change of two years ago.

The phenomenon of "money illusion" is clearly present during the first two time periods. Neither the current change in price level nor last year's change is completely identified by the consumer. For example, if these changes represent increases in the price level, the elasticities of $-.06$ and $-.29$ indicate that the consumer will *not*, in the first two years, increase his money outlays enough to offset the price increases. The result is a decline in real consumption. The overall effect of such price changes is to cause consumption expenditure to lag income formation.

The fourth variable in equation 1, $\Delta\dot{C}_{-1}$, is also a quasi-accelerator. It can be interpreted as an automatic readjustment to the rise or fall in consumption of the previous year,

19. Klock, p. 7.

or perhaps better, as a sort of second thought about last year's expenditures, i.e. an attempt by consumers to return to what they consider their normal spending habits.

The last variable in the consumption equation is the liquidity term, $\dot{c}^r_{-1}$, which has a favorable, although small, influence on consumption.

Investment equation. This equation of the model is

$$\text{(2)} \qquad \dot{I} = .82\,(\dot{Z}_{-1} - T''_Z) + .46\,\dot{p}_i + .80\,\dot{c}^r_{-1} - 7.18\,\Delta w_{l_{-\frac{1}{2}}} - \psi_i + 29.62.$$

Changes in investment are determined by changes in nonwage income (Z), taxes on nonwage income (T''_Z), the price index of investment goods ($\dot{p}_i$), liquidity ($\dot{c}^r$), the capacity variable (w_l), and the composite variable (ψ_i) explained below.

The investment equation is the most complicated equation of the entire model. Because autocorrelation was found when the trial equations were expressed in percentage changes, reformulation of the basic equation was necessary. As a result, the coefficients were not estimated from the equation above (the one which appears in the 1961 Plan) but from an equation expressing the variables as natural logarithms of their absolute value.

The estimating relationship has the following basic form:

$$I = (Z_{-1} - T_z)^{\alpha_1} p_i^{\alpha_2} q_{-\frac{1}{2}}^{\alpha_3} c_{-1}^{r\,\alpha_4}.$$

In this expression q is a proxy variable representing the nonlinear capacity ceiling (w_l). Taking the natural logarithms of both sides yields

$$\ln I = \alpha_1 \ln(Z_{-1} - T_z) + \alpha_2 \ln p_i + \alpha_3 \ln q_{-\frac{1}{2}} + \alpha_4 \ln c^r_{-1}.$$

By substituting the coefficients estimated by the Central Planning Bureau, the investment equation becomes:

$$\ln I = \underset{\substack{(.12)\\ .41}}{.46 \ln p_i} - \underset{\substack{(.26)\\ .04}}{.31 \ln q_{-\frac{1}{2}}} + \underset{\substack{(.08)\\ .50}}{.82 \ln(Z_{-1} - T_z)}$$

$R = .958 \qquad\qquad \sigma_y = .190$

$+ .80 \ln c^r_{-1} + 29.62.$

$(.13) \qquad (.34)$

$.05$

$\sigma_u = .055$

This equation expresses several variables in absolute terms while elsewhere in the model they are expressed in percentages, which necessitates further manipulation. First, each variable is written in terms of the logarithm of the variable in the base year, plus the difference between the logarithms of the base and current years, or $\ln I = \ln I_{-1} + \Delta \ln I$. Approximating the logarithmic terms by a Taylor expansion (*see* Appendix A.1) and multiplying by 100 yields

$$\begin{aligned} \dot{I} + 100 \ln I_{-1} &= \alpha_1[100 \ln(Z_{-2} - T_{z_{-1}}) + \dot{Z}_{-1} - 100\,\Delta(T_z/Z_{-1})] \\ &\quad + \alpha_2[\dot{p}_i + 100 \ln(p_i)_{-1}] \\ &\quad + \alpha_3[100\,\Delta \ln q_{-\frac{1}{2}} + 100 \ln q_{-1\frac{1}{2}}] \\ &\quad + \alpha_4[\dot{c}^r_{-1} + 100 \ln c^r_{-2}].^{20} \end{aligned}$$

The investment equation is further simplified by collecting

20. The term $[\ln (Z_{-2} - T_{z-1}) + \dot{Z}_{-1} - \Delta(T_z/Z_{-1})]$ was derived from $\ln (Z_{-1} - T_z)$ as follows: first add and subtract $\Delta Z_{-1}/Z_{-2}$, but since $\Delta Z_{-1}/Z_{-2} = \Delta \ln Z_{-1}$ (see Appendix A.1), $\ln (Z_{-1} - T_z) = \ln (Z_{-1} - T_z) + (\Delta Z_{-1}/Z_{-2}) - \Delta \ln Z_{-1}$. After expanding $\Delta \ln Z_{-1}$, $\ln (Z_{-1} - T_z) = \ln (Z_{-1} - T_z) + (\Delta Z_{-1}/Z_{-2}) - \ln Z_{-1} + \ln Z_{-2}$. Next add and subtract $\ln (Z_{-2} - T_{z-1})$ on the right-hand side. This gives

$$\begin{aligned} \ln (Z_{-1} - T_z) &= (\Delta Z_{-1}/Z_{-2}) - [\ln Z_{-1} - \ln (Z_{-1} - T_z)] \\ &\quad + [\ln Z_{-2} - \ln (Z_{-2} - T_{z-1})] + \ln (Z_{-2} - T_{z-1}). \end{aligned}$$

Note: The term $\ln (Z_{-1} - T_z) = \ln Z_{-1}[1 - (T_z/Z_{-1})]$, or

$$\ln Z_{-1} + \ln [1 - (T_z/Z_{-1})].$$

The latter can be written as $\ln Z_{-1} + (T_z/Z_{-1})$ since

$$\ln [1 - (T_z/Z_{-1})] \approx T_z/Z_{-1}$$

(see Appendix A.1). Thus $T_z/Z_{-1} = \ln Z_{-1} - \ln (Z_{-1} - T_z)$ and analogously, $T_{z-1}/Z_{-2} = \ln Z_{-2} - \ln (Z_{-2} - T_{z-1})$. By substitution one obtains $\ln (Z_{-1} - T_z) = \ln (Z_{-2} - T_{z-1}) + (\Delta Z_{-1}/Z_{-2}) - [(T_z/Z_{-1}) - (T_{z-1}/Z_{-2})]$, or $\ln (Z_{-1} - T_{z-1}) + (\Delta Z_{-1}/Z_{-2}) - \Delta(T_z/Z_{-1})$ which is the desired result.

all variables still appearing as levels into one term labeled ψ_i. (Note that all variables appearing as levels are lagged and are thus exogenous.) As a final step, natural logarithms are converted to common logarithms and the capacity variable w_l is substituted for (10) log q. (By definition $w_l = (10) \log q$; see Appendix 4). Thus

$$\begin{aligned} -\psi_i = {} & \alpha'(100) \log I_{-1} + \alpha_1'(100) \log (Z_{-2} - T_{z-1}) \\ & + \alpha_2'(100) \log p_{i-1} + \alpha_3'(23.0) w_{l-1\frac{1}{2}} \\ & + \alpha_4'(100) \log c^r_{-2}.^{21} \end{aligned}$$

The coefficients α_i' are the result of the conversion from natural to common logarithms, $\alpha_i' = 2.30\alpha_i$. The equation for I becomes:

$$\begin{aligned} \dot{I} = {} & \alpha_1\left(\dot{Z}_{-1} - 100\,\Delta\frac{T_z}{Z_{-1}}\right) + \alpha_2\dot{p}_i + \alpha_3(23.0)\,\Delta w_{l-\frac{1}{2}} \\ & + \alpha_4\dot{c}^r_{-1} - \psi_i, \end{aligned}$$

which is the form of the investment equation as it appears in the 1961 Plan.

Investment, as defined here, refers to gross investment exclusive of inventory change, residential construction, government investment, and investment by public enterprise. The first of these, inventory change, is explained by a separate equation. Residential construction is excluded because the government, through building permits, restriction of credit, or changes in building subsidies, effectively controls this area of investment; it is treated as an exogenous variable. Government investment and the investment of such public enterprises as the state-owned coal mines are also considered exogenous.

Investment is assumed to be dependent on $\dot{Z}_{-1}$, the percentage change in nonwage income lagged one year, minus T_z'', changes in the tax rate on nonwage income,

21. In the 1961 Plan, 100 was inadvertently dropped from the ψ_i terms. This explains the difference in this presentation and the published version.

which is defined as $T''_z = \Delta(T_z/Z_{-1})100$. Since T_z is measured in guilders, T''_z is the change in the incidence of direct taxes on nonwage income. This follows the general form of the other tax variables used in the model.

The investment equation introduces the nonlinearity referred to previously on the form of the capacity factor, w_l.[22] Literally w_l is a capacity ceiling whose effect becomes more pronounced as the economy moves toward full utilization of its reserve capacity. In the investment equation the capacity variable implies that positive changes in investment are promoted by movements in the direction of full capacity utilization. The need for such a variable developed out of the experience encountered with the economic boom of 1955. In retrospect, the Bureau found that the boom could not be explained by a linear function.

The capacity ceiling simulates a situation, such as occurred in 1955, in which aggregate demand outruns aggregate supply. Theoretically, three factors are recognized as being capable of causing output to fall behind demand: insufficient productive capacity, scarcity of raw materials, and labor shortage. In the case of the Netherlands, potential short supplies of raw materials can be overcome easily by imports from abroad. Insufficient productive equipment could be the cause of output restraint in the short run; however, such a shortage is difficult to determine because reliable figures on capital stock are not available. Fortunately, the lack of data on plant and equipment is probably not a serious defect in specifying the capacity equation. In view of the tight labor market that existed in the Netherlands since the mid-1950s, it is likely that scarcity of labor, rather than lack of capital, was the more significant cause of output lag. For this reason, the Bureau chose to focus on labor as the crucial element in determining capacity.

Thus, in the model, capacity (w_l) is assumed to be a function of unemployment (w). However, full employment

22. See Appendix 5 for a discussion of the definitional equation for w_l.

is not assumed to affect capacity abruptly; rather, the full employment ceiling is assumed to foreshadow its existence sometime before output has reached a maximum. This occurs through the use of a curvilinear relationship between capacity and unemployment. The function is specified such that as the level of unemployment increases, the level of unused capacity increases, although at a decreasing rate. On the other hand, when unemployment decreases and the economy moves toward full employment of its labor resources, each incremental decline in the unemployment rate reduces reserve capacity at an increasing rate. The parameters of the function were set a priori and not estimated simultaneously with the coefficients of the other behavioral equations.[23]

The third causal variable in the investment equation is $\dot{p}_i$, the change in the price index of investment goods. Although the sign of the coefficient is positive, it should not be interpreted as implying, from a behavioral standpoint, that increases in the price of investment goods have a favorable effect on total investment. The behavioral aspects of the price change are not directly indicated in the investment equation as it only shows the direct price effects as they influence the value of investment. However, the price elasticity of investment can be computed by using definitional equation 14, $\dot{I} = \dot{i} + \dot{p}_i$, and the coefficient of $\dot{p}_i$ in the behavioral equation for investment. The price elasticity (which turns out to be $-.54$) being less than 1, shows that *ceteris paribus* one can expect a price rise to reduce real investment.

The liquidity variable $\dot{c}^r$ again represents demand and time deposits of the commercial banking system. Unlike the influence of liquidity in the consumption equation, liquidity is seen to be a rather important determinant of investment because of its coefficient of .80.

23. The equation for capacity (w_l) is $q = w/.03(w - 1)$, where by definition, $w_l = (10) \log q$.

Stock formation equation. The third equation to be discussed is the stock formation equation:

$$(3)\ \dot{N} = .39\ \dot{v}' - 1.34 \frac{N_{-1}}{V'_{-1}}(100) + .96\,\Delta K + .18\,\dot{p}_m + .41\ t^*.$$

(.31)	(.17)	(.54)	(.16)	(.24)
.18	.18	.04	.44	.16

$R = .889 \qquad \sigma_y = .032 \qquad \sigma_u = .014$

* Period 1923–38.

In this equation $\dot{N}$, the dependent variable, is defined as $100(\Delta N/V'_{-1})$ rather than $100(\Delta N/N_{-1})$ because N_{-1}, as measured in the national income accounts, is already a change and thus could take on negative values. Negative N's lead to sign problems in computing $100(\Delta N/N_{-1})$, therefore, ΔN is taken as a percentage of V'_{-1}, which is always a positive quantity.[24] ΔN is defined as the net variation in inventories from the last period to the present $(N - N_{-1})$.

The variables $\dot{v}'$ and $100(N_{-1}/V'_{-1})$ represent, in part, the supposed influence of the level of output on stock formation and, in part, an accelerator effect. The hypothesized relationship is based on the assumption that there is a technically desired relationship between the value of stocks and the value of sales. Thus in the notation of the 1961 model, one may write the equilibrium condition, $N_b = \alpha V'$, where N_b represents the desired level of stocks and V' the level of output. However, the model forecasts changes in the value of inventory, a disequilibrium condition. Such a condition can be expressed as $N = \alpha V' - N_{b-1}$. In this case N_{b-1} is equal to the level of stock at the beginning of the period in which the disequilibrium occurs. Written in terms of first differences, the equation is $\Delta N = \alpha \Delta V' - \Delta N_{b-1}$. However, by definition, N_{-1}, the change in the level of

24. V'_{-1} equals total output less inventory changes and net invisibles. Net invisibles is defined as exports of services minus imports of services.

inventory, equals ΔN_{b-1}. Thus the above equation can be written as $\Delta N = \alpha \Delta V' - N_{-1}$, showing that the net change in inventory accumulation is a function of the change in sales and the inventory change of the last period. Dividing by V'_{-1} and multiplying by 100, one obtains an expression similar to the one in the original stock formation equation of the model; however, in the original equation sales are expressed in real terms rather than in value terms. Neglecting the price effect and substituting the coefficients of equation 3 into the model, the equation for $100(\Delta N/V'_{-1})$ may be written as:

$$(100)\frac{\Delta N}{V'_{-1}} = 1.34\,(100)\left[.29\frac{\Delta V'}{V'_{-1}} - \frac{N_{-1}}{V'_{-1}}\right].$$

Ignoring the 1.34 for the present, one notes that .29 is the same as α in the equation $\Delta N = \alpha \Delta V' - N_{-1}$, i.e. the desired ratio of stock to sales. Set a priori on the basis of independent studies of Dutch inventory practice, α implies that at any time the desired level of inventory is 29 percent of current sales. Such a desired ratio is not immediately achieved, however, due to the operation of the accelerator, i.e. the coefficient of 1.34. This coefficient, since it is greater than one, shows a tendency on the part of entrepreneurs to overstock (relative to the empirically observed level) when sales begin to accelerate; similarly, when sales fall, businessmen tend to reduce inventories below the technically desired level. On the basis of this equation, one expects inventory fluctuations to be of greater amplitude than accompanying fluctuations in the level of sales. This expectation is borne out in practice.

The third variable in the stock formation equation, ΔK, denotes the change in gross profit per unit of output, measured as a percentage of total output less stock changes and net invisibles. Thus $\Delta K = 100[(Z + F)/V']$ where Z is nonwage income, F is depreciation allowances, and V' is the total output less stock changes and net invisibles. The term ΔK may be interpreted as a straight-forward anticipatory effect, i.e. businessmen acting under the influence of rising profits increase their inventories in anticipation of even larger profits to come.

Stock formation is also assumed to be influenced by changes in $\dot{p}_m$, the level of import prices. From a behavioral standpoint, the influence of increases in import prices involves two expectations. The first of these is the fear of an even greater price increase, which leads users of imported raw materials to increase their stocks. On the other hand, the same price rise encourages domestic producers of import substitutes to enlarge their inventories in anticipation of a larger volume of sales.

The final term in the stock formation equation, t, is a decreasing trend. This trend was introduced to allow for an apparent decline in the relationship between the desired level of inventory and output over the time period covered by the observations. Starting with the base year of 1923 a straight linear trend was used. After 1938, the new desired relationship was considered to have been established and the trend factor was dropped.

Export equation. The next equation to be discussed is the export equation:

$$(4) \quad \dot{b} = \underset{\substack{(.10)\\ .57}}{1.46\, \dot{b}_c} - \underset{\substack{(.36)\\ .08}}{1.71\, (\dot{p}_b' - \dot{p}_b')} - \underset{\substack{(.32)\\ .07}}{1.11\, (\dot{p}_b - \dot{p}_b')_{-1}}$$

$$R = .973 \qquad \sigma_y = .170$$

$$- \underset{\substack{(.40)\\ .09}}{.64\, \Delta\dot{p}_v'} + \underset{\substack{(.33)\\ .19}}{1.42\, w_l} - \underset{(.38)}{7.52}.$$

$$\sigma_u = .039$$

The first causal variable in the export equation is $\dot{b}_c$. This is an index of the export trade of countries in close competition with the Netherlands in the world market. In each of the main foreign markets, the Bureau makes a comparison between Dutch sales and those of seven competing countries representing the bulk of the foreign competition: Belgium and Luxembourg, Denmark, France, Italy, the United Kingdom, the United States, and Western Germany. A triple system of weighting is used: first, in accordance with the average share held by each country in each market; second, in relation to the importance of each market relative to total Dutch exports; and finally in accordance with the composition of Dutch exports. Thus the weighting system has taken into account the importance of the importing country, the origin of the imported goods, and the importance of these goods relative to the overall composition of Dutch exports.

The weighting system indicates that changes in Danish exports usually have the greatest relative effect on Dutch exports. This is because the exports of Denmark go primarily to two of the largest Dutch markets, the United Kingdom and Western Germany, and because a large percentage of Danish exports to these two countries are agricultural and thus in direct competition with approximately 30 percent of Dutch exports. Therefore, Danish exports, in addition to going to one of Holland's main export markets, are directly competitive with one of the Netherlands' most important exporting sectors.

The coefficient of $\dot{b}_c$ is greater than 1, which indicates that Dutch exports, and consequently market shares, are more sensitive to changes in the level of international trade than are their competitors. In other words, reacting to the same external influences, Dutch exports rise or fall in greater measure than the overall world market demand for similar goods produced and exported by Dutch competitors.

The next causal factor, $\dot{p}_b - \dot{p}'_b$, is used to show the influence of changes in the Netherlands' export price level relative to the price levels of its most important competitors.

The variables $\dot{p}_b$ and $\dot{p}'_b$ are changes in the indices of Dutch export prices and of the export prices of competitors respectively. The coefficients of $\dot{p}_b - \dot{p}'_b$ is the elasticity of substitution of Dutch exports with respect to changes in the prices of Dutch export goods relative to the prices of their competition in the world market. Exports are also influenced by $\dot{p}_b - \dot{p}'_b$ lagged one year. The combined elasticity of the current plus the lagged price effect is -2.32. Thus changes in the relative price of Dutch exports have a substantial influence upon the world demand for these exports.[25]

The term $\Delta\dot{p}'_v$ is a quasi-accelerator similar to the one found in the consumption equation. Here $\Delta p'_v$ indicates that the impact of accelerating inflation on the level of exports is greater than suggested by the relative difference between the Dutch and the competitors' prices alone. The quasi-accelerator is used to show the effect of trade cycles on the demand for Dutch exports. It (the quasi-accelerator) accounts for the fact that changes in Dutch export demand occur even when the trade cycle is worldwide and Dutch and competitors' prices rise by like percentages. The quasi-accelerator retards exports during the upswing; its influence becomes zero just prior to the downturn, after which a falling price level reinforces export sales.

The reserve capacity factor, w_l, also affects the level of exports. Very low levels of unemployment, indicating full utilization of capacity, represent a potential loss in export sales because Dutch producers are not able to keep up with

25. This combined coefficient is not the simple sum of the two elasticities. The combined coefficient is called the total elasticity and is computed according to the formula: total elasticity $= (\eta_1 + \eta_2)(\alpha^2 + \beta^2 + \alpha\beta\rho)$, where η_1 and η_2 are the elasticities from the original export equation and α and β are simple weights,

$$\alpha = \frac{\eta_2}{\eta_1 + \eta_2}.$$

The factor ρ is the coefficient of serial correlation determined independently ($\rho = .308$). See P. J. Verdoorn, *De Verstarring der Productiekosten* (Haarlem, 1943), Appendix B.

the worldwide demand for their products. The effect of the capacity ceiling can be shown by applying the *ceteris paribus* assumption to all causal factors with the exception of the capacity variable and the trend constant. Under these conditions, exports can be expressed directly in terms of w, the unemployment percentage. This has been done by the Central Planning Bureau and the results are shown in Table 19.

TABLE 19. Effects of Various Unemployment Rates on Exports

Unemployment Percentage	Residual trend*
2	−3.67
3	−1.60
4	−.25
5	+.71

* Measures the *ceteris paribus* percentage change in exports associated with the unemployment percentage given in the first column.
Source: Central Economic Plan 1961, p. 119.

The entries in this table show that a rising level of unemployment, all other factors held constant, tends to increase the volume of exports. Fortunately, during the decade after the Korean War the overall upward trend in world trade was such that Dutch exports increased at a satisfactory rate, and the policy-makers did not have to examine the relationship between unemployment (capacity) and export volume in order to choose a "desirable level of unemployment."

Demand Equations for Factors of Production and Capacity

Import demand equation. The first equation showing the demand for a factor of production is the import demand equation:

$$\text{(5)} \qquad \dot{m} = \underset{\substack{(.20)\\ .11}}{1.24\,\dot{v}_m} + \underset{\substack{(.51)\\ .02}}{.29\,\Delta\dot{v}_m} + \underset{\substack{\\ .17}}{2.50\,\dot{N}} - \underset{\substack{(.37)\\ .26}}{.38\,\dot{p}_{m-v'}}$$

$$R = .982 \qquad \sigma_y = .142$$

$$\begin{array}{cccc} + .32\,\Delta\dot{p}_{v'} & - .30\,k & + .11\,k' & - .08. \\ (.59) & (.30) & (.60) & (17.75) \\ .09 & .18 & .17 & \end{array}$$

$$\sigma_u = .027$$

The dependent variable in the import demand equation is the volume of commodity imports. The first causal variable in the equation, $\dot{v}_m$, represents total output, less inventory and net invisibles, reweighted according to import content. This factor is obtained by weighting the four components of output by their import content. Thus $\dot{v}_m = .45\,\dot{c} + .15\,\dot{x} + .11\,\dot{i} + .29\,\dot{b}$,[26] where $\dot{c}$ is the percentage change in total private consumption, $\dot{x}$ is the percentage change in autonomous expenditure, $\dot{i}$ is the percentage change in investment, and $\dot{b}$ is the percentage change in the volume of commodity exports. The coefficients may be interpreted as the marginal import content of the corresponding output categories.

Output appears as a causal variable twice, once as a percentage change, and again as a quasi-accelerator. The quasi-accelerator may also be written as $\Delta\dot{v}_m = \dot{v}_m - \dot{v}_{m_{-1}}$. This definition can then be substituted for $\Delta\dot{v}_m$ in the original equation; thus the terms involving $\dot{v}_m$ may be written as $1.53\,\dot{v}_m - .29\dot{v}_{m_{-1}}$. This is (may be considered to be) the equivalent of $1.24\,\dot{v}_{m+\frac{1}{4}}$, i.e. a lead of imports over production by approximately three months. This seems reasonable when one recalls that a large proportion of

26. This definitional equation should be compared with the equation for $\dot{v}'$ (unweighted output, again excluding stock changes and net invisibles): $\dot{v}' = .59\,\dot{c} + .11\,\dot{x} + .08\,\dot{i} + .22\,\dot{b}$. The coefficients represent the average ratios of c/v, x/v, etc. (Their derivation follows that shown in Appendix 2.) Comparing the equation for $\dot{v}'$ with the the one for $\dot{v}_m$ shows that weighting by import content reduces the relative importance of consumer goods as an output component. From this, one may conclude that imports are less important to the consumer goods sector than to the government, investment, and export sectors.

Dutch industry is of the finishing and processing variety, dependent on imports for raw materials. The lead simply indicates that there can be no production until raw materials are available. The marginal propensity to import, with respect to output, computed on the basis of 1957 figures, is .43. On the whole, imports are quite sensitive to changes in output. Since the coefficient of the output variable is greater than 1, imports may be expected to fluctuate to a greater degree than output in the absence of other influences.

The influence of stock formation, $\dot{N}$, on the demand for imports is treated separately, having been excluded by definition from output, $\dot{v}_m$. In the Netherlands, inventory accumulation has a high import content because almost all building material must be imported. Thus $\dot{N}$, the third causal variable, shows the effect of changes in inventory on import demand.

The definition of the variable $\dot{N}$ has been given previously.[27] The coefficient of $\dot{N}$ was set a priori for the import equation. When the coefficient of $\dot{N}$ was estimated simultaneously with the other coefficients in the behavioral equations, the result was an unlikely marginal propensity to import for stock formation greater than 1. Therefore, the problem was worked backwards by starting with a marginal propensity to import for stock formation of .88 (determined from independent studies). Based on this figure, an elasticity of 2.50 was computed and then 2.50 N was combined with m, the dependent variable, for the purpose of estimating the remaining coefficients of the behavioral equations.

The fourth term, $\dot{p}_{m-v'}$, and the fifth term, $\Delta\dot{p}_{v'}$, of the import equation deal with price effects. The factor $p_{m-v'}$ is defined in equation 25 as $\dot{p}_{m-v'} = \dot{p}_m - \dot{p}_{v'_{-\frac{1}{2}}} + .06\ \dot{T}'_{k_{-\frac{1}{3}}}$, where $\dot{p}_{v'}$ is the change in the price index of total output (invisibles and inventory changes again being excluded), and $\dot{T}'_{k_{-\frac{1}{3}}}$ the percentage change in indirect taxes minus the percentage change in output.

27. See p. 210.

The coefficient .06 serves to approximate the import tax component of indirect taxes. $\dot{T}'_{k_{-\frac{1}{3}}}$ is lagged by one third of a year on the assumption that taxes affect imports at the time the contract is let rather than at the time goods cross the border, because on average, contracts are let approximately four months prior to delivery. The same rationale explains the lag given to the price term $\dot{p}_{v'_{-\frac{1}{2}}}$. The prices that affect the decision to buy or not to buy are assumed to be the prices that exist at the time the contract decision is made, which is assumed to be one-half year prior to delivery.

The coefficient of $\dot{p}_{m-v'}$ is the price elasticity of substitution between domestic and imported goods. This coefficient shows that, if the import price level increases by 1 percent relative to the domestic price level, imports will be approximately .4 percent less than they would have been if import prices and domestic prices had risen proportionately.

The final price term, $\Delta\dot{p}_{v'}$ is another quasi-accelerator. It has the same interpretation as in the export equation. Here the positive sign of the coefficient means that accelerating inflation encourages buying abroad.

The two k terms have to do with the quantitative import-control systems that operated during the prewar and immediate postwar periods. These restrictions have been removed, but the variables were included in the specifications in order to estimate more accurately the remaining coefficients. Finally, the negative constant term indicates that there exists a long-run trend for structural substitution of domestic production for imported commodities.

Labor demand equation. The second equation for factors of production and capacity is the relationship used to estimate labor demand:

$$(6) \quad \dot{a} = \underset{\substack{(.13)\\.38}}{.39\,\dot{v}_a} + \underset{\substack{(.48)\\.08}}{.76\,\Delta K} + \underset{\substack{(.59)\\.24}}{.07\,\dot{p}_{m-v'}} + \underset{\substack{(.32)\\.13}}{12\log\left(\frac{z}{a}\right)_{-1}}$$

$$R = .954 \qquad \sigma_y = .032$$

$$- 7 \log a_{-1} + .66.$$
$$(.46) \qquad (.78)$$
$$.17$$

$$\sigma_u = .010$$

Unlike the dependent variables in previous equations, which have been expressed either as current values or as volumes, the dependent variable of the labor demand equation is measured in man-years of employee time in private enterprise.

Causal factors in the employment equation that have not already been defined are log $(z/a)_{-1}$ and log a_{-1}. The first term represents the deflated level of profits per worker, lagged one year, and the second term represents the number of employees, also lagged one year. The two terms together represent the influence of the level of employment and the per worker profit rate on the demand for labor.

The variable $\dot{v}_a$ is total output, less inventory changes and net invisibles, reweighted according to its labor content. The definitional equation for $\dot{v}_a$ is: $\dot{v}_a = .46\,\dot{c} + .20\,\dot{x} + .16\,\dot{i} + .18\,\dot{b}$, where the coefficients represent the average labor content of the corresponding output categories.[28]

The coefficient of the import price margin, $\dot{p}_{m-v'}$, refers to the price elasticity of substitution of domestically produced goods for imported commodities. The greater the substitution effect between domestically produced goods and imported commodities, the greater the increase in demand for workers as domestic labor is substituted for foreign employment. For example, if the domestic price level should increase by 5 percent relative to the import price level, there would be a

28. This equation may be compared with the unweighted output definition: $\dot{v}' = .59\,\dot{c} + .11\,\dot{x} + .03\,\dot{i} + .22\,\dot{b}$. From this comparison, it appears that autonomous expenditures and investments are more labor-intensive than are consumption and exports. Construction, which is very labor-intensive in the Netherlands, probably accounts for the large shift in the coefficient of investment when weighted by labor content.

reduction of .35 percent in employment according to the price elasticity of substitution shown here.

The factor ΔK refers to changes in gross profits per unit of output and was discussed in conjunction with the stock formation equation. It signifies that increasing profit rates favorably affect the demand for labor.

The positive constant term implies a .66 percent annual increase in employment even if no other causal factors vary during the year. Such an increase is contrary to the normal expectation of employment trends. It is generally believed that structural changes, such as increases in capital intensity and the introduction of labor-saving innovations, tend to decrease the demand for labor when there is no increase in output. There are, no doubt, a number of unspecified factors left out of the equation for employment in the enterprise sector which would, if included, account for the positive trend. Among these are relative increases in the demand for services and the inclusion of a larger proportion of agriculture in the enterprise sector.

It should be noted that the labor demand equation does not provide a direct link between total output and employment because production for stock accumulation is excluded from the definition of $\dot{v}_a$. This exclusion is caused by the inability to distinguish between the domestic and imported content of inventory changes. Therefore $\dot{v}_a$ represents sales, not production. According to the specifications of the labor demand equation, systematic fluctuations in imports will not affect the demand for labor unless these fluctuations appear in sales and are not absorbed in inventory.

Unemployment equation. The final factor of production equation deals with the level of unemployment:

$$(7)\ \Delta w = -.42\,\dot{a} + .39\frac{\Delta P - \Delta a_0}{P_{B_{-1}}} - .04\,\Delta T_c + 1.68\left(\frac{P_{-1}}{P_{B_{-1}}}\right)^*$$

$$\begin{matrix} (.28) & (.35) & (.63) & (1.19) \\ .32 & .04 & .13 & .15 \end{matrix}$$

$$R = .923 \qquad \sigma_y = .017$$

$$+ 2.18\left(\frac{P_{-1}}{P_{B_{-1}}}\right)^{\dagger} - 4.49.$$

$$(.97) \qquad (1.01)$$

$$.36$$

$$\sigma_u = .006$$

* The ratio of the number of people of working age to the working population, 1923–38.

† The same ratio for 1949–57.

The dependent variable Δw is the change in the number of registered unemployed, measured as a percentage of the labor force. Thus $w/100 = U\gamma/P_B$, where P_B is the labor force and $U\gamma$ the number of registered unemployed. In addition, several other new terms are involved: ΔP is the change in working-age population, Δa_0 is the change in government employment, and T_c is the minimum temperature below 0° centigrade (T_c is based on the sum of the monthly averages: $\Delta T_c = T_c - T_{c-1}$).

The last two terms, Δa_0 and T_c, serve to correct for changes in the age structure and for changes in the composition of P_B. During the postwar years there has been an increasing tendency for larger proportions of the unemployed to register. As a result of this tendency, it was necessary to split the period into two parts, prewar and postwar, in order to account for this structural change.

The coefficient of a is less than 1, indicating that, *ceteris paribus*, a change in employment is less than proportionately transmitted to unemployment. While this is partially attributable to the fact that the two percentages are computed on different bases, it is also partially attributable to the fact that all persons willing to accept jobs did not register when unemployed. It is also known that some employers, even when faced with a labor surplus, do not discharge workers; they simply do not fill vacancies caused by normal turnover. These factors explain, in part, why the coefficient of $\dot{a}$ is less than 1, i.e. why fluctuations in unemployment are not as great as fluctuations in employment.

For this reason, sometimes called disguised unemployment, statistically determined employment figures may be too high on the short run. Over time, however, the artificially low unemployment figures may be expected to rise because new entries into the labor market will not find employment if vacancies are filled by the underemployed reserve.

The Price Equations

The four behavioral equations pertaining to prices cover consumption ($\dot{p}_c$), investment ($\dot{p}_i$), exports ($\dot{p}_b$), and autonomous expenditures ($\dot{p}_x$). The remaining price levels are either taken as exogenous or are defined as weighted averages of other prices.

Each price equation contains $\dot{H}$, the change in labor costs per unit of output, and an exogenous variable, $\dot{p}_m$, the change in the level of import prices. In three of the four price equations, prices are assumed to be determined mostly by the cost of the primary factors of production.

Labor costs are approximated by the following equation:

$$\dot{H} = \dot{l} - (\dot{v}' - \dot{a})_{-\frac{1}{2}} \tag{24}$$

where $\dot{l}$ is the percentage change in the wage level. This change is considered to be exogenous since wages are an instrument of government economic policy. The term $(\dot{v}' - \dot{a})$ represents labor productivity. According to the model, investment does not affect productivity; hence, all output changes are matched either by increases in employment or by gains in labor productivity. Labor productivity is incorporated in the formula with a lag of one-half year, while the wage rate appears with no lag. This is based on the assumption that prices react more rapidly to a change in the wage rate, which is easily recognized, than to changes in labor productivity, which are less easily observed.

All the price-determining relationships contain a distributed lag of one type of another. The use of distributed lags permits the effect of a given change in a causal variable to be spread over a number of years. The particular type of distributed lag used in the price-determining equations is one in which geometrically decreasing weights are assigned to earlier observations of certain of the causal variables.[29] The discussion below treats only the effects of these lags. The derivation of the distributed lag appearing in the equations for $\dot{p}_x$, $\dot{p}_i$, and $\dot{p}_b$ is contained in Appendix 6; the lag in the equation for $\dot{p}_c$ is discussed in Appendix 7.

The consumption price equation. The assumption underlying this equation is that entrepreneurs fix prices almost solely on the basis of costs. Thus changes in the consumer price index ($\dot{p}_c$) are assumed to be determined by changes in four cost components: unit labor costs ($\dot{H}$), import prices ($\dot{p}_m$), indirect taxes ($\dot{T}_k'$), and the rate of interest (Δr_k); no allowance is made for demand factors. In addition, changes in the import content of production, $(\dot{v}' - \dot{m})_{-\frac{1}{2}}$, is assumed as a causal variable. An increase in the share of imports causes consumer prices to rise, while a decrease in import content causes them to fall.

Because of the particular form of the distributed lag in the consumer price equation, it contains variables expressed in both percentage changes and lagged levels. The equation in the form in which it was estimated is shown below. However, in the model as published in the 1961 Central Economic Plan, and as it appears in Table 17, the consumer price equation was split into two parts: the lagged terms were collected into one term, Λ, which is separately expressed in equation 38.

29. See L. M. Koyck, *Distributed Lags and Investment Analysis* (Amsterdam North-Holland Publishing Co., 1954).

The consumption price equation is:

$$\dot{p}_c + 83 \log p_{c_{-1}} = \underset{\substack{(.52)\\ .01}}{.21}\, \dot{H} + \underset{\substack{(.08)\\ .50}}{56} \log H_{-1}$$

$$+ \underset{\substack{(.17)\\ .38}}{.20} \left(\dot{p}_{m_{-\frac{1}{2}}} + 83 \log p_{m_{-1\frac{1}{2}}}\right)$$

$$- \underset{\substack{(.19)\\ .04}}{.42} \left[(\dot{v}' - \dot{m})_{-\frac{1}{2}} + 83 \log \left(\frac{v'}{m}\right)_{-1\frac{1}{2}}\right]$$

$$+ \underset{\substack{(.21)\\ .06}}{.17} \left(\dot{T}'_{k_{-\frac{1}{3}}} + 83 \log T'_{k_{-1\frac{1}{3}}}\right)$$

$$+ \underset{\substack{(.28)\\ .01}}{1.82} \left(\Delta r_{k_{-\frac{1}{2}}} + .36\, r_{k_{-1\frac{1}{2}}}\right) - \underset{(.31)}{2.26}.$$

$$R = .981 \qquad \sigma_y = .056 \qquad \sigma_u = .011$$

The lagged term expressing changes in labor costs is clearly the most significant causal variable. This is true in both a statistical sense, the coefficient being seven times its standard error, and with regard to the amount of explained variance attributed to the presence of H_{-1} in the equation. In the latter case, H_{-1} is responsible for 50 percent of the explained variance in $\dot{p}_c$. The equation also contains a distributed lag in H. This lag, however, is assumed to start only after the first year since the first-year effect of $\dot{H}$ in explaining variations in $\dot{p}_c$ is only 1 percent.

Next to labor productivity, changes in import prices is the most important factor in causing consumer prices to change.

This term, $\dot{p}_m$, is lagged one-half year. Although there is no distributed lag with respect to $\dot{p}_m$, the effects of changes in $\dot{p}_m$ are spread over two years because of the half-year lag. Thus one half of the influence of $\dot{p}_m$ on $\dot{p}_c$ is attributed to the first year effect and one half is assumed to be a lagged effect.

The tax variable, $\dot{T}'_k$, is lagged one third of a year. The lags of one year for H and one half and one third year for the other cost factors ($\dot{p}_m$ and $\dot{T}'_k$) imply that entrepreneurs are quicker to recognize changes in import prices and fixed costs, such as taxes, than they are to note changes in labor costs per unit of output.

The export price equation. This is the only price-determining equation to contain a demand factor. The price of competing exports, $\dot{p}'_b$, appears both as a percentage change ($\dot{p}'_b$) and as a quasi-accelerator ($\Delta\dot{p}'_b$). In addition to changes in the price of competing exports, Dutch export prices are assumed to be determined by changes in unit labor costs ($\dot{H}$) and by changes in import prices ($\dot{p}_m$). Thus changes in export prices are largely governed by exogenous variables, i.e. import prices and the prices of competing exports.

$$\text{(10)} \qquad \dot{p}_b = \underset{(.50)}{.43}\,(.75\,\dot{H} + \dot{p}_m) + \underset{(1.07)}{.23}\,\dot{p}'_b + \underset{(.58)}{.25}\,\Delta\dot{p}'_b + \underset{(.87)}{.15}\,\dot{p}_{b_{-1}} - \underset{(.69)}{.65}.^{30}$$

$$R = .984$$

The investment price equation. Changes in the index of investment prices are assumed to be determined by changes in unit labor costs ($\dot{H}$) and by changes in the cost of imports ($\dot{p}_m$). Both factors are assumed to have a distributed lag.[31] The causal variables have previously been discussed and therefore will not be elaborated here.

30. The percentages of variance explained, σ_y and σ_u, were not available for the export price equation.

31. See Appendix 6.

$$(9) \qquad \dot{p}_i = \underset{\substack{(.54)\\ .10}}{.41}\,\dot{H} + \underset{\substack{(.15)\\ .65}}{.39}\,\dot{p}_m + \underset{\substack{(.27)\\ .25}}{.33}\,\dot{p}_{i_{-1}} + \underset{(.45)}{1.03}.$$

$$R = .953 \qquad \sigma_y = .081 \qquad \sigma_u = .024$$

The autonomous price equation. Autonomous expenditures are defined as net government current expenditures (not including wages and salaries), government investment, investment of government enterprises, and residential construction. Two cost factors are assumed to effect changes in the price level of autonomous expenditures: changes in unit labor costs ($\dot{H}$) and import price variations ($\dot{p}_m$). It is assumed that both effect the price of autonomous expenditure with a distributed lag.[32] The autonomous price equation is very similar to the investment price equation, the only difference being the size of the coefficients. In each equation the most significant variable is $\dot{p}_m$, both in terms of explained variance and statistical significance. The coefficients of the distributed lags are .33 for the investment price equation and .27 for the autonomous price equation. The average time lag is measured as the so called "half life," the time in which the first half of the total influence of the variable concerned has worn off, and amounts of .6 and .5 years respectively.[33]

$$(11) \qquad \dot{p}_x = \underset{\substack{(.28)\\ .18}}{.69}\,\dot{H} + \underset{\substack{(.15)\\ .58}}{.31}\,\dot{p}_m + \underset{\substack{(.29)\\ .24}}{.27}\,\dot{p}_{x_{-1}} + \underset{(.29)}{1.22}.$$

$$R = .974 \qquad \sigma_y = .082 \qquad \sigma_u = .019$$

DEFINITIONAL EQUATIONS

The remainder of the model consists of definitional equations. Some of these have already been mentioned,

32. See Appendix 6.
33. Central Economic Plan 1961, p. 124.

specifically those relationships between value and volume variables that have the form $\dot{C} = \dot{c} + \dot{p}_c$, the expenditure totals for $\dot{v}'$, $\dot{v}_a$, and $\dot{v}_m$, the equation defining change in labor costs ($\dot{H}$), and the equation for the margin between import prices and domestically produced goods ($\dot{p}_{m-v'}$). Other definitional equations discussed previously were the two tax equations, one for $\dot{T}_k$ and another for T''_z; the income definitions for $\dot{L}^B$ and $\dot{Z}^B$; and the definitions of the lagged influences collected from the investment, labor demand, and consumption price equations (ψ_i, ψ_a, and Λ).

Among the remaining equations the most interesting are the balance equation for total output, the equation for the price indices p_v and $p_{v'}$, the relationship used to derive ΔK, the rate of profit, and the equation for the percentage change in nonwage income. Each of these is discussed briefly below.

The percentage change in total output, $\dot{V}$, is simply the sum of the percentage changes in its component parts, when each component is weighted according to the ratio of the base-period value of the factor to the base-period total output.

$$\dot{V} = \frac{C_{-1}}{V_{-1}}\dot{C} + \frac{X_{-1}}{V_{-1}}\dot{X} + \frac{I_{-1}}{V_{-1}}\dot{I} + \frac{V'_{-1}}{V_{-1}}\dot{N}^{*} + \frac{B_{-1}}{V_{-1}}\dot{B} + \frac{D_{-1}}{V_{-1}}\dot{D}.$$

* Because $\dot{N}$ has a special meaning, its coefficient was determined by the ratio of V' to V.

By substituting 1957 values for the lagged variables, the coefficients may be computed and the equation written as it appears in the 1961 Plan.

$$(22) \quad \dot{V} = .44\,\dot{C} + .13\,\dot{X} + .10\,\dot{I} + .92\,\dot{N} + .25\,\dot{B} + .06\,\dot{D}.$$

The coefficients of definitional equation 18 for $\dot{v}'$ are derived in a like manner: the ratios of the lagged variables are replaced by corresponding averages for the sample period.

Definitional equation 21 concerns the price index of

output, defined as total output less stock formation and net invisibles. It is interesting to note that while $\dot{p}'_v$ may be written as a linear combination of the percentage changes in its component price indices, $\dot{p}_c$, $\dot{p}_x$, $\dot{p}_i$, and $\dot{p}_b$, as was done in the model, it may also be written as a linear combination of the percentage changes in the prices paid for the factors of production: $\dot{l}$, $\dot{p}_m$, $\dot{T}'_k$, and ΔK. In this equation, l is the wage rate, p_m is the import price index, T'_k is the incidence of indirect taxes, and ΔK is the change in the rate of profit. Thus,

$$\dot{p}_{v'} = \frac{L_{-1}}{V'_{-1}}\dot{l} + \frac{M_{-1}}{V'_{-1}}\dot{p}_m + \frac{T'_{k_{-1\frac{1}{3}}}}{V'_{-1}}\dot{T}'_{k_{-\frac{1}{3}}} + \frac{Z_{-1} + F_{-1}}{V'_{-1}}\dot{K}.$$

As used here, F is depreciation, and $Z + F$ represents gross profits. Gross profit per unit of output is defined as $K = 100(Z/V' + F/V')$, and $\dot{K}$ as $100(\Delta K/K_{-1})$. The coefficient of the $\dot{K}$ term, however, is simply equal to $K_{-1}/100$. Therefore, $K_{-1}/100$ and $100(\Delta K/K_{-1})$ may be substituted in the equation for $\dot{p}_{v'}$, which is then written as:

$$\dot{p}'_v = \frac{L_{-1}}{V'_{-1}}\dot{l} + \frac{M_{-1}}{V'_{-1}}\dot{p}_m + \frac{T'_{k_{-1\frac{1}{3}}}}{V'_{-1}}\dot{T}'_{k_{-\frac{1}{3}}} + \Delta K.$$

After replacing the value ratios by their 1957 numerical values and transposing, the equation becomes

$$\Delta K = \dot{p}_{v'} - .27\,\dot{l} - .30\,\dot{p}_m - .06\,\dot{T}'_{k_{-\frac{1}{3}}}$$

This is the definition for ΔK that appears in the model as equation 26.

The final equation to be discussed here is the definitional equation for nonwage income:

$$(31) \quad \dot{Z} = 3.77\,\dot{V} - 1.06\,\dot{L} - .24\,\dot{T}_k - 1.23\,\dot{M} - .24\,\dot{F}.$$

This equation is obtained by expressing V, the total output, as the sum of: Z, nonwage income; L, wage income; T_k, indirect taxes; M, imports; and F, depreciation. Thus, $V = Z + L + T_k + M + F$. The coefficients are determined by the procedure shown above and in Appendix 2. The expression can then be written as:

$$\dot{V} = \frac{Z_{-1}}{V_{-1}}\dot{Z} + \frac{L_{-1}}{V_{-1}}\dot{L} + \frac{T_{k_{-1}}}{V_{-1}}\dot{T}_k + \frac{M_{-1}}{V_{-1}}\dot{M} + \frac{F_{-1}}{V_{-1}}\dot{F}.$$

Numerical coefficients are obtained by replacing the value ratios shown here by their 1957 numerical values and solving for Z.

CHAPTER 8

Accuracy Analysis of the Models of the Central Planning Bureau

A model cannot be a useful tool for quantitative economic analysis unless it can accurately forecast future values of the endogenous variables and predict the probable effects of alternative economic policies. Tests of the accuracy of a model are called accuracy analysis, and a variety of test methods can be applied to the Dutch models.

The accuracy of the model as a forecasting device is assessed by measuring the variation of the forecasts around the actual values as they become known with the passage of time. The simplest and most straightforward approach to accuracy analysis is to take the predicted values of the endogenous variables and compare them with the realized values. However, in models such as those described here, the accuracy of the forecasts of the endogenous variables depends, in large measure, on whether the values assumed for the exogenous variables were, in fact, realized in the prediction period.

If the assumed values of the exogenous variables differ materially from the realized values, the forecasts of the endogenous variables will miss their mark. Therefore, a better method of determining the accuracy of a model is to re-estimate the endogenous variables, using the realized values of the exogenous variables. Then the re-estimated values of the exogenous variables may be compared with their realized values. This process involves using the model in its reduced form.[1] The observed values of the exogenous variables are inserted in each equation of the reduced form; the

1. The model can be solved so that each endogenous variable is expressed as a function of the exogenous variables, the parameters, and the constant terms of the model. This is referred to as the reduced form of the model.

endogenous variables are then recomputed. The result is a conditional forecast, i.e. conditioned by the realized values and the exogenous variables. This procedure serves as a measure of the accuracy of the specifications of the model as a whole.

A third way to ascertain accuracy is to investigate the structural specifications of individual equations. This is done as follows: the observed values taken by the explanatory (casual) variables during the prediction period, both endogenous and exogenous, are inserted in the structural equation. A new value of the dependent variable is then computed. The result is again a conditional forecast, but conditional upon the endogenous variables that appear in the equation as well as the realized values of the exogenous variables.

This third method may not be used to assess the accuracy of the model as a whole, since it can only be used to validate each equation taken individually. It is therefore of little use in determining whether or not a given model is useful as a policy-making tool because it requires the substitution of ex-post endogenous variables, the forecasting of which is in itself one objective of the model.

On the other hand, the first method, the simple ex-ante–ex post comparison, shows the accuracy of the forecasts at the time policy decisions were being made. This method of accuracy analysis can therefore be indicative of the usefulness of the model to the policy-maker.

The second method is also useful in that it assists in determining if the cause of faulty prediction is the inaccurate prediction of the exogenous variables, rather than the model itself. When such is the case, the need for improved methods of estimating those variables that are forecast independently of the model is emphasized.

Over the years, there have been several studies of the accuracy of the Dutch economic forecasts. The most recent was conducted by Pieter de Wolff and C. A. van den Beld.[2] Most of the statistical data presented in this section

2. De Wolff and van den Beld, "Ten Years."

was taken from their study. Their basic data are shown in Tables 20 and 21. In some cases, the forecasts of the endogenous variables have been corrected for unanticipated changes in government economic policy that took place after the plan forecasts were made. Such a policy change occurred in March 1961 with the revaluation of the Dutch guilder. Corrections were also made for a general and unforeseen wage increase in 1956 and several unanticipated changes in the tax rate that occurred at other times during the ten-year period covered by the report.

The comparison of predicted and realized values of the endogenous variables can be shown graphically by plotting the actual changes in the variables against the predicted changes. The accuracy of the estimates of several exogenous variables and the accuracy of the predictions of certain of the endogenous variables are plotted in this manner in Figures 2 and 3. Perfect forecasts would fall on the dashed line. Points in the second and fourth quadrants indicate turning-point errors, that is, differences in sign between the predicted change and the actual change.

Figure 2 presents the scatter diagram of four important exogenous variables. The first two are the wage level in industry and an aggregate variable called the impulse government budget. The aggregate variable represents government expenditures (computed net of changes in tax revenues) on wages, consumption, and investment. The wage level in industry and the impulse government budget are considered to be instruments of government policy. The Central Planning Bureau estimates these variables on the basis of what is understood to be the government program for the year ahead. The other two exogenous variables are changes in the volume of world trade and changes in the price level of imports. These variables are completely outside the control of the Dutch authorities, and are predicted on the basis of the Central Planning Bureau's estimates of world economic conditions.

TABLE 20. Forecasting Accuracy of the Netherlands Central Economic Plans, 1953–62: Actual Results (R) Versus Forecasts (F)[a] of Exogenous Variables
(in percentages)

		1953	1954	1955	1956	1957	1958	1959	1960	1961	1962
Wage level in industries	R	3.7	8.8	8.6	8.2	10.6	4.4	2.1	9.4	5.3	8.0
	F	2.2	7.2	4.8	7.6	6.7	3.0	3.0	7.5	5.0	6.0
Government wage bill	R	7.8	16.7	13.1	11.3	12.8	4.9	3.1	9.9	8.1	13.5
	F	7.3	9.5	8.6	6.7	13.8	7.0	3.5	11.0	8.0	11.7
Other public consumption	R	10.5	9.9	10.1	15.9	0.8	−11.0	−5.9	12.8	5.4	11.6
	F	21.1	−.2	2.4	8.0	−5.7	−5.8	−2.0	5.0	8.9	10.9
Public investment	R	56.6	−8.2	9.2	14.9	20.2	−6.8	13.8	9.0	13.9	11.7
	F	23.2	2.5	−7.5	19.3	−7.5	−1.4	14.5	11.5	12.9	10.2
Volume of residential construction[b]	R	18.1	11.2	−9.5	12.1	13.5	9.5	5.7	−1.7	−1.0	−5.7
	F	8.5	3.6	2.4	19.6	10.8	1.9	5.4	−.7	2.9	3.1
Price of commodity imports	R	−10.0	−2.5	1.6	3.4	4.8	−5.4	−3.1	−.3	−1.4	−1.5
	F	−12.0	−6.7	.0	1.0	4.0	−2.0	−1.0	2.0	−4.0	.0
Volume of world trade	R	3.8	9.3	11.9	7.1	7.2	−.8	9.4	12.3	5.2	6.0
	F	7.0	.0	4.0	7.5	5.0	3.0	3.5	6.0	6.0	4.0
Competitive price abroad	R	−4.2	−2.7	1.4	3.9	1.6	−2.8	−2.5	1.2	−3.2	1.0
	F	—	—	.0	1.0	3.0	−1.0	.0	2.0	−1.7	.0

a. Given in percentage changes. b. Percentage of gross national product in base year.
Source: De Wolff and van den Beld, "Ten Years", Appendix A.

TABLE 21. Forecasting Accuracy of the Netherlands Central Economic Plans 1953–62: Actual Results (R) Versus Forecasts (F)[a] of Endogenous Variables
(in percentages)

		1953	1954	1955	1956	1957	1958	1959	1960	1961	1962
Production in industries	R	8.3	7.7	8.2	5.1	2.8	– .2	5.3	10.0	2.3	3.7
	F	6.8	3.8	2.2	3.3	1.0	–1.9	3.6	5.9	4.4	4.0
Employment in industries	R	1.5	2.4	2.1	2.0	1.0	– .9	1.4	1.8	1.7	2.5
	F	1.6	1.8	1.1	1.3	.3	– .5	1.1	1.8	1.5	2.0
Unemployment[b]	R	–1.5	–1.1	– .8	– .5	.4	1.6	– .7	–1.0	– .5	.0
	F	–1.0	– .8	.3	– .3	.8	2.1	.0	– .7	– .1	.2
Volume of private consumption	R	5.9	7.0	7.5	8.9	.1	– .2	4.7	6.2	4.4	4.5
	F	4.6	6.1	2.7	4.1	1.7	1.0	3.4	5.5	4.6	4.0
Volume of industrial investment[c]	R	11.7	24.3	21.6	12.6	2.8	–15.6	13.7	15.8	7.7	4.9
	F	–1.2	4.8	2.4	4.4	2.2	–10.1	–1.0	19.0	7.1	7.9
Volume of commodity exports	R	12.7	13.5	10.2	3.1	5.4	10.2	12.1	14.4	3.1	7.0
	F	4.0	6.3	4.8	6.6	6.7	3.0	6.0	8.0	7.8	4.0

Volume of commodity imports	R	19.5	24.7	8.1	13.6	2.9	−5.9	13.7	17.2	7.2	5.5
	F	24.2	10.7	1.2	9.7	.0	−5.6	9.0	15.4	10.5	4.5
Inventory[d]	R	.7	4.7	− .9	.4	.3	−3.0	.9	2.9	− .2	−1.4
	F	4.9	.9	−1.4	−1.8	−2.2	−4.2	1.7	1.6	.0	− .8
Price of private consumption	R	− .9	3.7	1.3	1.3	5.5	2.2	1.0	2.2	1.6	2.5
	F	−2.3	2.3	1.2	1.2	4.5	.9	−1.0	2.0	.5	2.0
Price of industrial investment	R	−2.9	.6	3.7	7.0	6.5	2.5	−1.5	0.9	1.3	2.5
	F	−7.1	−2.6	1.1	2.6	3.2	− .5	1.0	1.5	− .3	2.5
Price of commodity exports	R	−8.3	−1.8	1.8	2.4	2.9	−4.2	− .2	− .7	−1.7	−1.0
	F	−6.9	−4.5	.0	2.1	2.9	−1.0	−1.0	2.0	−2.3	.0
Nonwage income	R	9.0	12.3	14.6	6.3	7.0	−3.1	8.7	12.4	−2.9	.0
	F	.8	2.7	.3	3.8	6.4	−5.6	1.9	4.9	3.3	3.3
Current account of balance of payments[d]	R	−1.7	−4.6	2.0	−5.1	.5	6.0	.7	−1.5	−1.6	.0
	F	−5.4	−1.3	1.1	−1.3	2.2	4.2	− .7	−2.8	− .2	.2

a. Given in percentage changes. b. Percentage of working population in base year.
c. Residential construction not included. d. Percentage of gross national product in base year.
Source: De Wolff and van den Beld, Appendix A.

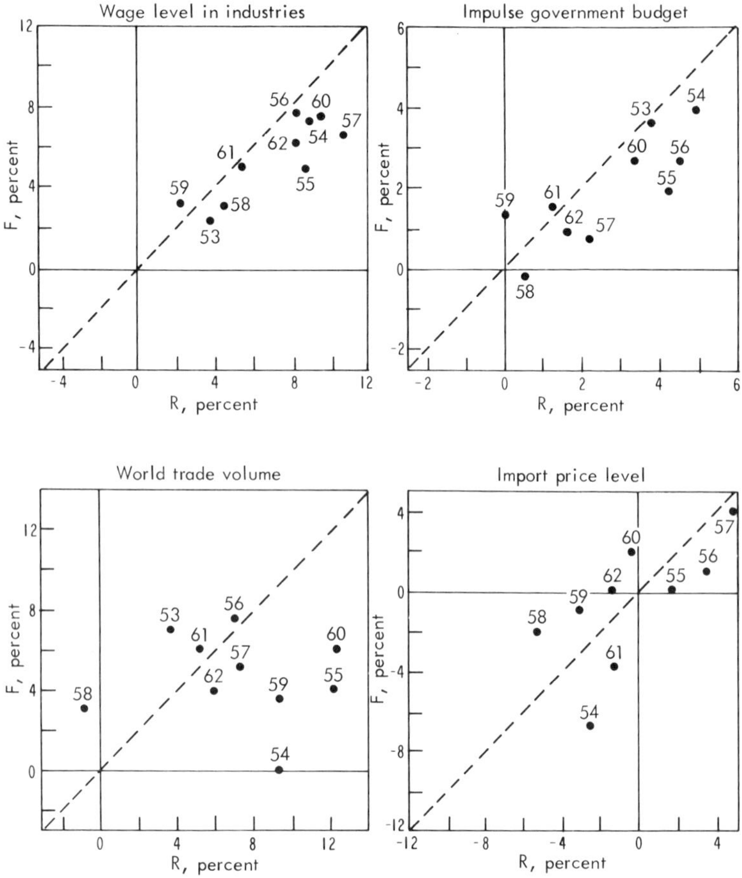

FIGURE 2. Forecast (F) versus Realization (R) of Exogenous Variables

Source: Van den Beld, "Short-term Planning Experiences in the Netherlands," p. 144.

In Figure 3, the forecasts of four endogenous variables are plotted against their realized values. These four variables are targets of Dutch economic policy inasmuch as their realization is particularly important to policy makers. They are: unemployment, the volume of investment in fixed

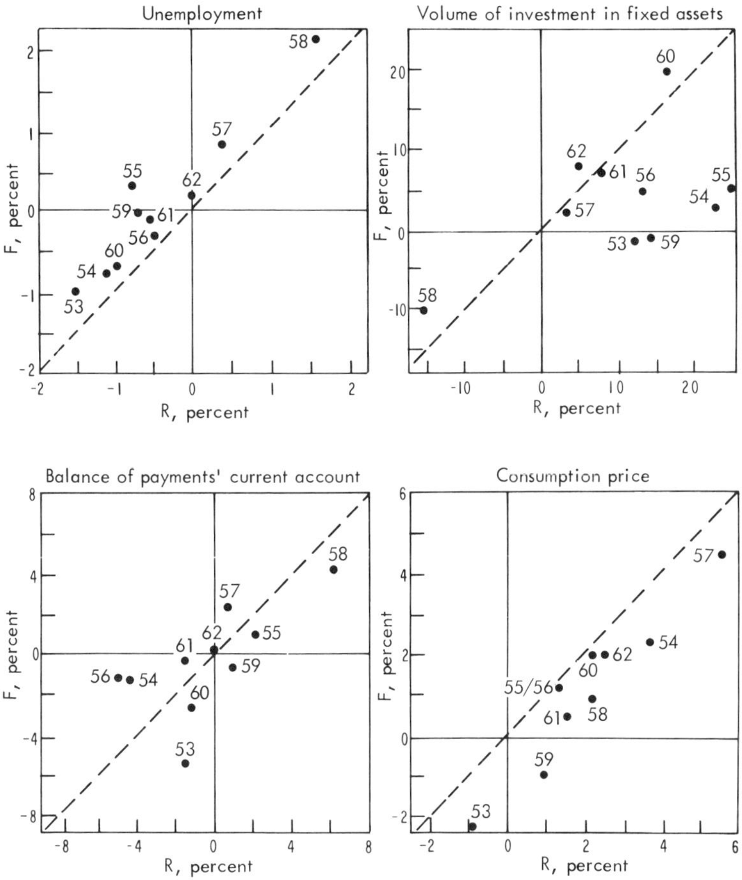

FIGURE 3. Forecast (F) versus Realization (R) of Endogenous Variables

Source: Van den Beld, p. 145.

assets, the current account of the balance of payments, and the consumption price level.

Figure 4 shows the accuracy of certain of the variables that were forecast by the models in 1954, 1956, 1958, and

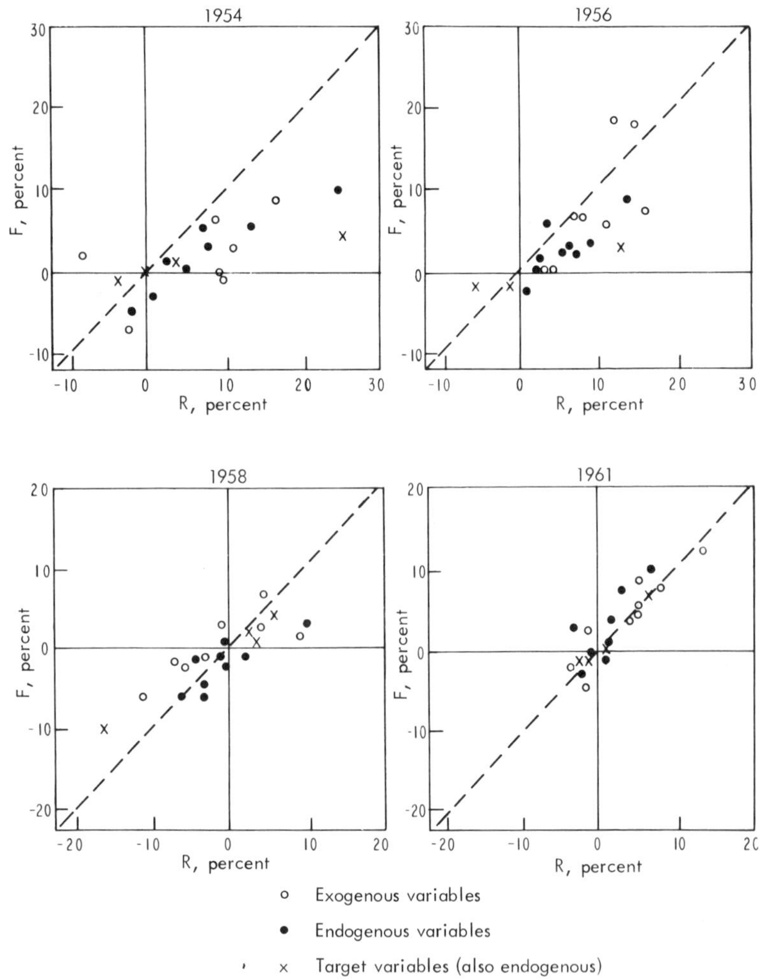

FIGURE 4. Forecast (F) versus Realization (R) of Central Economic Plans

Source: Van den Beld, p. 147.

1961. Each graph in Figure 4 contains plots of a selected set of forecasts.[3] The variables plotted are: (a) a number of

3. Since different versions of the Central Planning Bureau model were used in each of the yearly forecasts, Figure 5 also serves to show the improvement of later versions of the model over the earlier versions.

exogenous variables, (b) the four targets mentioned above, and (c) the remainder of the endogenous variables.

Although a general impression of the degree of forecast reliability can be obtained from the graphs, the graphic presentation gives only a visual picture of the distribution of the forecasting errors about the realized values. Inspection is not sufficient to evaluate accurately the correspondence between forecasts and realizations. What is needed is a numerical index of the performance of the model. The classical standard error of the residuals of the forecasts is of little use inasmuch as it measures the dispersion of the errors around their average value. This would not be objectionable if the average is zero, but a brief inspection of the graphs shows that this is not the case. There is generally a significant bias toward over or underestimating changes. The standard error, therefore, although it may be small, is not a good indication of the accuracy of the forecast.

One solution is to measure the deviation of the predicted values from the realized values themselves. This can be called the forecasting error and defined by the symbol $u_{i(t)}$. It is written as

$$u_{i(t)} = F_{i(t)} - R_{i(t)},$$

where $F_{i(t)}$ stands for the forecast of the ith variable in time period t and $R_{i(t)}$ for the realized value of the ith variable in time period t. The second moment of the forecasting error, defined as $u^2_{i(t)}$, that is, the moment about $R_{i(t)}$, is found as follows:

$$u^2_{i(t)} = \sum_t \frac{1}{T} (F_{i(t)} - R_{i(t)})^2.$$

This statistic measures the deviation of the forecast values of a particular variable about a zero forecasting error, i.e. the realized value. It is given for eight exogenous variables and thirteen endogenous variables in Table 22.

TABLE 22. The Deviation of the Forecast Values about the Realized Values ($u^2_{i(t)}$), 1953–62

	$u^2_{i(t)}$
EXOGENOUS VARIABLES	
Wage level in industries	4.59
Government wage bill	9.99
Other public consumption expenditure	49.53
Public investment expenditure	134.37
Volume of residential construction	50.98
Price level of commodity imports	5.80
Volume of world trade	26.04
Competitive price level on foreign markets	3.99
ENDOGENOUS VARIABLES	
Employment in industries	.29
Price level of consumption	1.19
Volume of private consumption	5.73
Volume of commodity imports	32.63
Volume of production in industries	8.57
Price level of exports	3.18
Unemployment	.25
Volume of commodity exports	33.64
Balance of payments, current account	5.40
Volume of industrial investment	126.38
Price level of gross investment	8.29
Nonwage income	52.07
Stock formation	4.77

Source: Computed from data given in de Wolff and van den Beld, Appendix A.

Such a measure, while useful, is not a complete measurement of the quality of the predictions. It can be improved by taking into account the difficulty of forecasting large, relative to small, changes in the predicted variables. Such a procedure recognizes the fact that large changes are harder to forecast accurately than small changes. For example, when there is no change in the realized value from one year to the next, even a small forecasting error should be considered serious. However, when the realized value changes on the order of 15 percent, a forecast of 13 or 14 percent might be considered to be quite good indeed.

The difficulty of forecasting relatively large changes can be taken into account if a measure of the distribution of successsive differences is incorporated into the overall measure of forecasting accuracy. Successive differences are the changes in the realized values from one period to the next. This is done by dividing the square root of $u^2_{i(t)}$ by the root mean square of the observed changes in the ith variable, taken from zero.

$$\sqrt{\frac{1}{T}\sum_t R_{i(t)}}$$

This statistic represents the normal intensity of change of the variable during the period of observation. Analogous to this is the problem of showing the relative difficulty of forecasting a variable that changes very little during a particular time period to that of predicting another variable that changes by a significant amount.

Following the procedure outlined above, two summary measures, called inequality coefficients, can be derived.[4] The first describes the quality of the forecast of a *given* variable over the *total* period covered by the observation.

$$u'_i = \sqrt{\frac{\sum_t u^2_{i(t)}}{\sum_t R^2_{i(t)}}}$$

The second, which measures the quality of a number of forecasts of *different* variables in a *given* period of time, is

$$u'_{(t)} = \sqrt{\frac{\sum_i u^2_{i(t)}}{\sum_i R^2_{i(t)}}}$$

Perfect forecasts occur when u'_i or $u'_{(t)}$ equals zero. When

4. For a more complete discussion of the inequality coefficients, see Verdoorn and van Eijk, pp. 59–80; and Ferber and Verdoorn, *Research Methods in Economics and Business*, pp. 476–82.

TABLE 23. Inequality Coefficients ($u'_{(t)}$) by Central Economic Plans, 1953–62

	1953	1954	1955	1956	1957	1958	1959	1960	1961	1962
Exogenous Variables										
Controlled	.71	.74	.91	.54	1.06	.46	.18	.38	.23	.42
Noncontrolled	.43	1.06	.69	.76	.38	.68	.78	.57	.50	.34
All exogenous	.63	.85	.83	.63	.87	.55	.50	.46	.36	.39
Endogenous Variable										
Targets[a]	.67	.90	.89	.66	.39	.50	.77	.28	.37	.18
All endogenous	.86	.93	.84	.66	.50	.53	.58	.48	.36	.22
All variables	.79	.90	.84	.65	.67	.54	.55	.47	.36	.28

a. Balance-of-payments current account, unemployment, volume of investment, and consumption price level.
Source: De Wolff and van den Beld, p. 19.

the coefficient equals 1, the forecasting errors are as great as the changes in the realized variables. At this point the forecasts must be considered rather poor.

In Table 29 the inequality coefficient $u'_{(t)}$ is given for the years 1953 through 1962. Variables are grouped as exogenous or endogenous, and are subdivided according to their status as controlled exogenous, noncontrolled exogenous, or target endogenous variables.

In general, the forecasts tend to be less accurate in periods of rapid expansion. Such periods occurred in 1954–55 and 1959–60. This illustrates the fact that large changes are more difficult to forecast than small ones. The data bear this out inasmuch as relatively good predictions appear during years of little expansion, such as in 1956–57 and 1961.

In Table 24, the first two columns show the root-mean-square deviations of the realized values for the ten-year period and also for the last five years taken separately. From the table, it can be seen that there was a slightly slower rate of expansion during the latter five years than for the period taken as a whole. One could expect that forecasting during the last five years was slightly easier and, therefore, that the inequality coefficients should be lower. The last two columns of the table give the inequality coefficient u'_i and show that indeed this was the case. Table 24 shows also that prediction improved substantially, probably in greater measure than could be accounted for by the fact that there was less change to be predicted. This additional improvement in forecasting is undoubtedly the result of three factors: better statistical information, better models, and cumulative experience.

The general cause of errors in the forecasts of endogenous variables lies in inaccuracies in the prediction of the exogenous variables. The volume of world trade was consistently underestimated in periods of rapid expansion, such as 1954–55 and 1959–60, and the forecast of the price level of foreign competition has frequently been in error. This is also true in the case of forecasts of government expenditures.

TABLE 24. Root-Mean-Square Deviations and Inequality Coefficients

	Root-mean-square deviations of the realizations (in percentages)		Inequality coefficients (u'_i)	
	1953–62	1958–62	1953–62	1958–62
Exogenous Variables				
Wage level in industries	7.4	6.4	.29	.20
Government wage bill	10.9	8.7	.29	.12
Other public consumption expenditure	10.2	9.8	.69	.47
Public investment expenditure	12.6	11.4	.92	.22
Volume of residential construction	10.2	5.6	.70	.54
Price level of commodity imports	4.3	2.9	.56	.56
Volume of world trade	8.1	7.8	.63	.54
Competitive price level on foreign markets	2.7	2.3	.74	.68
Endogenous Variables				
Employment in industries	1.8	1.7	.30	.18
Price level of consumption	2.6	2.0	.42	.46
Volume of private consumption	5.7	4.5	.42	.16
Volume of commodity imports	13.6	11.0	.42	.20
Volume of production in industries	6.1	5.4	.48	.38
Price level of exports	3.3	2.1	.54	.59
Unemployment	.9	.9	.56	.48
Volume of commodity exports	10.0	10.2	.58	.57
Balance of payments, current account	3.1	2.9	.75	.44
Volume of industrial investment	14.6	12.4	.77	.50
Price level of gross investment	3.6	1.9	.80	.53
Nonwage income	8.8	7.0	.82	.64
Stock formation	2.1	2.0	1.04	.44

Source: De Wolff and van den Beld, pp. 9–15.

Poor forecasts of government expenditures can, however, be explained in part by the fact that the government budget is an authorization budget rather than a performance budget, and there may be unaccounted delays between authorization and expenditure.

Inaccurate predictions of another exogenous variable, the world price level, have been the chief cause of the relatively high inequality coefficients of the forecasts of the volume of exports. Contributing to the poor quality of the export predictions in 1956 and 1961 was the influence of capacity constraints, which were not, until lately, taken into account in the model. Because of the interaction among the variables in the model, such errors are in a sense cumulative. This general underestimation of export possibilities has been the main cause of the continual underestimation of domestic production and of the surplus in the balance of payments.

The forecasts of the industrial wage level also exhibit an underestimation bias. As this is an important factor in the price equations, the latter were also generally too low. In addition, the quality of the predictions of nonwage income has been very uncertain, which is explained partially by the fact that nonwage income is calculated as a residual term in the model. Errors in the forecasts of total production do not appear to be transmitted in their entirety to the forecasts of labor demand. Presumably, changes in production are absorbed, at least initially, by changes in labor productivity. As a result, the inequality coefficients for employment tend to be better than those for production.

The forecasts of changes in the level of unemployment constitute an interesting case. There is a definite, positive bias over the ten-year period. Either increase in the level of unemployment were overestimated or decreases were underestimated, with the result that the forecasted level of unemployment was always too high.

The data show a marked improvement in the quality of the forecasts of the exogenous variables in the government sector over the last five years. There has been also a significant improvement in the quality of the forecasts of consumption, investment, and stock formation. These improvements have in turn resulted in better forecasts in the important balance of payments account.

Throughout the period, signs have been predicted relatively well, i.e. turning-point errors are relatively few in number. De Wolff and van den Beld report that about 80 percent of the turning points that occurred in the endogenous variable were predicted correctly.[5] It must be noted, however, that about 20 percent of the turning points predicted by the model did not in fact occur. If the movement of endogenous variables during the period 1953–62 is divided according to whether a slow down, an acceleration, or a turning point occurred, the data show that out of a total frequency of 129 changes, 84, or 65 percent, were predicted correctly. The main contributor to faulty prediction was in forecasting acceleration. Only 29 out of 49 accelerations were predicted correctly.

The general conclusion to be drawn from this analysis is that the forecasts have generally been good and, in particular, improved over the years 1960–65. Further improvement would seem to rely upon better forecasts of the exogenous variables.

5. "Ten Years," pp. 18–19.

CHAPTER 9

Planning and Economic Policy

The object of this study has been to show how the formulation of economic policy in the Netherlands is a combination of the political process and the technical process. The Dutch political process decides upon economic policy objectives and selects means to obtain them. The technical process provides information and analysis relating to the main issues facing policy-makers: it produces accurate and up-to-date statistics on the Dutch economy, identifies problems of economic policy by forecasting short-term and long-term economic developments, and predicts the probable effects of alternative policy proposals prior to their adoption.

The Dutch have been forerunners in the development of a planning approach in which the decision-making process is subjected to objective study and quantitative analysis. In recent years more and more countries have shown an interest in the type of economic planning exhibited by the Netherlands. In the Netherlands, as pointed out throughout the text, this approach relies heavily on the conditional forecasts made with the aid of econometric models. In a sense, it can be said that the models give organization to the discussion of policy decisions.

Two reasons have been given for the relatively influential position of the technical process in the Netherlands. First, because the political process is colored by religious controversy, often at the expense of current issues, important matters are frequently not decided through normal parliamentary channels. Second, the Dutch authorities have pursued a purposeful wage and price policy designed to affect domestic cost levels. In implementing this policy, the government has relied heavily on the quantitative analysis supplied by technical bureaus. In large measure the contrasts of the conditional forecasts made with the aid of econometric models and the annual Central Economic Plans. The models and the plans, particularly in the preparatory stages, give organization to the discussion of policy decisions. It has been pointed out that the plans are not, however, plans in the strictest sense of the word, but rather forecasts of future (short-run) economic developments. Over the years, these bureaus and several extra-parliamentary organizations have acquired increased importance in matters of economic policy, while the power of parliament has declined.

In assessing Dutch economic planning, it is important to note that the objectives have been sought and policy developed in the light of the economic conditions existing in Western Europe at the time. The Western European economies have become more closely interdependent since 1950. Trade between them has become freer of quantitative controls, and other trade barriers have been progressively reduced. In particular, the use of tariff policy as a means of attaining economic objectives has been severely curtailed. Changes in exchange rates have also been tacitly rejected as instruments of policy, except in dire emergency.

These considerations have strongly affected the means or instruments by which the objectives of Dutch economic policy can be realized. Specifically, the instruments have been restricted to: a centralized income policy by which wage and price developments are negotiated between employers, employees, and the government; control of certain strategic points, mainly through the use of monetary and fiscal measures that influence the general level of economic activity; and certain selective taxes and subsidies by which market preferences within the domestic economy are altered to a limited extent.

One purpose of this study has been to show that Dutch economic planning is based in large measure on quantitative analyses of the issues involved, and that even the approximate quantification of the relationships between economic variables makes it possible to estimate with some accuracy the repercussions of various contemplated policy measures both in the short run and to forecast their implication with regard to the future course of economic events.

It might be worthwhile to point out that, technically, there is a difference between planning and forecasting. Forecasting, by definition, involves the future. To forecast is to predict some future condition or event, but a simple forecast does not, like a plan, necessarily involve a predetermined course of action on the part of the authorities or anyone else. Planning, as the term is used in the Netherlands, describes a process that goes a step beyond simple forecasting in that it hypothesizes a course of action on the part of those involved in the economic process both in the Netherlands and abroad. However, as pointed out in Chapter 5, the Dutch plan, although it is an essential part of the planning process, does not ensure that a particular course of action will actually be followed. In fact, there is no central executive planning agency charged with implementing the plan. Implementation of economic policy is entirely in the hands of the cabinet ministers. Thus, the forecasts of the Central Planning Bureau might turn out to be erroneous for the additional reason that the assumptions about government policy used by the Bureau in drawing up the plan, insofar as they pertain to action by the government during the plan year, may turn out to be incorrect.

The Influence of the Central Planning Bureau and the Central Economic Plans

The effect of the Central Planning Bureau's activities is mainly limited to influencing the climate of thought. The Bureau is not, from an organizational standpoint, a powerful agency—to a considerable extent its work is scientific and research-oriented. However, its function as ad hoc staff for the Social and Economic Council and the latter's important role in the political environment of the Netherlands tend to make the Bureau an influential body. The fact that the executives of the Bureau have been persons of some renown has also contributed to its influence.

In general, the work of the Bureau is held in high regard throughout the Netherlands. According to Willem Hessel, who spoke as Director of the Scientific Bureau of the Netherlands Federation of Trade Unions, "During the years of its existence, the Central Planning Bureau has created much goodwill and confidence by its objectiveness and capability, both at the side of employers' organizations and the side of the trade unions." He went on to emphasize the importance of this confidence. "Otherwise," he said, "any detail and any implicit assumption [involved in the forecasts made by the Bureau or in its staff work for the Social and Economic Council] would become disputable."[1]

As stated previously, the Bureau is not responsible for executive coordination of economic policy. That is, the Bureau does not concern itself with the administration and implementation of the plans and programs; it assists in preparation. However, it appears that the different government agencies and departments charged with formulating economic policy do, in fact, make policy decisions against the Bureau's assessment of forthcoming economic events. In this respect the plan serves the government as a bench mark for government policy. Although the Bureau offers only an advisory coordination, most observers regard this as an improvement over the prewar period when such a basis for coordinated policy did not exist. At that time each department presumably made policy decisions only in light of its own assessment of the future economic situation.

Although the government does not accept responsibility for the achievement of the forecasts that appear in the plans,

1. W. Hessel, "Quantitative Planning of Economic Policy in the Netherlands," p. 165.

by releasing the plans for publication the government has in a sense validated the policy assumptions underlying them. The responsibility for the forecasts, which make up the body of the plans, remains with the Central Planning Bureau. The main value of the plans, as far as the government is concerned, is that economic policy is subjected to a thorough analysis during the formulation of the annual plans. Their worth as pieces of published research is, in effect, a by-product of their preparation. The first step taken in constructing each plan is to describe economic development under the assumption that government policy is left unchanged, i.e. that the Dutch economy is affected only by expected changes in external variables not under the control of the policy-makers. If it is clear to the policy-makers that "no change" in government policy leads to unfavorable developments, alternative drafts of the plan are prepared to analyze the implication of various policy changes. Although nothing has been proved on this point, one can assume, in principle at least, that the government chooses the policies that are expected to lead to the most desirable results in terms of the general objectives of its overall economic policy.

The published plans are not designed to represent government policy, but a plan does have an influence on events after its publication. For example, suppose the Bureau indicates, by forecasting a low unemployment rate, that the coming year will show a tight labor market. This prediction will assist those ministers who want to stress economy in matters of government expenditures. If the Bureau foresees a surplus in the balance of payments, the position of those who want to take measures to increase the level of national expenditures will be strengthened. If the plan shows that a rise in wage rates will have only a slightly adverse effect on the price level, trade unions will not be slow to use the argument in future wage negotiations. Hence many persons look to the forecasts published in the central economic plans for support of their arguments, and, in spite of the original intent, the plans become important, if indirect, policy documents.[2]

THE EFFECTS OF FORECASTING ERRORS ON THE DIRECTION OF ECONOMIC POLICY

While no one has yet established any definite connection between the forecasts of the Bureau and the policy action of the government, in a recent study C. A. van den Beld of the Central Planning Bureau undertook to chart the anticyclical and procyclical aspects of government economic policy and to compare these with the forecasts of the Bureau.[3] When compared with movements in the level of unemployment, budgetary policy until 1958 was procyclical rather than anticyclical. Van den Beld also found that up to 1956 monetary policy was procyclical as well. He attributes the procyclical budgetary and monetary policy to the fact that a higher weight was placed upon restoring balance-of-payments equilibrium (in 1951–52 and 1957–58) than upon reducing the level of unemployment. His analysis, which extends through 1962, shows that policy in recent years has been more consistent: policy actions have been inflationary when unemployment has been rising, and deflationary when unemployment has been falling. According to van den Beld, the fact that policies corresponded more closely with the situation in the early sixties "has some connection with the improvement in the forecasts."[4]

2. The direct influence of the plan in the private sector is not clear. Presumably the plan is useful to the larger industrial concerns and to other individuals or groups, including international organizations, who have a need to be informed about economic events.

3. C. A. van den Beld, *Conjunctuurpolitick in en om de jaren vijftig* (Short-term Policies in the Fifties), Central Planning Bureau Monografie No. 8 (The Hague, 1963). This analysis is reported in brief in his contribution to Hickman, ed., *Quantitative Planning of Economic Policy*, pp. 134–62.

4. C. A. van den Beld, *Conjunctuurpolitick in en om de jaren vijftig* (Short-term Policies in the Fifties), Central Planning Bureau Monografie No. 8 (The Hague, 1963). This analysis is reported in brief in his contribution to Hickman, ed., *Quantitative Planning of Economic Policy*, p. 151.

The accuracy of the forecasts published in the annual central economic plans has been discussed in Chapter 8. Several measures of forecasting accuracy were described. Among these were the simple differences between the forecasts and their realizations. Also discussed were a series of inequality coefficients.

Ideally, each forecast should be evaluated in the light of how well it served the purpose for which it was designed, rather than by some measure of the degree to which actual events agreed with the predictions. A rigorous analysis of this issue appears to be impossible due in part to the lack of data and of detailed accounts by those actually involved in the policy-making process as to the effects of the forecasts on the final decision. There is no unique correspondence between the individual forecasting errors or the inequality coefficients described in Chapter 8 and the actual effect of forecasting errors on policy decisions.

Strictly speaking, the preliminary economic projections used by government policy-makers are not forecasts, since at least in the preliminary versions they are intended to lead to decisions during the forecast period. However, one can look at those years in which the final forecasts indicated the appropriate direction for government policy and those in which policies based on the forecasts would have tended to be destabilizing. For example, in 1955 the forecast of the loss of reserves that would take place in 1956 was underestimated by a factor of four. The Bureau's prediction of the employment opportunities likely to be generated in 1956 was also too pessimistic. The expansionist policy followed by the government in 1956, which contributed to the balance-of-payments crisis that followed, may have resulted from these erroneous forecasts.

Unemployment increases were always overestimated and decreases underestimated, and therefore the predicted level of unemployment was always too high. According to de Wolff and van den Beld, "This may have caused too expansionist policies in periods of upswing, like 1953–56 and 1959–61, in particular in 1955 when unemployment was expected to rise when it actually fell."[5]

During the recovery from the recession of 1957–58, the forecasts of improvements in the balance-of-payments account were too pessimistic, which may have led to a less than optimum expansionist policy on the part of the government. However, because there were offsetting errors (for example, in the unemployment forecast, where the decrease in the level of unemployment was greater than predicted), the overall effects of the 1958 forecasts may have been neutral.

Throughout 1950–65 the Central Planning Bureau consistently underestimated export possibilities. One effect of this was that increases in wages were probably regarded as more serious than was perhaps warranted. In spite of this, the Bureau's forecasts of the annual increases in wages was usually underestimated. As a result, consumer price changes were also underestimated with the result that the annual increase in prices was usually in excess of those forecast by the Central Planning Bureau. One might conclude that a more rigorous price policy might have been pursued had the Bureau's estimates been more accurate.

In view of the discussion on the Dutch model's accuracy contained in Chapter 8, it is not unreasonable to say that the gross characteristics of the most important policy variables are adequately described by the Dutch model. The model provides a good approximation of the actual behavioral relationships that exist in the Netherlands' economy and offers a systematic, quick, economical (after the initial investment in its construction), impartial, and relatively clear-cut approach to the analysis of problems of national economic policy. Nevertheless, definite conclusions concerning the relationship between forecasts and policy actions cannot be drawn without more information regarding the actual

5. De Wolff and van den Beld, "Ten Years," p. 16.

influence of the forecasts, whether correct or incorrect, on the policy-makers in any particular instance.

The institutional arrangements that have facilitated the rise of the technical process to its position of importance in the Netherlands and that continue to facilitate its functioning as part of the economic planning process came about directly after the war. At the start these institutional arrangements were informal, in the sense that they are superimposed on the traditional government system. Over the years, however, most of the early postwar experiments were given more formal existence, either by statute or by custom.

As pointed out in Chapter 3, the Dutch economic and social order is influenced by religious convictions. One might conclude that one factor leading to the emergence of the technical process was the need to minimize the effect of nonrational elements, such as the Catholic-Protestant dichotomy, on political debate regarding economic issues. One may hypothesize, although not prove, that the potential for political instability such as that existing between Catholic and Protestant and between religious and nonreligious elements in the Netherlands might be a significant precondition to the recognition of the potential contribution that quantitative analysis can make to the formulation of economic policy.

It should be noted however that, although the various social, economic, and political groups in the Netherlands do not agree on ultimate values, there is a high degree of consensus on the broad rules for society. During the period covered by this study it seems these groups were, for the most part, able to agree on what to do under the changing circumstances of the day. In some measure this was due to the system described in the previous chapters, a system that characterizes Dutch economic, social, and political life as a neatly built up fortress of separate *Weltanschauungen* within which the parties haggle endlessly over substance but keep the system going via sacrosanct ways of procedure.[6]

6. In Dutch, a *verzuiling* system.

At the end of 1965 the government was trying desperately to keep this system, within which its income policy functioned, intact. However, many labor and management leaders who had participated in policy-making since the war had passed from the scene. They were being replaced by younger men whose loyalties to the system were not conditioned by memories of the depression and of the reconstruction period. And, as is well known, the value of a system such as has been built up in the Netherlands is proscribed by the commonsense observation that to ride together in a bus while wanting to go to different places may be all right provided that the destinations are not too different from each other.

The institutional arrangements that have been developed to analyze and effect the government's economic policies have also helped create a situation in which the traditional boundaries between state and society are no longer easy to distinguish. Some see such a situation as dangerous to the democratic process. Pieter de Wolff, current director of the Central Planning Bureau, has spoken out against this apprehension in these words, "I do not think that central economic planning directed to the realization of certain aims and within limits set by the available instruments can be regarded as hostile to democracy so long as the aims and instruments are provided by normal democratic procedures."[7]

The influence of short-term central economic planning on economic developments in a democratic society such as the Netherlands is probably overestimated by both proponents and opponents of the system. In Western society the freedom of action of the authorities is severely limited by both domestic and external economic forces. The government's ability to take action is also affected by social and political forces that operate through normal parliamentary as well as extra-parliamentary channels. Even the Dutch system of

7. De Wolff, "The Scope, Methods and Tools of Planning," p. 5.

wage direction, which on the surface has the appearance of a formal autonomous government process, is in reality a means of applying the government's sanction to wage agreements mostly reached within industry itself. In recent years the system's main effect has been to reduce irregular wage increases.

Finally, in a country such as the Netherlands, the government has at its disposal only a very restricted number of instruments, and because economic activity is, for the most part, freely determined, these instruments are not as effective (in the sense that they are capable of influencing the target variables) as they are in a centrally directed economy. In addition, the short-run outlook is largely determined by forces that are already in being. Therefore there is much room for forecasting but relatively little room for planning.

Nevertheless, few countries have gone as far as the Netherlands in attempting to quantify economic relationships, to forecast economic conditions, and to evaluate the consequences of alternative policy actions on the part of the government. Since World War II, the Dutch have been developing what appears to be useful tools for the solution of problems of economic policy. These tools are essentially pragmatic in character: they are designed to provide knowledge about how the economy works. When properly used, few will doubt that such knowledge contributes to more consistent price, wage, fiscal, and monetary policies. The 1950–65 planning process in the Netherlands was based, in large measure, on the belief that analysis is the main ingredient for sound economic policy.

APPENDIX

Aspects of the 1961 Model

This Appendix contains seven sections, each dealing with a particular aspect of the econometric development of the 1961 model. The seven sections are:

While the material contained in these sections is not essential for an understanding of the main thrust of the text, the reader interested in pursuing further the econometric development of the model will find the material in these appendices useful.

Appendix 1

Linearization and the Taylor Series Expansion

The definitional equations that show the relation between volume measurement and value measurement result from a linearization procedure common to the models of the Central Planning Bureau. For the benefit of the non-econometrician, one such relationship is derived in detail below. The example chosen is the consumption equation $\dot{C} = \dot{c} + \dot{p}_c$, which is the linear approximation of the nonlinear expression $C = cp_c$. The latter can be written in natural logarithms as:

$$(1.1) \qquad \ln C = \ln c + \ln p_c.$$

Since $\Delta C = C - C_{-1}$, then $\Delta \ln C = \ln C - \ln C_{-1}$, and the left-hand side of 1.1 can be written as: $\ln C = \Delta \ln C + \ln C_{-1}$. Furthermore, since $\ln c = \Delta \ln c + \ln c_{-1}$ and $\ln p_c = \Delta \ln p_c + \ln p_{c-1}$ by substitution $C = cp_c$ or $\ln C = \ln c + \ln p_c$ becomes $\Delta \ln C + \ln C_{-1} = \Delta \ln c + \ln c_{-1} + \Delta \ln p_c + \ln p_{c-1}$. But since $\ln c_{-1} = \ln c_{-1} + \ln pc_{-1}$, the lagged terms cancel from both sides, and $C = cp_c$ becomes

$$(1.2) \qquad \Delta \ln C = \Delta \ln c + \Delta \ln p_c$$

The left-hand side of 1.2, $\Delta \ln C$, can be developed as follows:[1]

By definition $\Delta C = C - C_{-1}$. Transposing, one obtains $C = C_{-1} + \Delta C$, which can be written as $C = C_{-1}[1 + (\Delta C/C_{-1})]$. Taking logarithms of both sides gives

$$(1.3) \qquad \ln C = \ln C_{-1} + \ln(1 + \Delta C/C_{-1}).$$

Transposing $\ln C_{-1}$ from left to right one obtains $\ln C - \ln C_{-1} = \ln [1 + (\Delta C/C_{-1})]$, and since $\ln C - \ln C_{-1} = \Delta \ln C$, then $\Delta \ln C = \ln [1 + (\Delta C/C_{-1})]$.

By definition, $\dot{C} = 100(\Delta C/C_{-1})$. Thus, $\ln [1 + (\Delta C/C_{-1})] = \ln [1 + (\dot{C}/100)]$. The latter is a special form of the general expression $\ln (1 + \alpha)$. The expansion of this series, known as the Taylor Series, is $\ln (1 + \alpha) = \alpha - \frac{1}{2}\alpha^2 + \frac{1}{3}\alpha^3 - \ldots$.

If α is small, a condition satisfied in the case of $\dot{C}/100$, the leading term is a good approximation of the sum of the series. Thus, $\ln[1 + (\dot{C}/100)] \approx \dot{C}/100$, or $\Delta \ln C \approx \dot{C}/100$. The terms $\Delta \ln c$ and $\Delta \ln p_c$ can be developed in a like manner to obtain $\Delta \ln c = \dot{c}/100$, and $\Delta \ln p_c = \dot{p}_c/100$.

Substituting these expressions in 1.2 and multiplying by 100 yields the desired result: $\dot{C} = \dot{c} + \dot{p}_c$.

1. An alternative development of 1.2 is $\Delta \ln C = \ln C - \ln C_{-1}$. However, the right-hand term can be written as: $\ln [(C/C_{-1})]$. By adding the term $(C_{-1} - C_{-1})$ to the numerator, one obtains: $\ln(C + C_{-1} - C_{-1}/C_{-1})$ which also can be written as: $\ln[1 + (\Delta C/C_{-1})]$.

Appendix 2

The Derivation of the Coefficients That Are Not Estimated Statistically

In general, the derivation of the coefficients that are not estimated statistically takes the following form.[2] Consider the familiar income equation,

$$Y = C + I. \tag{2.1}$$

After taking lags and subtracting, 2.1 can be written as

$$\Delta Y = \Delta C + \Delta I. \tag{2.2}$$

Dividing 2.2 by Y_{-1} yields $\Delta Y/Y_{-1} = \Delta C/Y_{-1} + \Delta I/Y_{-1}$, which, after multiplying the numerator and denominator of the consumption term by C_{-1} and the numerator and denominator of the investment term by I_{-1}, may be written as

$$\frac{\Delta Y}{Y_{-1}} = \left(\frac{C_{-1}}{Y_{-1}}\right)\frac{\Delta C}{C_{-1}} + \left(\frac{I_{-1}}{Y_{-1}}\right)\frac{\Delta I}{I_{-1}}. \tag{2.3}$$

Multiplying 2.3 by 100, one obtains

$$\dot{Y} = \left(\frac{C_{-1}}{Y_{-1}}\right)\dot{C} + \left(\frac{I_{-1}}{Y_{-1}}\right)\dot{I}. \tag{2.4}$$

Substituting in equation 2.4 yields coefficients such as those that appear in the 1961 model in the equations whose coefficients are not estimated statistically. Note that equation 2.4 is a linear relation in C and I with known (since they are functions of lagged variables) coefficients. Note also that the coefficients add to unity and that the coefficients vary depending on the base year chosen.

Appendix 3

The Derivation of the Coefficients of the Equations for $\dot{L}^B$ and $\dot{Z}^B$

The procedure for deriving the coefficients of the equations for

2. See Appendix 3 for the main exception to the derivation presented here.

changes in disposable wage and nonwage incomes differs from that shown in Appendix 2.

The equation for disposable wage income, L^B, is

$$L^B = L + O'_L. \tag{3.1}$$

In terms of first differences, 3.1 becomes

$$\Delta L^B = \Delta L + \Delta O'_L. \tag{3.2}$$

By definition, $\dot{L}^B = 100(\Delta L^B/L^B_{-1})$, $\dot{L} = 100(\Delta L/L_{-1})$, and $\dot{O}'_L = 100(\Delta O'_L/L_{-1})$. Transposing each of the above one obtains, $\Delta L^B = (L^B_{-1}/100)(\dot{L}^B)$, $\Delta L = (L_{-1}/100)(\dot{L})$, $\Delta O'_L = (L_{-1}/100)(\dot{O}'_L)$. Substituting these expressions in 3.2, and multiplying by 100 and dividing by L^B_{-1} yields $\dot{L}^B = (L_{-1}/L^B_{-1})(\dot{L}) + (L_{-1}/L^B_{-1})(\dot{O}'_L)$. By substituting the 1957 values of the lagged variables, one obtains the coefficients that appear in the model. Note that these coefficients vary, depending on the values of the variables in the base year chosen.

Appendix 4

The Relationship Between w_l and q

In explaining the investment equation in the body of chapter 7, a term q was introduced. This variable is a function of the capacity variable w_l. In the generalized investment equation q appears in the term $\alpha_3[100\ \Delta \ln q_{-\frac{1}{2}} + 100 \ln q_{-1\frac{1}{2}}]$.

The relation between q in natural logarithms and q in common logarithms is $\ln q = 2.30 \log q$. Therefore, after converting to common logarithms, the capacity term may be written as $\alpha_3[23.0(10)\ \Delta \log q_{-\frac{1}{2}}] + \alpha_3[23.0(10) \log q_{-1\frac{1}{2}}]$ or after factoring out α^3 (23.0), as $\alpha_3(23.0)[(10)\ \Delta \log q_{-\frac{1}{2}} + (10) \log q_{-1\frac{1}{2}}]$. However, since $\Delta \log q_{-\frac{1}{2}} = \log q_{-\frac{1}{2}} - \log q_{-1\frac{1}{2}}$, one may write $\log q_{-\frac{1}{2}} = \Delta \log q_{-\frac{1}{2}} + \log q_{-1\frac{1}{2}}$. Therefore, $\log q_{-\frac{1}{2}}$ may be substituted for $\Delta \log q_{-\frac{1}{2}} + \log q_{-1\frac{1}{2}}$ in the expression $\alpha_3(23.0)[(10)\ \Delta \log q_{-\frac{1}{2}} + (10) \log q_{-1\frac{1}{2}}]$ to obtain $\alpha_3(23.0)(10)\log q_{-\frac{1}{2}}$.

The capacity variable w_l is defined in terms of q as $w_l = (10) \log q$, or $w_{l_{-\frac{1}{2}}} = (10) \log q_{-\frac{1}{2}}$. Since $w_{l_{-\frac{1}{2}}} = \Delta w_{-\frac{1}{2}}$

$+ w_{l_{-1\frac{1}{2}}}$, therefore $\alpha_3(23.0)(10) \log q_{-\frac{1}{2}}$ may be written as $\alpha_3[(23.0)\ \Delta w_{l_{-\frac{1}{2}}} + (23.0) w_{l_{-1\frac{1}{2}}}]$.

This expression contains the same variables as the investment equation appearing in the published versions of the 1961 model. In the published investment equation the coefficient of $\Delta w_{l_{-\frac{1}{2}}}$ and $w_{l_{-1\frac{1}{2}}}$ is 7.18. Then since α_3 (23.0) equals 7.18, α_3 is .31. Thus the elasticity of investment with respect to the capacity variable w_l, as expressed in the model, is .31.

Appendix 5

The Definitional Equation for w_l

In the published version of the 1961 model of the Central Planning Bureau, the equation defining w_l, the capacity variable, appears as

(5.1) $$w_l = 10 \log w - .30\ (w - 1).^3$$

In this equation, w is the number of registered unemployed expressed as a percentage of the dependent working population, which is defined as those persons who are employed by someone else, i.e. the self-employed are excluded.

The equation used to define w_l in the working version of the 1961 model is

(5.2) $$w_l = .43\ \dot{w}' - .300\ \Delta w + 1.000\ w_{l_{-1}}.$$

The variable w' is a proxy variable for which an additional definitional equation is added to the working version of the model. This is equation 29 in the list of equations, and equation 5.2 is number 27 on the list. The definitional equation for w' is

(5.3) $$\dot{w}' = 7.299\ \Delta w.$$

By definition, $\dot{w} = (\Delta w / w_{-1})100$. In 1960, w_{-1}, the unemployment rate, was 1.375 percent. Substituting 1.375 for w_{-1} in

3. The form of this equation is such that if $w_l = (10) \log q$ (see Appendix 4), then $10 \log q = 10 \log w - .30\ (w - 1)$, or $q = w/10^{.03(w-1)}$.

the equation above yields $\dot{w} = 72.99\ \Delta w$. Substituting $\dot{w} = 10\ \dot{w}'$ in this equation gives $\dot{w}' = 7.299\ \Delta w$.

The factor w_{-1}, representing the assumed rate of unemployment in the base year, is both an exogenous variable in the reserve capacity–unemployment relationship and a determinant of the coefficient of the definitional equation for $\dot{w}'$. This variable introduces some difficulties in the solution of the model because each time a different initial level of unemployment is chosen, w_{-1} changes. This affects not only w_{-1} as a predetermined variable but also the coefficient of the $\dot{w}'$ definitional equation. A new coefficient for $\dot{w}'$ therefore must be computed. This in itself is not difficult, but the calculation of the effect of this coefficient change on the other endogenous variables in the system involves quite a bit of computational effort. Methods have been worked out to cope with the situation by deleting w_l from the class of endogenous variables and including it among the predetermined variables.[4]

The remainder of this appendix shows how 5.2 is derived from 5.1. Equation 5.1 can be written as $w_l = 10 \log w - .30\ w + .30$. After lagging, this becomes $w_l - w_{l_{-1}} = 10 \log w - .30\ w + .30 - 10 \log w_{-1} + .30\ w_{-1} - .30$, or after cancelling and collecting

$$(5.4) \qquad w_l - w_{l_{-1}} = 10 \log w - 10 \log w_{-1} - .30\ \Delta w.$$

By transposing $w_{l_{-1}}$, 5.4 can be written as $w_l = 10\ \Delta \log w - .30\ \Delta w + w_{l_{-1}}$. If one then converts to natural logarithms, the term $10\ \Delta \log w$ becomes $4.34\ \Delta \ln w$. However, $\Delta \ln w$ is equal to $\dot{w}/100$ (see Appendix 1). Thus,

$$(5.5) \qquad w_l = 4.34\ \dot{w}/100 - .30\ \Delta w + w_{l_{-1}}.$$

At this point the proxy variable $\dot{w}'$ is introduced. In terms of $\dot{w}'$, $\dot{w}$ is defined as $\dot{w} = 10\dot{w}'$. By substituting $\dot{w} = 10\dot{w}'$ in 5.5, one obtains the desired result: $w_l = .434\ \dot{w}' - .30\ \Delta w + w_{l_{-1}}$, which is equation 27 of the model as presented in Table 17 and the actual capacity equation used in the working version of the 1961 model.

4. See P. J. Verdoorn and J. J. Post, "Capacity and the Short-term Multiplier," paper presented to the 25th meeting of the European Econometric Society, Copenhagen, July 1963.

Appendix 6

Distributed Lags in the Equations for Changes in Autonomous Prices and Investment Prices

Each price equation has a distributed lag. The distributed lag is determined by applying geometrically decreasing weights to one or more of the causal variables in each successive preceding year of the sample period. The lags in the autonomous price equation, p_x, and the investment price equation, p_i, are assumed to pertain to all of the causal variables appearing in these equations. In this appendix the development of these equations is explained, using the autonomous price equation p_x as an example.

The assumptions underlying the export price equation, p_b, and the consumption price equation, p_c, are such that the distributed lag is not assumed to pertain to all of the causal variables. For example, in the export price equation a distributed lag is assumed for labor costs, H, and import prices p_m, but not for changes in the competing export price level, p_b', the third causal variable appearing in equation 10. When a distributed lag is assumed with regard to one or more variables but not for others in the equation, the estimator equation is no longer linear in the coefficients. Independent estimates of the coefficients and of the lag are therefore impossible, and reasonable values for the lag must be assumed. Presumably, the lag selected is the one that maximizes the coefficient of multiple correlation, providing the estimates of the coefficients of the causal variables are acceptable.[5] As an example, the development of the equation for changes in consumer prices, $\dot{p}_c$ is shown in Appendix 7.

Turning to the development of the equation for changes in the price of autonomous expenditures, one finds that when the variables of the autonomous price equation, $\dot{p}_x$, are expressed in terms of natural logarithms of the original data, geometrically decreasing weights lead to the following result:

$$(6.1) \quad \ln p_x = \alpha \ln H + \alpha\lambda \ln H_{-1} + \alpha\lambda^2 \ln H_{-2} + \dots + \beta \ln p_m + \beta\lambda^2 \ln p_{m_{-1}} + \beta\lambda^2 \ln p_{m_{-2}} + \dots .$$

5. See Robert Ferber and P. J. Verdoorn, *Research Methods in Economics and Business* (New York, Macmillan, 1962), pp. 341–48 and 372–78; and Verdoorn and van Eijk, "Experimental Short-term Forecasting Models," pp. 37–40.

However,

$$(6.2)\quad \ln p_{x_{-1}} = \alpha \ln H_{-1} + \alpha\lambda \ln H_{-2} + \ldots + \beta \ln p_{m_{-1}} + \beta\lambda \ln p_{m_{-2}} + \ldots .$$

Multiplying 6.2 by λ yields $\lambda \ln p_{x_{-1}} = \alpha\lambda \ln H_{-1} + \alpha\lambda^2 \ln H_{-2} + \ldots + \beta\lambda \ln p_{m_{-1}} + \beta\lambda^2 \ln p_{m_{-2}} + \ldots$, which, with the exception of $\alpha \ln H$ and $\beta \ln p_m$, is the right-hand side of 6.1.

Therefore, after substitution, one can write

$$(6.3)\qquad \ln p_x = \alpha \ln H + \beta \ln p_m + \lambda \ln p_{x_{-1}}.$$

After lagging, 6.3 can be written as $\ln p_x - \ln p_{x_{-1}} = \alpha(\ln H - \ln H_{-1}) + \beta(\ln p_m - \ln p_{m_{-1}}) + \lambda(\ln p_{x_{-1}} - \ln p_{x_{-2}})$ or $\Delta \ln p_x = \alpha\Delta \ln H + \beta\Delta \ln p_m + \lambda\Delta \ln p_{x_{-1}}$.

Following the procedure shown in Appendix 1, equation 6.4 can be written as

$$(6.5)\qquad \dot{p}_x = \alpha\dot{H} + \beta\dot{p}_m + \lambda\dot{p}_{x_{-1}}.$$

Equation 6.5 is the equation for changes in autonomous prices as it appears in the 1961 Plan.

Appendix 7

The Distributed Lag in the Consumption Price Equation

Of the four price equations in the 1961 Plan, each of which contains a distributed lag of one sort or another, the most complicated lag appears in the consumption price equation. As in the investment equation, the equation for changes in consumer prices was estimated with variables expressed in both percentage changes and in lagged levels of the initial variables.

In its basic form, the consumer price equation may be written

$$(7.1)\quad \ln p_c = \beta_1 \ln H + \beta_2 \ln H_{-1} + \rho\beta_2 \ln H_{-2} + \rho^2\beta_2 \ln H_{-3} + \ldots + \beta_3 \ln p_{m_{-\frac{1}{2}}} + \beta_4 \ln\left(\frac{v'}{m}\right)_{-\frac{1}{2}} + \beta_5 \ln T'_{K_{-\frac{1}{3}}} + \beta_6 .01\, r_{k_{-\frac{1}{2}}}.$$

To derive the equation as it was estimated by the Central

Planning Bureau, one first subtracts $\rho \ln p_{c_{-1}}$ from both sides of 7.1 (see Appendix 6). This gives

$$(7.2)\quad \ln p_c - \rho \ln p_{c_{-1}} = \beta_1 \ln H + (\beta_2 - \rho\beta_1) \ln H_{-1} + \beta_3(\ln p_{m_{-\frac{1}{2}}} - \rho \ln p_{m_{-1\frac{1}{2}}}) + \beta_4\left\{\ln\left(\frac{v'}{m}\right)_{-\frac{1}{2}} - \rho \ln\left(\frac{v'}{m}\right)_{-1\frac{1}{2}}\right\} + \beta_5(\ln T'_{K_{-\frac{1}{3}}} - \rho \ln T'_{K_{-1\frac{1}{3}}}) + \beta_6\, .01(r_{k_{-\frac{1}{2}}} - \rho r_{k_{-1\frac{1}{2}}}).$$

After adding and subtracting $\ln p_{c_{-1}}$, the left-hand term of 7.2 may be written as $\Delta \ln p_c + (1 - \rho) \ln p_{c_{-1}}$. By treating the right-hand terms in a like manner, one may write 7.2 as

$$(7.3)\quad \Delta \ln p_c + (1 - \rho) \ln p_{c_{-1}} = \beta_1\Delta \ln H + \{\beta_2 + \beta_1(1 - \rho)\} \ln H_{-1} + \beta_3\{\Delta \ln p_{m_{-\frac{1}{2}}} + (1 - \rho) \ln p_{m_{-1\frac{1}{2}}}\} + \beta_4\left\{\Delta \ln\left(\frac{v'}{m}\right)_{-\frac{1}{2}} + (1 - \rho) \ln\left(\frac{v'}{m}\right)_{-1\frac{1}{2}}\right\} + \beta_5\{\Delta \ln T'_{K_{-\frac{1}{3}}} + (1 - \rho) \ln T'_{K_{-1\frac{1}{3}}}\} + \beta_6\, .01\, \{\Delta r_{k_{-\frac{1}{2}}} + (1 - \rho)\, r_{k_{-1\frac{1}{2}}}\}.$$

Following Appendix 1, the Δ ln terms may be replaced by the percentage change in the variable divided by 100. Finally, if natural logarithms in equation 7.3 are converted to common logarithms ($\ln X = 2.30 \log X$) and the equation multiplied through by 100, the equation may be written as

$$(7.4)\quad \dot{p}_c + 2.30\,(1 - \rho) \log p_{c_{-1}} = \beta_1\dot{H} + 2.30\,\{\beta_2 + \beta_1(1 - \rho)\} \log H_{-1} + \beta_3\,\{\dot{p}_{m_{-\frac{1}{2}}} + 2.30\,(1 - \rho) \log p_{m_{-1\frac{1}{2}}}\} + \beta_4\left\{(\dot{v}' - \dot{m})_{-\frac{1}{2}} + 2.30(1 - \rho) \log\left(\frac{v'}{m}\right)_{-1\frac{1}{2}}\right\} + \beta_5\{\dot{T}'_{K_{-\frac{1}{3}}} + 2.30\,(1 - \rho) \log T'_{K_{-1\frac{1}{3}}}\} + \beta_6\{\Delta r_{k_{-\frac{1}{2}}} + (1 - \rho) r_{k_{-1\frac{1}{2}}}\}.$$

Equation 7.4 is the form in which the coefficients were estimated. The constant ρ was set a priori at .64.

After substituting the coefficients shown in the 1961 Plan, 7.4 may be written

$$(7.5)\quad \dot{p}_c + 83 \log p_{c_{-1}} = .21\,\dot{H} + 56 \log H_{-1} + .20\{\dot{p}_{m_{-\frac{1}{2}}} + 83 \log p_{m_{-1\frac{1}{2}}}\} - .42\left\{(\dot{v}' - \dot{m})_{-\frac{1}{2}} + 83 \log\left(\frac{v'}{m}\right)_{-1\frac{1}{2}}\right\} + .17\{\dot{T}'_{K_{-\frac{1}{3}}} + 83 \log T'_{K_{-1\frac{1}{3}}}\} + 1.83\{\Delta r_{k_{-\frac{1}{2}}} + .36\, r_{k_{-1\frac{1}{2}}}\}.$$

In the 1961 Plan, the variables in equation 7.5 expressed in levels were collected into a single term labelled Λ.[6] Thus,

$$(7.6)\quad \Lambda = -83 \log p_{c_{-1}} + 56 \log H_{-1} + 17 \log p_{m_{-1\frac{1}{2}}} - 35 \log\left(\frac{v'}{m}\right)_{-1\frac{1}{2}} + 14 \log T'_{K_{-1\frac{1}{3}}} + .65\, r_{k_{-1\frac{1}{2}}}.$$

6. In equation 38 for Λ published in the 1961 Plan, a factor of 100 was inadvertently dropped. This explains the difference between 7.6 and the equation found in the 1961 Plan.

Selected Bibliography

ALLEN, R. G. D., *Mathematical Economics*, London, Macmillan, 1956, Chap. 20.

ANDRESSEN, J. E., "Economic Development in the Netherlands," *Planning and Development in the Netherlands, 1* (1962), 29–36.

BASMANN, R. L., "A Generalized Classical Method of Linear Estimation of Coefficients in a Structural Equation," *Econometrica, 25* (1957), 77–83.

BAUCHET, PIERRE, *Economic Planning, The French Experience*, New York, Praeger, 1964.

BOS, H. C., *A Discussion on Methods of Monetary Analysis and Norms for Monetary Policy* (Rotterdam, Netherlands Economic Institute, 1956).

BRANDES, P., "The Netherlands Labor Foundation," mimeo. The Hague, Netherlands Labor Foundation, 1955.

BUSSINK, W. C. F., "De gevolgen van de recente revaluaties voor 1961," mimeo. The Hague, Central Planning Bureau, March 1961.

DAALDER, HANS, "Parties and Politics in the Netherlands," mimeo. The Hague, Institute of Social Studies, 1960.

DAHL, ROBERT H., "The Politics of Planning," *International Social Sciences Journal, 11* (1959), 340–50.

DE WOLFF, PIETER, "Central Economic Planning in the Netherlands," *Weltwirtschaftliches Archiv, 92* (1964), 181–207.

———, "The Scope, Methods and Tools of Planning," *Planning*, paper read at the Conference of Business Economists, New College, Oxford, April 1962.

———, and C. A. VAN DEN BELD, "Ten Years of Forecasts and Realizations," paper presented to American Statistical Institute Conference, Ottawa, August 1963.

———, and J. SANDEE, "Recent Experiences in the Application of Econometric Policy Models in the Netherlands," paper read at the 21st meeting of the European Econometric Society, Amsterdam, September 1959.

DREES, WILLIAM, *On the Level of Government Expenditures in the Netherlands after the War*, Lieden, H. E. Stenfert Kroese N.V., 1955.

DROR, YEHEZHEL, "The Planning Process: A Facet Design," *International Review of Administrative Sciences, 29* (1963), 46–58.

"Econometric Analysis of the Dutch Economy," mimeo. Report A-10, 1960, The Hague, Central Planning Bureau, 1960. 32 pages.

Economic Quarterly Review, old series, Nos. 128–147, June 1960 March 1965, Amsterdam Bank N.V.; new series, beginning June 1965, Amsterdam-Rotterdam Bank N.V.

FELLNER, WILLIAM J., et al., *The Problem of Rising Prices*, Paris, Organization for European Economic Cooperation and Development, 1961.

FERBER, ROBERT, and P. J. VERDOORN, *Research Methods in Economics and Business*, New York, Macmillan, 1962.

FRIEDMAN, JOHN, "Introduction," *International Social Sciences Journal, 11* (1959), 327–38.

GEARY, R. C., ed., *Europe's Future in Figures*, Amsterdam, North-Holland Publishing Co., 1962.

HAAVELMO, TRYGVE, "The Probability Approach to Econometrics," *Econometrica, 12* Supplement (1944).

HARTOG, F., "Economic Policy in the Netherlands," in E. S. Kirschen, ed., *Economic Policy in Our Time*, Amsterdam, North-Holland Publishing Co., 1964.

HESSEL, WILLEM, "Quantitative Planning of Economic Policy in the Netherlands," in Bert G. Hickman, ed., *Quantitative Planning of Economic Policy*, Washington, D.C., The Brookings Institution, 1965.

HOFSTRA, H. J., "De revaluatie van de Gulden," *Economisch-Statistische Berichten*, March 15, 1961.

HOLTROP, M. W., "Method of Monetary Analysis Used by De Nederlandsche Bank," *International Monetary Fund Staff Papers, 5*, February 1957, 303–16.

HOOGERWERF, A., "Latent Socio-Political Issues in the Netherlands," *Sociologia Needandica, 2* (Summer 1965), 161–77.

International Monetary Fund, *International Financial Statistics Supplement to Issues 1964/65*, Washington, D.C., 1965.

KEYNES, J. M., "Professor Tinbergen's Method," *Economic Journal, 49* (September 1939).

KLEIN, L. R., *A Textbook of Econometrics*, Evanston, Ill., Row, Peterson, 1953.

KLEVE, J. G., "The National Income and Product Accounts of the U.S. in the Netherlands Arrangements," *Review of Economics and Statistics, 40* (November 1958), 375–83.

KLOCK, T. A., "Comparative Survey of Two Econometric Models," mimeo. Rotterdam, Netherlands School of Econometrics, 1962.

KOOPMANS, TJALLING, "When Is a System Complete?" *Statistical Inference in Dynamic Economic Models,* Cowles Commission Monograph No. 10, Chicago, 1950.

KOYCHK, L. M., *Distributed Lags and Investment Analysis,* Amsterdam, North-Holland Publishing Co., 1954.

———, and G. K. BOON, "Post War Holland and the Impact of the Common Market," *The Common Market Economies,* London, District Bank Limited, 1962.

LIPS, J., and D. B. J. SCHOUTEN, "The Reliability of the Policy Model Used by the Central Planning Bureau," *Income and Wealth,* Series VI, London, Bowes and Bowes, 1957.

MARRIS, R. L., "The Position of Economics and Economists in the Government Machine: A Comparative Critique of the United Kingdom and the Netherlands," *Economic Journal, 64* (December 1954).

Netherlands Bank N.V., *Annual Reports,* 1955–64.

Netherlands Central Bureau of Statistics, *Jaarcijfers voor Nederland 1959–1960* (Statistical Yearbook of the Netherlands), The Hague, 1961.

———, *Monthly Bulletin of Social Statistics,* The Hague.

———, "National Accounts of the Netherlands," *Statistical Studies,* No. 11 (December 1961).

———, *Netherlands Central Bureau of Statistics,* The Hague, 1960.

Netherlands Central Planning Bureau, *Centraal Economisch Plan* (Central Economic Plan), The Hague, published annually; cited as *Centraal Economisch Plan* if it is available only in Dutch and as Central Economic Plan if it is available in an English translation.

———, *Comparison Between the Central Planning Bureau's Forecasts and Actual Economic Developments, 1949–1953,* CPB Monograph No. 4, The Hague, 1955.

———, *Monetary Statement and Monetary Analysis,* CPB Monograph No. 7, The Hague, 1959.

———, "Revaluatie van Mark und Guilden," mimeo. The Hague, July 1960.

———, *Scope and Methods of the Central Planning Bureau*, The Hague, 1956.

———, *Toeneming en besteding van het nationale inkomen in de Komende vier jaren*, CPB Monografie No. 9, Den Haag, 1963.

Netherlands Government Information Service, *Digest of the Kingdom of the Netherlands, Social Aspects*, The Hague, 1962.

Netherlands Ministry of Economic Affairs, *Memorandum on the Industrialization of the Netherlands*, translation of Annex IV to the Explanatory Memorandum to Chapter X (Economic Affairs) of the 1950 Budget, The Hague, September 1949.

———, *Netherlands Economic Bulletin for the Foreign Press*, Economic Information Service, No. 319 (April 1961), No. 348 (June 1962), No. 356 (October 1962).

Netherlands Social and Economic Council, *Advies inzake de bestedingen*, Publikaties van de Sociaal-Economische Raad, Den Haag, 1956.

———, *Advies inzake het in 1958 en 1960 Te Voeren Sociaal-Economisch* Belied, Publikaties van de Social-Economische Raad No. 2, Den Haag, 1959.

Organization for Economic Cooperation and Development, *Policies for Price Stability*, Paris, OECD, 1962.

Organization for European Economic Cooperation, *Statistical Bulletin*, No. 6, Paris, OEEC, 1955.

Pedersen, Jorgen, "The Control of Wages and the Value of Money: The Dutch Experience," *Banca Nazionale del Lavoro Quarterly Review*, *40* (March 1957).

Pels, R. J., *Industrial Relations in the Netherlands*, Trade Union Research and Information Service, European Productive Agency, Paris, OEEC, n.d.

"Quarterly Economic Review" (Annual Supplement on the Netherlands), *The Economist*, London, May 1964.

Ravenswaaij, C. A., "The Changing Face of Dutch Politics," *The Scholars Magazine*, The Hague, Netherlands Institute of Social Studies, July 1963.

Roberts, B. C., "National Wage Policy in the Netherlands," *Economica*, *25* (1957).

SANDEE, J., ed., *Europe's Future Consumption*, Amsterdam, North-Holland Publishing Co., 1964.

———, "A Long-Term, Phased Policy Model for the Netherlands," paper read at the Boston meeting of the Econometric Society, December 1963.

SCHOUTEN, D. B. J., "The Wage Level, Employment of Economic Structure," *International Economic Papers, 2* (1952).

SPENGLER, JOSEPH J., *Economics and Public Policy*, Washington, D.C., The Brookings Institution, 1955.

STONE, RICHARD, "Model Building and the Social Accounts," *Income and Wealth, Series IV*, London, Bowes and Bowes, 1955.

TELDERSSTICHTING, B. M., *The Public Industrial Organization in the Netherlands*, The Hague, Martinus Nijhoff, 1957.

THEIL, HENRI, "The Aggregation Implications of Identifiable Structural Macrorelations," *Econometrica, 27* (January 1959).

———, *Economic Forecasts and Policy*, Amsterdam, North-Holland Publishing Co., 1958.

———, *Linear Aggregation of Economic Relations*, Vol. 12 of the series, *Contributions to Economic Analysis*, Amsterdam, North-Holland Publishing Co., 1954.

———, *Optimal Decision Rules for Government and Industry*, Amsterdam, North-Holland Publishing Co., 1964.

———, "Survey of Foreign Postwar Developments in Economic Thought," *American Economic Review, 54*, Supplement, Part 2 (March 1964).

———, "Who Forecasts Best?" *International Economic Papers, 5* (1955), 194–99. Original article in Dutch was published in *De Economist*, February 1954, under the title "Wie Voorspelt Het Best?"

TINBERGEN, JAN, *Central Planning*, New Haven, Yale University Press, 1964.

———, "Central Planning in the Netherlands," *Review of Economic Studies, 15* (1947–48), 70–77.

———, *An Econometric Approach to Business Cycle Problems*, Paris, Hermann et Cie, 1937.

———, *Economic Policy, Principles and Design*, Amsterdam, North-Holland Publishing Co., 1964.

———, *On the Theory of Economic Policy*, Amsterdam, North-Holland Publishing Co., 1952.

———, *Statistical Testing of Business Cycle Theories*, Vol. 1: *A Method and Its Application to Investment Activity*, Vol. II: *Business Cycles in the U.S. 1919–1932*, Geneva, League of Nations, 1939.

United Nations Economic Commission for Europe, *Economic Survey of Europe*, Geneva, 1951 and 1959.

Van den Beld, C. A., *Conjunctuurpolitick in en om de jaren vijftig*, Centraal Planning Bureau Monografie No. 8, Den Haag, 1963.

———, "The Procedures Followed by the Central Planning Bureau in Drawing Up the Central Economic Plan," *Economic Quarterly Review*, No. 128 (June 1960).

———, "Short-term Planning Experiences in the Netherlands," in Bert G. Hickman, ed., *Quantitative Planning of Economic Policy*, Washington, D.C., The Brookings Institution, 1965.

Van den Bogaard, P. J. M., and J. Versluis, "The Design of Optimal Committee Decision," *Statistica Neerlandica, 16* (1962), 271–89.

———, and A. P. Barten, "Optimal Macroeconomic Decision Rules for the Netherlands," Report 5915 of the Econometric Institute of the Netherlands School of Economics, mimeo. 1959.

Van de Panne, C., "De voorspellingskwaliteit van de Centrale Economische Plannen" (The Predictive Quality of the Central Economic Plans 1949–1956), *De Economist*, No. 107 (1959), pp. 91–123.

Van Eijk, C. J., and J. Sandee, "Quantitative Determination of an Optimum Economic Policy," *Econometrica, 27* (1959), 1–13.

Verrijn, G. M. S., "Economic Policy in the Netherlands," *Lloyds Bank Review* (January 1953), pp. 34–43.

Verdoorn, P. J., and C. J. van Eijk, "Experimental Short-term Forecasting Models, mimeo. The Hague, Central Planning Bureau, 1958.

Von Holenbalken, B. and G. Tintner, "Econometric Models of the OEEC Member Countries and the U.S. and Canada and Their Application to Economic Policy." *Weltwirtschaftliches Archiv, 89* (1962).

Vermeulen, A., "Collective Profit Sharing," *International Labor Review, 67* (June 1953).

Wittersen, H. J., "Revaluatie, De Wisselkoers als instrument van structuurpolitick," *Economisch Statistische Berichten*, March 22, 1961.

Zoeteweij, B., "National Wage Policy: The Experience of the Netherlands," *International Labor Review*, *71* (February 1955).

Index